Passport to A

The final stage of a twenty five year
around the world circumnavigation
from Cyprus to England.

Passport to Adventure

The final stage of a twenty five year around the world circumnavigation from Cyprus to England.

by Shirley Billing

Bosun Publications

Published by Bosun-Publications
Email: fbarter@bosunpress.com

Passport to Adventure.
The final stage of a twenty five year around the world
circumnavigation from Cyprus to England.
Copyright © 2011 Shirley Billing

ISBN: 978-0-9561210-3-5

A CIP catalogue record for this book is available from
the British Library.

Printed in England by: Ian Allan Printing Ltd

CONTENTS

Dedicated to:

PAUL, NOEL & ANDREA AND THEIR
CHILDREN

With gratitude to our family for letting us go
and then welcoming us back when we came home

and to our supportive sisters:
SHEILA, HILARY AND LIZ

and to PETER

'Here is the sailor, home from the sea.'
R.L.S.

Other books by Shirley Billing
Red Sea Peril
Seize the Day

INTRODUCTION

WHATEVER TYPE of boat you go on, you will have adventures. Often the smaller the boat, the bigger the adventure.

Few sensations exceed the excitement of anticipating the open space just waiting to be explored: around the next bend in the river, the next cove along the beach, or the next ocean. Stepping onto land on the far shore having arrived under your own power feels a great achievement, be it the river bank, the next harbour along the coast, a foreign country or even another continent.

Can you resist the smell of the sea? The ozone from a rocky shore as the tide goes out? The roar, or soft lapping of the waves? Sitting watching the power of the ocean as breakers crash against cliffs? Or the call of boats gently rocking in the harbour? The sound of a gale screaming through the rigging or the gentle flap, flap, as the ensign slaps its pole? Swimming in a blue lagoon where the water is so clear it takes an act of faith to dive overboard – if the boat is floating it must be there, but all you can see is the bottom and the furrows made by the anchor chain as it dragged across the sand.

Paddling a canoe, rowing your boat, or sailing a dinghy is like riding a bike before you drive a car. You learn the rules of the road, the power of the sea, the effect of currents and tides and the hazards of going aground.

It's twenty five years since we started our circumnavigation, before personal computers, email, mobile phones, Global Positioning Systems (GPS) credit cards and cash machines. In 1983, for ordinary yachts, there were few reliable sail roller-reefing systems. It wasn't usual to have an electric anchor winch and few British boats had freezers or radar – or double beds! No Kevlar sails or graphite masts and of course no laptops with tide tables or weather faxes. There have been many clever introductions for safer easier voyages.

However the sea hasn't changed. It still demands respect and seamanship. Personal relationships haven't changed either – you must continually consider the other person's feelings in such a small space or it could end in murder or a push overboard, or even giving up yourself and jumping into the sea. You still can't quit mid-ocean or escape from close quarters with your partner or crew.

You start a world voyage and hope you will complete it, but apart from the actual glorious sailing the spin offs are beyond imagination. For us the opportunities to work in Asia allowed us to be involved in fascinating cultures and yearly home-leave flights which enabled us to visit parents in Australia, son Paul in the USA as well as the rest of our families in the UK.

We made mistakes – there isn't a sailor alive who hasn't thought 'Ooops! That wasn't clever!' In spite of all the problems we made it – JUST!

Burton Ferry August 2010

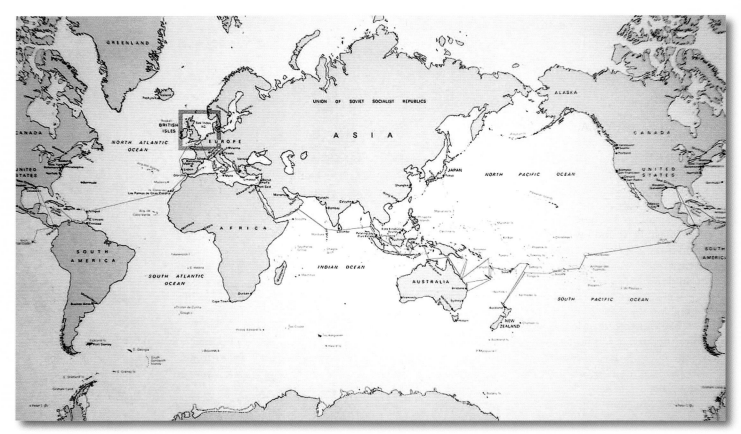

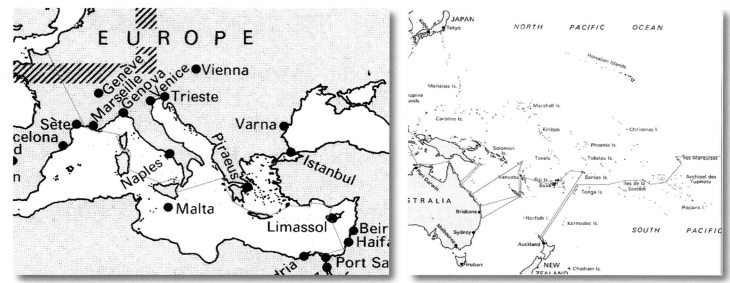

8

CHAPTER ONE | THE ANGRY SEA

THE ANGRY SEA, as the Ancients called it, lies between the south western Turkish coast and Crete, where, we found out later, the sea floor suddenly drops from 200 metres to the abyss of 5,000 metres, causing underwater turbulence and up-wellings.

We paid for our ignorance.

At last! Peter and I were about to enter Europe again in our Endurance 35' ketch CLYPEUS after twenty years sailing and working our way west around the world. Yippee!

We had seen and learned so much - but not enough!

"We will keep the Mediterranean until we're older," I had said. But now, we were worried - had we spent too long playing around the historic, scenic and sunny, Turkish coast? Had we passed our 'sell by' date?

It was our first overnight voyage for three years and we had been lulled into complacency, spending the summers day-sailing along the fantastic southern Turkish coast where the brisk mid-day breezes and calm, warm, nights gave ideal cruising conditions.

At 10.30 on the 12th of June 2003, we left the pastel coloured Venetian style homes, gracing the pavements around Kastellorizo's aquamarine harbour for Crete and motored out into the calm dark blue Mediterranean. Sitting astride the bowsprit I admired a field of sparkling diamonds set in a sapphire sea. The bow-wave created white foam bubbles which swirled up and tumbled as though searching for more air to breathe. I was conscious of the phut phut and burble of the engine, the creak and rattle of the sails and the graunch and whine of the auto-helm as it steered us west.

As we motor-sailed along with the breeze ten

At 10.30 on the 12th of June 2003, we left the pastel coloured Venetian style homes gracing the pavements around Kastel-lorizo's aquama-rine harbour for Crete and mo-tored out into the calm dark blue Mediterranean.

degrees off the bow, a pair of trawlers towing colourfully ballasted nets, slowed down in our path and then seemed to be following. They weren't trying to catch us? Were they? We took a wide deviation around them. Later, a shining white fender bobbed into view, CLYPEUS circled and I hooked it out and tied it on the rail alongside the others.

All through the cloudless day, CLYPEUS dipped and bounced up each wave ready to curtsey again in the trough. (When we first bought CLYPEUS in 1982 we found the name difficult to pronounce or remember – it is the Greek entomological word for the carapace of an insect, particularly the hard outer shield protecting the forehead. The previous owner had named her and we thought it appropriate for a concrete hull. (He suggested 'cycle clips' was a good 'aide memoire' for the pronunciation.)

After lunch the staysail was hoisted and Peter slept to ward off seasickness, which we hadn't experienced for at least five years. We both suffer, but I lose my last meal early and usually feel better while Peter just hangs on and can feel rotten for days. At 6.30 p.m. a pod of seven bottlenose dolphins diverted from their course to come and leap, swoop and play around our bow for ten minutes. They had grey backs with white bellies, a few scars but no particularly distinguishing marks. We had always believed we were in no danger if dolphins were near.

Then the romance of the day began to wane. Although we were going fast at 5.5 knots, the motion was extremely bumpy. The waves fought like two hostile armies colliding and spurting crests reached for the sky. Eventually we were making little headway against wind and sea and every wave sent sheets of spray up into the cockpit and against our faces. Our salt-caked cheeks felt as though covered in sand. We grimly remembered our ocean crossings when we often felt really ill for long, long days, and would encourage ourselves with "Togetherness, is being seasick holding hands."

The wind and sea gradually grew. In the open cockpit of a small yacht, you are in very close contact with the elements. By nightfall we were motoring but with sails still up to steady the boat. As CLYPEUS dipped and rolled we wished we were somewhere else. Uneasily we ate our supper. The horizon, which looked so flat, belied the continuous heaving swell which lifted, then plunged our boat into the next trough of the over-riding short steep sea. The wavelets didn't seem to know which way to go, they suddenly gathered themselves into untidy lumps to crash against our hull.

Peter said "I'm feeling sick. I think I'll go below and try and sleep."

Three hours on watch, three hours off, we have found over the years, suits us. I wrote in the log:

"I lie in the cockpit with the kitchen pinger beside me set to 15 minutes so that I can stand up and scan the horizon to make sure no other shipping is around". When I feel seasick I always try and lie in the first aid 'recovery position' – but it didn't work this time. Clypeus ducks and weaves through the waves. By nightfall we are still motor sailing. The cross swell combines a twist and dip as we corkscrew towards Crete. The cresting wave-tops keep gathering themselves into one huge wave as though they are trying to tip us over".

Off watch trying to sleep in the cabin I was conscious of the gurgling sound of water close against my ear as it seethed and foamed along the hull. I concentrated on the sounds of the creak of ropes, the jingle of jam jars and tinkle of swaying sauce bottles, and tried to emulate Patrick Ellam and Colin Mudie in their book *Sopranino* in which they describe being able to distinguish the clink-clunk of the tomato ketchup against the Marmite jar, from the clunk-click of the Worcester sauce against the marmalade.

On watch again the one metre swell from the North collided with a half-metre swell from the West. My stomach continually sank, then lifted to hit my diaphragm before subsiding again; I timed it, as though giving birth.

Thank God for the Perkins 4108 diesel which is so reliable – not like the Vire petrol engine we had in the 70's in our Folkboat, SARKA. Mid-voyage it would perform reasonably well, but as soon as we closed land it would give up, ensuring, if there was no wind, that we drifted with the tide past our hoped-for destination. I could never start the Vire, it needed the knuckle-busting starting handle turned with power and persistence. When it did fire, it would squash Peter's fingers against the engine casing. The Perkins always starts first turn of the key - I can do that.

However, tonight, with no warning, but with a cough and splutter, the engine died - no real problem, we were bouncing and bucking along in the light wind and managed to avoid an oncoming tanker.

"I can't even try and see what's wrong in this sea" Peter moaned. (Our engine is beneath the saloon floor and the five foot square slab of parquet flooring is difficult to stow safely in rough weather.)

"Have a sleep and think about it," I consoled. "I'll stay on watch - Dan is managing well. (Dan is our Helmsman autopilot, so named because it has a black belt!)

The watch was endless and awful. Hanging over the side I said goodbye to my dinner and worried that my lower teeth would go with it, but didn't have the energy, or a spare hand, to remove them - sailing for pleasure doesn't get much worse.

Lights were coming toward us, a lower white light to the right - what did it mean? "Peter, wake up, come and help me, I can't tell if the ship's going to hit us and I'm busy being sick."

"You go below. I've had a sleep."
As my head sank on the pillow it jarred against the bulkhead as CLYPEUS hit each oncoming wave. It was like banging my head against a brick wall. After two hours of blissful oblivion. Splat, water landed on my sleeping head and arms. The hatch hadn't been closed securely. It was 03.00 a.m. I stepped out onto the soggy carpet and tightened the hatch closure but there was a lot of water sloshing and dripping from its surrounds. 'Not enough to sink us. It can wait' I thought but the boat does seem to be sluggish and wallowing. Stuff: pillows, books, Scrabble pieces, fruit, all rolled and slid across the main cabin floor. They hadn't been stowed carefully enough.

In the cockpit, the compass light lit a haggard, tight-lipped Peter, his shoulders hunched. He seemed to have aged overnight. The motion was awful, CLYPEUS ducked into a wave, scooped up water and then, like an enraged bull, tossed it back down the side decks where it sloshed its way to the stern coaming, splattering some into the cockpit before it swished to the gunwales, usually colliding with the next torrent cascading down the deck. I put on my safety harness and handed Peter his, which he reluctantly struggled into.

"Wind's dropping - the auto-helm can't work with the staysail up. I'll go and take it down." He worked at the mast then went forward to tie the staysail to its boom. Clipping and unclipping himself to the safety lines he slowly returned and said grimly, "The spare anchor warp has slipped off the deck and 180 feet of rope is dragging in a bight behind us. Worse still, the Genoa has come loose from its ties on the bow rail and we are trying to pull a huge bag of water with us. I'll go and assess the situation." He came back again with further bad news, "the Avon dinghy forward compartment has filled with water - you didn't close the valve; and a leg of the pulpit has been pulled way from the bowsprit by the sail dragging in the water."

In our yellow oilskins we crawled forward together, clipping and unclipping the double lines of our safety harnesses to the steel cable life-line. When we reached the bow we knelt, both holding on with one hand and surveyed the sorry situation. Over the side the ballooned-out foresail looked as though a huge white whale was swimming beside us. It had been pulled from its ties on the bow rail by the constant dipping in and out of the sea. We slowly, carefully, hauled it up onto the deck then rolled it, as well as we could, and retied it firmly along the guard rails. Fortunately it wasn't torn.

Then, as Peter pulled in the 60 metres of 20mm multi-plait nylon warp, I carefully coiled the thick rope and to ensure it didn't slip again, secured the 60 lb CQR anchor on top. Nothing could be done about making the Avon ready for a quick 'abandon ship'. We would have to rely on the buoyant fibre glass dinghy which had a foam filled seat and was always kept ready for an emergency with our survival gear strapped into it. Quick release catches meant it could be let go in seconds.

Back in the cockpit, he said sorrowfully "We can't keep on doing this you know - we're getting too old and making silly mistakes". I had to agree. Later he groaned, "I must lie down". When I went below to check on him he looked so sick and worn and lay still, his hands clasped across his chest as though in a coffin. The sea continued its sickening multi-sided rolling and CLYPEUS continued to bash into every wave then lift and shake her head, but we were going nowhere. I sat in the cockpit feeling a bit better on an empty stomach. Every ten minutes when the alarm pinged, I stood up and scanned with the binoculars, gradually turning around. Then…
Oh God!...

A container ship bearing down on us at full speed, just minutes away. We couldn't move out of its way with no engine and no wind.

"Peter quick," I screamed. "A ship nearly on us. Call on the VHF. Call on the VHF. Quick. Quick." By the time he had woken up, turned the radio on, selected channel 16 and started speaking, I could see its name towering above us.

"It's called MEDITERANNÈE LOCO". I yelled above the roar of its engines. Even in the dark I could easily read the name on the high bow slicing towards us as it threw up hills of phosphorescent foam which tumbled away from the towering steel hull cutting through the sea. The thump of its engines pounded in my ears as I watched the high blaze of lights approach. How could it have come up on us so quickly. It must be doing thirty knots. Breathing stopped…

I could hear Peter's voice in the cabin calling on Channel 16 on the VHF.

"MEDITERRANEAN LOCO, MEDITERRANEAN LOCO, this is sailing yacht CLYPEUS. We are immediately in your path. We are immediately in your path. MEDITERRANEAN LOCO, we are directly in your path. MEDITERRANEAN LOCO…"
It was going to hit us…
It was going to shave us…
It was going to miss us… Just!
I was able to call out. "Its OK, it's going behind us by about 20 yards. Hang on!

HOLD ON. HOLD ON!" I shouted as a wall of grey steel swept past. "It will be a huge wake." CLYPEUS rolled, falling off the bow wave, the lee combing swishing through the foam under water, then she righted herself to be tossed aside again. Then it was over.

We were OK. We were going to survive.
I looked up, back towards the bridge side wings and

waved: not a soul, or a motion acknowledged me. How did it miss us? Either your God is with you or he isn't! Where was the watch keeper? Probably watching a video. They wouldn't have even felt a bump as they smashed our boat under.

Peter came up and we held hands and watched the lights of Mediterranean Loco disappear to the East.

"I've had enough," he said. "We haven't got to put ourselves through this you know." We stood and hugged each other as the moon cast a pewter pathway across the black sea.

Peter re-programmed our course on the GPS for the closer island of Karpathos. I made a hot drink, then we sat in the cockpit warming our hands on our hot mugs while our hearts returned to their normal beat. Gradually the motion lessened enough for him to take up the saloon floor and investigate. He tried each logical cause for the engine stoppage in turn: replaced the diesel filter, tightened every nut, bolt and clip. It proved to be an air leak in the fuel pipe to the filter. While he bled the engine I steered under sail at 1-2 knots with the sea now dying. He started the engine.
"All OK."

On watch again the new day dawned with an encircling pale misty horizon rising to a clear azure dome above. Karpathos mountain tops appeared ahead. It wasn't calm until we entered Pigadia Harbour at 4 p.m., laid a bow anchor and tied the stern to the wall which was too high to climb. We launched the Avon and Peter rowed round to the Chef du Port to book in.

The fishing harbour had pyramids of yellow nets and was surrounded by pretty white and cream arched and balconied houses which looked charming. Terraced bars and restaurants lined the harbour side and two typical blue domed white

Greek chapels looked down benignly upon on us.

A pilaff filled our empty stomachs. Peter hadn't actually been sick but he hadn't eaten for 24 hours. Pigadia was a friendly clean town. Prices were reasonable in euros and nobody hassled us to buy or eat (a contrast to the ever resourceful and persistent Turks). A restaurant, festooned with vines and bougainvillea, looking down over the harbour beckoned. The white marble-topped tables and blue wooden chairs with woven straw seats looked perfect. The menu boasted that today's specials were calamari in wine sauce, spinach pie and home baked lamb or moussaka.

A caraffe of retsina, and lunch was eaten while looking out over the sparkling harbour to our dear boat – our life seemed privileged again, but was it worth the trauma of the last 36 hours? We must tighten up our skills. Three years of day-pottering has made us forget the minute attention to detail needed for ocean voyaging. We'd been told of the Med's Angry Sea, but hadn't realised just how undisciplined it is. It has the wave-length and flow of a front loading washing machine.

Thoroughly chastised by the pitiless sea, Peter decided it was time to end our 20 year circumnavigation. However, Karpathos wasn't the right place to sell CLYPEUS, we must head further west.

The rest of the summer was a delight and calmed our nerves and outlook as we explored Crete's northern coast, and continued to Kithera, then up the west coast of mainland Greece to Methoni, Olympus, Zakynthos, Levkas and Preveza.

I wrote the following poem for my hero:

TO A DYING DREAM

By Shirley Billing 2003

Unbidden tears roll down her face,
She tries to understand with grace,
Their dream to sail around the world
Is over, Sails will now be furled.

On their way for twenty years
Challenging gales and coral spears.
Red Sea arrest for no good cause.
Melded together, skills and flaws.

Now age is taking up its toll
It's time to let the good times roll
Away, return home, settled down
With memories that none can crown.

Thank you dear for all you've done
To give me time beneath the sun.
To live the vagrant life and share
The paradise of those who dare.

CHAPTER TWO | CATCH UP - Our Sailing Story so far

AN EMPTY NEST, overwork, and a car accident in 1980, helped us decide to sell up and sail away around the world.

We both loved sailing. In 1938, before the second World War, when on holiday in Frinton with his parents, Peter had been given 2/6d (two shillings and six pence) to hire a sailing dinghy at Clacton. He stepped into it and was able to sail away immediately after having avidly read and learned how to sail from Arthur Ransome's stories.

My father had always owned a boat, usually a motor cruiser as he wasn't prepared to trust in the wind to be back in his office on time. Some of my earliest memories are of being on his motor yacht BEATRIX on the Grand Union Canal, curled up with my sisters in the triangular forward bunk with a mug of hot, sweet, tea made with Nestles Condensed Milk. When my children were small, Dad let us use his motor cruiser THE VENTUROUS on Milford Haven. The boys wore life jackets but we tied them on with fishing twine as well.

In 1968 we had returned from a business contract in Australia on an ocean liner ELLENIS which called at Tahiti. "Wouldn't it be wonderful to sail here one day in our own boat," I had said, never dreaming we would actually do it.

Together, we had sailed dinghies in England and Australia before we upgraded to our 26'

Folkboat, SARKA, For thirteen years between 1969 and 1982 we sailed for all holidays and racing weekends with our three children. As they grew up it became quite a squash as I became the smallest person on board.

On THE BEATRIX, my father offers me a biscuit from the tin as I rest my back on Auntie Muriel. Mother and my sisters sit on the deck below – Uncle Charlie is steering!

Paul, Noel and Andrea strategically placed to keep the bow down when racing.

When our children had left home, life lost its purpose, Peter was unhappy at work, and then a car accident made us realise we should 'Seize the Day' and follow our dream. Our faithful Jeremy Rogers Folkboat and house were sold and we bought a ferro-cement Endurance 35, CLYPEUS. One third of our accumulated capital bought the boat and two thirds were invested as income.

It took us three years to prepare to sail away. In 1982, it was traumatic giving up jobs, salaries, pensions, insurances, clubs, committees, family and friends. We attended First Aid and navigation classes and I gained my Yacht Masters Certificate, so that although Peter is the better sailor, I am the better qualified - I don't mind him being Captain, as long as I'm Admiral.

We had medical check ups and minor operations were sorted. We also asked our Doctor what we should do if one of us died mid-ocean? He said "make sure you keep a log of what has happened so you have some proof that you didn't just push him, or her, overboard. Your biggest problem will be getting a dead body out of the cabin. Think about it, and devise a way of lifting 10 or 12 stone up and out through the narrow hatch."

We moved on board in Portsmouth Harbour on 18th October 1982, Peter's 51st birthday and sailed from Porchester Marine to St. Katharine's Dock to live on CLYPEUS for six months before leaving. We needed to make sure we could exist together in a space smaller than one of our previous bathrooms.

I honed our plans for a three year circumnavigation using the Cruising Association Library in Ivory House while Peter carried on electronic consultancy work. The CA Library and lectures gave us first hand information – there were no World Cruising Guides then, we had to rely on the old sailing ships

bible: 'Ocean Passages of the World' and Admiralty Pilots. We became used to snow-covered decks and cosy confined living, with the comforting glow of the oil lamps on the red velvet upholstery.

At our sailaway party on 19th March 1983, the

Vicar of All Hallows by the Tower blessed our boat as he had done for Sir Francis Chichester. Amidst the party poppers and our friends' spirited rendition of Rule Britannia we set off down the Thames - too early in the year and met cold winds, gales, rain and snow. Wishful thinking that we would soon be safe and warm encouraged us to surf into a French commercial harbour which we thought was Dieppe – it wasn't, it was Le Treport which dries out. The scend in the harbour was terrifying. The lock into the inner calm commercial basin had just closed as the tide had started going out. Frogmen zoomed around us in an inflatable.

"Bonjour," I called. "A quelle heure ouvert le port, s'il vous plait?"

"Douze heure," a voice shouted

"Ah" deux heure" Peter breathed a sigh of relief. "It will open at two; must be that now."

"No. No. He means douze, twelve o'clock. Midnight. Another ten hours away."

"Bloody Hell!"

The frogmen tried to help us by tying CLYPEUS fore and aft between two anchored cruisers. Our eleven tons of concrete was tossed around like a tennis ball and our bowsprit crashed through a cabin window. Eventually the water calmed as the entrance dried out and we were able to moor up to the quay wall until the lock opened at 2 a.m. Next day we tried to find the owner of the damaged boat to pay him and found out that he hadn't paid his harbour dues and nobody knew where he was, so "pas de problem".

Arriving in St Peter Port a month later we continued fitting out. Peter installed a new Perkins 4108 diesel engine, an Aries wind self steering gear, a Walker Sat Nav and re-designed and made a new rudder. When giving the hull a last polish before setting off for Spain, I noticed the expensive new epoxy paint was blistering. If we wanted it re-done free, under guarantee, we must return to the Hamble. So, the six weeks we should have been swanning down the Portuguese and Spanish coast were actually spent in a dirty boat shed near Southampton while the hull was re-ground and re-painted.

Eventually we started again down to the Mediterranean. Biscay was rough and we decided 'togetherness is being seasick holding hands.' The warmth and wine of the Spanish Coast and then a visit with our daughter to Alicante, Formentara and Ibiza restored our spirits.

November 26th 1983 saw us setting off across the Atlantic from Teneriffe proud of our up-to-date Walker SatNav which gave a fix every 90 minutes or so. Peter continued to take sextant sights and work out our position each day as, being an electrical engineer, he doesn't trust electronics to survive in the sea's hostile environment. He kept our boat

Crossing the Atlantic, Peter regularly took sextant sights.

simple, so that he could repair everything himself – no refrigerator, (just a cool box) no electric anchor winch, no self-furling jib. Our only communication was the VHF with a range of 20 miles. How different from today's modern equipment, mobile phones and GPSs but, consequently, we have never had to have 'the man' on board, to fix any problems.

Crossing the Atlantic I baked bread, sometimes light, sometimes like a small, hard, Elizabethan brick. A gale struck and broke the wind vane and steering wires. Peter made temporary repairs. However one day as he was coming back into the cabin after checking that the jury rig was still working well, a huge wave broke above us and swept him down into the saloon filling the bilges and bringing sea water almost up to the engine starter motor. Furious baling managed to avert disaster.

After thirty days at sea, as the anchor rumbled out in Antigua Harbour a young woman rowed up and called out "Hello Shirley. I met you in the Cruising Association Library." Trish and Ray of RALPH ROVER, had taken a gap year to sail around the Atlantic with their two small daughters, and have remained life-long friends. Flying the Cruising Association's blue ensign defaced with a red anchor was the only introduction needed.

Why has our voyage taken so long? Well, our boat was robbed three times in the Caribbean which meant we couldn't afford to fly to see our eldest son Paul who lived in New Orleans, so our first deviation was to sail to Louisiana to see him via the Mayan ruins on the Yucatan Peninsula. Our first sight of the USA was just a post in the Ocean, one of the markers of the Inter Coastal Waterway. After staying with Paul for a month during the hurricane season we bought a car, rented a tent and drove 8,000 trouble free miles around the States meeting nothing but kindness and hospitality. The mild, wild, manatees in Florida were gentle and unaggressive.

Through the Panama Canal in 1985.

Through the Panama Canal in 1985, where the young lady Pilot Advisor gave Peter orders, much to his annoyance. The Pacific was idyllic and we did manage to venture off the beaten track: Uninhabited Cocos Island then on to the Galapagos Islands where we laughed at the completely unafraid boobies and marine iguanas, Peter posted cards into the informal mail box in Post Office Bay. It had been set up by the old whalers and the cards did eventually reach their destination. Then we made for the Marquesa Islands and Tuamotos before reaching Tahiti and visited many other remote South Pacific tropical islands which fulfilled all our dreams. As Captain Cook said "The Polynesians are a beautiful people with a pleasant disposition". My parents flew from Australia to spend a month with us. They stayed in hotels in Tahiti and Moorea and sailed with us between the islands. A wonderful time when my parents were just our friends before they returned to Rockingham.

A family who lived on a small island off Huahine befriended us. The father, Noel, came for a sail with the youngest four of his thirteen children. He worked on a local trading sailing vessel and was competent, gentle and charming. In the Cook Islands, on Nuie, we were thrilled to explore down into secret beaches but apprehensive about our ability to climb back up. Being able to explore such exciting places made us feel less guilty about having escaped the rat race while we were still young enough to take full advantage of opportunities.

Throughout the twenty four hours we shared most tasks: each taking three hour watches, navigating, sail changing, but Peter is responsible for going up the mast while I do all the diving under the keel, or any underwater work. I cook, he does the dishes. He looks after hull, engine and electronics, I look after cabins, stores and sail mending. One of the minor advantages of our boat are the mast steps on both masts which makes adjusting aerials, flags and navigations lights relatively easy tasks. Hoisting a heavy man in a 'bosun's' chair isn't always practical, but with the steps I just needed to make three turns of the rope attached to Peter's harness around the main winch on the mast and gradually control his up or down climbing, ready to jamb it if he fell. The wide arc made by the top of the mast in heavy seas is still a major hazard of course.

There were dangers and problems. In Mid Pacific, a floating rope became entangled and wrapped itself tightly around the propeller and shaft which meant I had to dive down and try and cut it free in three-mile-deep ocean. I filled a hat with sponges in case CLYPEUS crashed down on my head in the swell, tied a rope around my waist in case she tried to sail away without me, and rubber gloves to protect my hands from the barnacles on the propeller as I clung to it to hold me down. Worried, in case a shark, or other sea monster, flashed by and bit off the lower half of my body! It took many dives to saw through the rope with the bread knife but the engine had to be ready for any future crises.

The South Pacific was glorious. All we ever expected: swaying palms, coral islands, beautiful kindly people and calm seas. During the ocean crossings, we saw nobody except each other for thirty days, I did miss my children desperately. Wives seem to suffer homesickness and loss of family contact much more than men. Our second son Noel, was taking care of our post and finances.

Arriving in New Zealand for Christmas, we realised we were rushing too quickly through this once in a lifetime experience and decided to slow down. During the 80's we would have had difficulty finding jobs, but we were managing on our investment interest. Each six month cyclone season we have spent either travelling inland or flying home to see our growing family. At Opua Yacht Club we studied for American Radio Ham licences and had a Kenwood Single Sideband Radio delivered which has been a source of many friendships and information as well as weather forecasts. Sharing a hire car with an American couple we toured North and South Islands to West Coast Glaciers then on to Milford Sound where the

landmarks have the same names as our Welsh Milford Haven. A Pembrokeshire sailor, Captain Gronow, sailed a whaling ship and named these southern New Zealand valleys, peaks and waterfalls after familiar places in his home county: Lawrenny Peak, Pembroke Mountain etc.

Polynesians are a beautiful people with a pleasant disposition.

1986 took us back north to Tonga, where we were invited to a traditional wedding. On to American and Western Samoa, Wallis and then to Fiji – to join the Fiji to Vanuatu fun race. The rules delighted us: handicap points were given to boats floating 6" below their waterline, had children on board, photo-copied charts or pot plants. Penalties were imposed on superior yachts with rod rigging, bloopers, bow thrusters, or crews wearing matching oilskins. The use of engines was encouraged. Prizes were awarded for the oldest crew, youngest crew, biggest fish, smallest bikini, first and last to cross the winning line and the winner to be drawn out of a hat. The 'Live Figurehead' Competition was won by an Australian Captain Bligh with his bare breasted wife slung below the bowsprit. Our effort was 'Musket Cove's entry for the America's Cup' which was to be held in Australia the following year. We finished 22nd of 32 yachts in the 800 mile race and were given a prize for "the boat which has sailed the greatest distance to join the Race." There were no other British Yachts in the fleet. In fact there were very few British boats in the Pacific then.

We explored Vanuatu's many islands and made friends with the local people who invited us into their homes, reminding us that the poorer the people, the more generous they are. Everyday empty containers for us, are magic for them: screw top mayonnaise and jam jars, plastic bags, biscuit tins, all help keep bugs and animals out of their food. While I taught Meri to knit, Peter tried to mend a radio but sand and dead cockroaches in the works defeated him. The Islanders were clever craftspeople and spoke many local languages as well as English and French. After a short visit to New Caledonia we eventually arrived in Australia where my parents and sister live. In 1987 we were able to watch the America's cup with them when Connors retrieved the trophy for America, leaving West Australian enthusiasts in deep mourning.

Before we left Australia I had to have surgery and we decided it should be a light sailing year. Anchored off an uninhabited island in New Caledonia, we received a short radio message from our daughter:

"I got married today and I'm so happy.

Love Andrea"

She hadn't even said who to?

I was devastated as I had never imagined our daughter getting married without us. We rushed to the nearest inhabited island, rowed ashore, walked three miles and found a telephone box from which we could direct dial her home. Being able to talk to her helped and we were reassured enough to organise a beach barbecue with the other yachties to celebrate her wedding. It was a stern lesson that you can't have everything. Life is a series of choices, you just hope you make the right ones.

We wanted to revisit the gentle Vanuatuans. I had given talks to Church groups in Australia and with the money collected we were able to take books, pencils and paper for the School on Awok Island where the children could only write every other day as there were not enough pencils to go round. However it wasn't a good year weather-wise. El Nino was disrupting normal weather patterns. We explored up to the Banks and Torres Islands, once again enjoying hospitality from isolated people. Victor took us to a secret cave where his parents had imprisoned visitors before eating them and left their sculls as trophies.

"Why did they kill these people? I asked.

"Because they came," he said.

Victor steered Clypeus to a secret cave where his parents had imprisoned visitors before eating them, sculls were still evident.

"They would only have come for our land, food or women, but we are Christians now." My respect for Missionaries grew. The uninhabited reefs of northern New Caledonia abounded with wild life. The turtles took no notice of us as they lumbered

up the beach to find a safe place to lay their eggs.

Eight hundred miles out, on the way back to Australia, we hit an uncharted reef off Chesterfield Reef and holed CLYPEUS. After eight hours of pumping to assist the electric bilge pump we beached her on a sand bank. Four Australian yachts were in the lagoon and they filled sacks with sand to make a wall on which to rest our hull. Peter mended the hole with the Portland Cement and Sika Quick Setting Solution which we carry for just such an emergency. We sailed back to Australia and, very chastened, spent the cyclone season flying to USA and UK to see our children and first grandchild, Laura. This was the only real problem in our lives, being away from our children and grandchildren and missing their growing years. All of our six grandchildren were born while we were on the other side of the world and it's my only real regret. I did send them audio tapes of bedtime stories and songs which helped, but I'm not as close

to them as I would like to be. The other problem, which thanks to modern technology is now solved, was keeping in touch. Letters were carefully forwarded from port to port and many eventually caught up with us in Coffs Harbour, which was great, but hadn't spared us the worry of why a family member hadn't written. Was something wrong? Were they ill? International telephone calls from phone boxes were so expensive, apart from finding enough local coins to feed into the pay boxes. How modern mobile phones and texts have changed so many travel worries.

In 1988 The Great Barrier Reef and the Louisiade Archipelago of Papua New Guinea provided marvellous lonely cruising with exotic dancers on some islands and then a calm Coral Sea to return to Queensland. The 1989 Darwin to Ambon Race arranged easy entry into Indonesia and we took the advantage to anchor off and visit Suluwesi, Bone Rate, Komodo, where we watched the dragons. On to Lombok and Bali, a beautiful island where dancing and temple processions are a way of life. Then on to Java, Sumatra and Borneo. In Singapore CLYPEUS was hauled out for five years while we went back to work.

During our voyage Peter's previous employers offered him three two year contracts to help set up joint manufacturing ventures in busy Taiwan, clean, green Singapore, and burgeoning Shanghai. We took advantage of the opportunities to refill the cruising kitty and to buy a 'house to let' in Wokingham, extremely pleased to get ourselves back on the housing ladder: Our home in Wokingham which we had sold in 1982 for £84,000 had been resold, unchanged, for £250,000 only four years later. I took full advantage of the Company's generous 'home leave' flights and was able to spend time with our growing family.

The turtles took no notice of us as they lumbered up the beach to find a safe place to lay their eggs.

Life in superficially squeaky clean Singapore still has to sometimes come to terms that it is still tropical jungle country. An amusing article in the Straits Times told of a python which frequently came up the lavatory bowl in an old people's home. It took many days to catch it. Another story told of a Golf Pro who had his testicles bitten by a python while sitting on the loo. It was a sufficiently serious injury for him to need stitches in Hospital. That article also pointed out that the gentleman was using the ladies' loos because they are cleaner than those of the men.

The east and west coasts of Malaysia and Thailand provided stunning scenery and easy, cheap living. Elephants were part of every day life and these babies, only one and two years old, were

Elephants were part of every day life and these babies were gentle loving creatures.

gentle, loving creatures. We did start out for home from Phuket in 1995 but three days out decided to return to this wonderful cruising ground for another year. It allowed me to spend time in Australia with my aging parents and be with my 85 year old Mother when she died. Peter stayed on board anchored in the Ding Dings River and did serious maintenance including replacing the chain plates which secure the rigging.

Crossing the Indian Ocean to Sri Lanka, the Maldives, Oman, and Yemen showed us the Muslim way of life, some of it benign and some very restrictive and harsh, particularly for the women.

Leaving Aden in 1996 we sailed up the Red Sea with Australian and American buddy boats to lessen the risk of piracy, and when we didn't appear on the usual radio schedule they knew something had happened to us. Off the Eritrean coast we had been taken from our boat at gunpoint by the Eritrean military and were detained for nearly a month under suspicion of spying. The worst moment was when bundled onto a plane from Assab to Asmara, the capital, for further interrogation, we realised our tickets were under false names and only one way! It looked as though when they realised we were only very ordinary sailors they may shoot us and dump us in a ditch somewhere. Then, once after being questioned yet again by a particularly sharp and zealous interrogator, he left the room with a vicious

"Do not lie to us. We know everything." What did they know? What were we supposed to have done? Had we been framed for something? Or were we hostages for some international incident about which we knew nothing?

Thanks to our sailing friends' persistent telephoning of the authorities, family, and English friends, the Media became involved and four weeks later we were freed.

In Egypt we were fortunate to travel to the Valley of Kings then, Israel, Palestine and Petra in Jordan before the politics got out of hand.

CLYPEUS was hauled out in Larnaca in Cyprus while we flew to Shanghai for Peter to work for his old company and I taught 'English as a Second Language' in commercial companies and at the University.

THE TIMES THURSDAY APRIL 4 1996

Retired couple on 13-year voyage are held captive after yacht is boarded by Eritreans

Round-the-world pair arrested in Red Sea swoop

By Stephen Farrell

A BRITISH couple appealed for help yesterday after the Eritrean navy interrupted their 13-year circumnavigation of the globe by boarding their yacht and putting them under house arrest.

Peter Billing, 64, and his wife, Shirley, 61, have been held prisoner for 16 days. The Eritreans claim that their 35ft ketch *Clypeus* strayed into a restricted zone near the Hanish islands in the Red Sea, which are the subject of a territorial dispute with Yemen. The crew of a naval patrol vessel boarded the twin-masted boat as it lay at anchor two days out of Aden, and took the couple to a desert military camp. They were questioned and flown to the capital, Asmara, with a French couple, arrested in similar circumstances. They are now being held at an hotel but cannot leave their room or make outgoing calls.

The Billings, who are experienced navigators from Wokingham, Berkshire, say that they had consulted other yachtsmen before passing through the area and had received no warning when they left Aden. Mrs Billing said yesterday that they had been woken by armed men who forced them to navigate dangerous shallow waters at night, then took their passports, charts and cameras.

She and her husband, an electronics engineer, were kept in a mice-infested hut at gunpoint. "We were in fear of our lives for the first three days. We just had no idea what was going on and were not allowed to speak to anyone," Mrs Billing said. "They seemed to think we were spies, which is ridiculous. We are grandparents and so are the French couple.

"The problem seems to be that it is difficult to explain to people who have been at war for 30 years that you have enough leisure time to go off and cruise around the world on your own. They just do not understand it and they probably think we are mad."

The couple set off around the world on March 19, 1983, after selling their home. Their

... the Galapagos Islands, the South Pacific, South-East Asia, Oman and Yemen. They spent four years in Taiwan and Singapore where Mr Billing worked for the engineering firm of which he was formerly a director.

On Sunday, after nearly a fortnight in captivity, they were given access to the honorary British consul, whom ... thinks it's better to play the thing quietly, but the softly, softly approach has gone on long enough," Mrs Billing said.

Habtom Gebremichael, Consul-General at the Eritrean Consulate in London, said last night. "It will be sorted out. I gather they are about to be released. This should have taken place on Tuesday, but it ... claimed last night that initially the Eritreans had been reluctant to grant access, but had allowed the honorary consul to visit after officials in Addis Ababa "underlined our concerns" by letter. "The consul reports they are in good spirits and we understand there is a likelihood they may be released very shortly," a spokesman said last night ... until Friday. Their daughter Andrea Lowther-Harris said she had feared the worst until she talked to them on the telephone at the weekend.

"They are bored but all right. Knowing my mother will have ...

Peter and Shirley Billing, who are both in their 60s, were interrogated in a desert camp on suspicion of spying

I found I wanted to tell the world of the beauty of our planet and the kindness of strangers and the freedom a boat offers. I kept a journal and had started writing articles for international sailing magazines. Two of my books have been published, *Red Sea Peril* in England and the USA, and *Seize The Day* in 2005 by Bosun Press.

Now it's time to tell the story of the last seven years of our voyage from Larnaca Marina in Cyprus to our home in Wales.

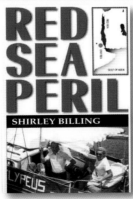

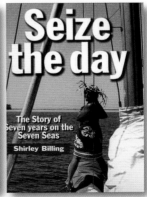

RED SEA PERIL — SHIRLEY BILLING

Seize the day — The Story of Seven years on the Seven Seas — Shirley Billing

CHAPTER THREE | UP, UP and AWAY -
1999-2001 Shanghai – Cyprus – preparations – Tasucu – Kappadokia

LEAVING SHANGHAI full of excitement and anticipation, after three years ashore, at last, we were off. Up, up, up and away through the grey smog, up above the shimmering silver clouds into the bright sun-filled atmosphere. The Boeing 777 turned east into the rising sun towards USA and then the UK for family visits before heading for Cyprus. It was 1999 and we were in our late sixties. Were we both going to survive long enough to complete our quest to circumnavigate the world in our own boat? Peter had had a hard time in China, working conditions were appalling in the foundries he visited to design, install and sometimes repair the power electronics. The air pollution and unsanitary facilities had undermined his health. Hopefully the sea would restore him.

At last we landed in Cyprus but the excitement of being reunited with our beloved boat was a little diminished when we actually saw her, trussed up and resting on her cradle. The paint on her white topsides was flaking like dandruff, the red antifouling paint was a blotchy orange resembling a bad case of shingles. I couldn't resist picking at it to reveal the cream expanse of epoxy resin - the Altex Devoe paint applied in New Zealand in 1985 looked in good smooth order. The interior was fresh and the air sweet, thanks to the two four inch computer fans, attached to a solar panel, which Peter had fitted into the forward hatch.

As soon as the Customs office opened in the Marina we were told us must see the Chief of the Port Authority as we were in default of payment.

"Your import extension is three months overdue. Why did you not review on time? Peter stuttered our excuses.

"Because you have been in China I will only fine you £50, it should be £150 as £50 a month is the usual fine. Come back on 24th June."

We sat, ashamed. We didn't have £50 CYP (Cyprus pounds) on us, but £40 and US$20 was sufficient and we were allowed to leave.

Formalities completed, we were able to start serious work on CLYPEUS. Peter chip, chip, chipped away at the anti fouling and managed a few square yards in five hours hard work. I took away the dusty tarpaulins which had covered the gritty and dirty boat. It was great sloshing warm sea water and detergent and scrubbing them. They weren't white any more but not too bad. Would one fit as an awning?

Beyond the harbour the sea looked blue and rough; white caps rolled in from the south west. It was time to start seriously noticing the weather again. The sun blazed down from a cloudless sky and glittered on the dancing harbour water.

Larnaca was a good place to be based, both for the necessary spares and equipment, but also for the Marina social life: weekly barbecues, Sunday morning book swap, Quiz evenings supported by local and visiting yachts' people; an early morning exercise class, two Bridge sessions a week. There was Line dancing on Thursday evenings and I started an aqua-aerobics class in pool of a nearby hotel. Friendships blossomed and I was given a memorable 65th birthday party.

We leased an apartment near the old fishing harbour and the landlord rented us his old Suzuki van for another £100 a month. We wondered why our arrival sometimes caused laughter until it was explained that the Greek writing on the sides advertised porcelain toilet bowls and sanitary ware. By the end of a summer's hard work CLYPEUS still wasn't ready for sea, so in September we covered her up again and flew back to move into our new home beside Milford Haven estuary in

Left hand page: The paint on her white topsides was flaking like dandruff, the red antifouling paint was a blotchy orange resembling a bad case of shingles.

Friendships blossomed and I was given a memorable 65th birthday party.

Pembrokeshire and enjoy the Millennium celebrations. In 1998 while on home leave from Shanghai staying with my sister Sheila I saw a bungalow for sale fronting on to Milford Haven Estuary. The kitchen, dining room and lounge all faced south towards the sparkling water. I knew it was within our budget so emailed Peter 'please come home and bring your cheque book. I think I have found the house where we could happily spend the rest of our lives'. He did, and within two weeks the house was ours and tenants had been arranged for the first year.

Our whole family gathered together for the first

Peter removed the rudder and found what he thought was probably the problem, a crack, which he filled and epoxied.

time for Easter 2000. I was reluctant to leave all the house and garden jobs which needed attention, and grandsons needed looking after during a family crisis, so I stayed in the UK during 2000. Peter spent three months on his own in Larnaca working on the boat and living on board. Up the ladder, down the ladder, twenty times a day. He refitted the diesel engine injectors after they were serviced and a hundred and one other things a thirty year old boat needs after 60,000 miles and four years ashore. The sails were sent for overhaul and her load lightened by giving away extra ropes and equipment no longer needed.

We planned the remainder of our voyage using our comprehensive library which encouraged us from the shelf: Pilot books for Turkey, Crete, Greece, Sicily, Sardinia, Corsica, France, Spain. The essentials were all on board: Charts, and Pilot Charts, which tell us the average wind strengths and from what quarter it had blown for the last 100 years, plus sailing stories and novels. (see appendix 5 on page 205).

It was May 2001 before CLYPEUS was finally anti-fouled and ready to go back to sea. Even before we set sail I felt an amazing sense of freedom, of space, getting away from the clutter of modern life. It was wonderful to be in charge of our own destiny again and to rekindle our complete trust in each other's skill and abilities. When you set off across the ocean if something goes wrong it is serious. There is little hope of rescue and you will probably die. We had been sailing for over twenty years before we made our decision to sell up and sail away in 1983. We knew how dangerous it could be.

Slings were placed beneath the keel, chocks were knocked away, our boat was raised and lowered into the water where she curtsied, then lifted her clipper bow ready to be off. BUT within

four hours, still tied up, we had a problem – the automatic bilge pumps had started working – there was a leak. We looked everywhere and examined every orifice but couldn't find it. Hauled out again Peter removed the rudder and found what he thought was probably the problem, a crack, which he filled and epoxied. Back in the water, £200 pounds poorer, the bilge pumps started up again every four hours. It was only a fine trickle but we couldn't see where it was coming from. We decided to start for Turkey and home anyway. Surely the Mediterranean shouldn't be too difficult. Even if we make some silly mistakes and founder, it would have been worth it. We have seen and done undreamed of, wonderful things.

After taking on fuel and booking out with the Harbour Master, Police and Customs, we prepared to leave at dawn.

On Friday 15th June 2001, at last we were off to Turkey. We knew so little about this country which has had 13 successive civilizations dating back to 6,500 BC. What would it be like? At 6 a.m. the red waking sun began to lick the haze off the water, a flicker of wind came from the west and by 7 a.m. the bright sun was in our eyes, as we headed east towards Cap Greco on the south east corner of Cyprus.

The following wind breathed into our sails the life of the open sea, with the mainsail and Yankee boomed out wing and wing CLYPEUS dipped and rose in the sparkling water. The world was ours. Barefoot and scantily clad, away from land, work, problems, authority and exhaust fumes. No time-table, no tickets, free to take our time and explore as we wish. This time we were not going to ruin a cruise by hurrying as we had done when crossing the South Pacific from Louisiana to New Zealand in ten months. All bills were paid, Wills made, our affairs were in order. As our son Noel had written earlier in the voyage when we were fretting about not seeing any bank statements "What's the point of leaving the rat race, if you take the cage with you." As we left the land anxieties fell away infecting us with bubbling gaiety. Our well used clichés sprang to life again – 'I see no ships', 'the relentless tide' (none at the moment), 'fraught with danger', 'the tyranny of the tiller', 'I keep thinking it's Tuesday', and although I don't think I ever said it 'The Captain's steady hand is on the wheel, his calm weather beaten face makes my heart grow strong.' The land, crags and coves of Eastern Cyprus slid by, the only noise was of water chuckling beneath the bow, sails and creaking ropes stretching after their five year rest. If there is one place in the world for romance it is under the warm Mediterranean skies in a sailing boat.

We returned to our three hours on, three hours off watch routine, which works well for us. Two bottle-nosed dolphins visited in the afternoon and played in our bow-wave as it sliced through the slippery surface. The sun reflected in golden shafts from the snowy peak of Mt Olympus. It was wonderful to take the midnight to 3 a.m. watch again. To sit in the cockpit and contemplate the night which was dark with no moon but a million stars twinkling in a firmament of deep blue velvet while listening to the fragile violin melody of Beethoven's Violin Concerto soaring to the heavens.

It is a complete world in itself, just yourself and the boat and the sea – a way of life almost, for you are on your own, entirely self sufficient. Why do people do it? It's not just to get to the other side, the way a mountaineer thinks of getting to the top.

The following wind breathed into our sails the life of the open sea, CLYPEUS dipped and rose in the sparkling water.

And this sort of day and night sailing is far removed from just "messing about in boats." I think it is the challenge, the exhilaration of using and sometimes fighting the elements, the sense of achievement when you have made your landfall and brought your boat safe into a foreign port; above all, the peace of being away out of reach and on your own in a world that has become too crowded.

This was so easy compared with our second start in July 1983, when our first heated argument occurred in the Solent. We had eventually left the Hamble River where the hull had been repainted due to chemical reaction between paint and concrete. When only two hours out we were making for the Needles in a turbulent, gunmetal sea and found ourselves in the shallow Shambles turmoil. After two hours at the helm steering carefully through the confused tumbling grey and white water, I handed the wheel to Peter and picked up the new and expensive Tamaya binoculars.

"Don't drop them," he cautioned, once too often.

"Of course I won't drop them. You trust me with your life and then admonish me in case I drop the binoculars. I'm not a six year old. If you ever say 'don't drop them' again I'll throw your blasted binoculars into the sea. Here, have your bloody binoculars." I thrust them at him and retired below to fume and feel unappreciated. This was supposed to be a partnership, not a parent/naughty child relationship and now we only had each other.

Now, as we glided past Cyprus, on this warm and beautiful night the Aries wind self-steering gear kept us on course but it was essential to keep a good lookout, to stand up and scan right around the horizon every fifteen minutes. Merchant ships can no longer be trusted to be alert for other shipping. It is said that more ocean yachtsmen die crushed under the bows of careless merchant vessels than from their own mistakes.

As I contemplated the stars I once again realized that this was one of the greatest gifts of our voyage – time: all twenty four hours were ours. There was time to reminisce about children, parents, friends, places we have been: Galapagos, Tahiti, Komodo, Borneo, China and its draconian laws.

I was still mentally reeling from an incident in Shanghai when an American friend lost? her purse in a central market. As it contained her credit cards plus about $20 in yuan, she reported it to the Tourist Police who were patrolling, then cancelled her cards by telephone as soon as she got home and forgot about it. Two weeks later she received a phone call from the Police. "We have your purse madam. When would you like to come and collect it?"

"Oh! Thank you. Would tomorrow be convenient?"

"Yes Madam. And do you wish to witness the execution?"

It turned out a 15 year old boy had pinched her purse and was to be executed for the crime. With the Olympics coming up the government were particularly determined that China would be safe for tourists. The Americans, who had a son of similar age, asked the American Embassy to plead for mercy, but they were told it wasn't possible to intervene in the justice system of a host country. The family just couldn't cope with the situation and asked to be repatriated. There were many reasons why we were happy to leave China. Apart from the major problems, they couldn't understand why anyone would want to go to sea for fun!

In the rising sun, my walk around the deck revealed a couple of flying fish which had, like

Icarus, flown too high and expired in the dawn. I fried them for breakfast – tasty, but boney.

At 8 a.m. Peter sighted land – the white cliffs of Turkey at 36.19'N, 33. 52'E. Tasucu (Tashucoo) Harbour gradually became obvious - crowded ferries were leaving for Northern Cyprus. We anchored surrounded by a green park with bright flowers and birds singing in the trees. Hurriedly the Avon dinghy was pumped up and, wearing clothes which covered our elbows and knees, so as not to offend local Muslims, we rowed ashore to be met on the beach by a young Turk dressed in a white short sleeved shirt and cotton sarong.

"My name Duran", he said. "Like British Pop Group Duran Duran. I show you round. I show you where to go."

"Okay. First to a bank, we need money to book in." In the bank Peter asked for a hundred million Turkish lira (L100,000,000). We grinned at the thought, that at last, we were millionaires. We found the huge numbers difficult to deal with and were pleasantly surprised when shopkeepers handed back the odd hundred thousand we overpaid. The Turks seemed very honest.

Bumptious Duran had given the impression that he knew exactly where to take us, but he didn't. He took us to seven offices altogether – some of them twice. The Port Captain took almost half our money but did supply the necessary transit log for the Turkish coast. Then Duran led us into the gated Port itself for the Customs Office. While we queued for attention we noticed our confident guide, who had been standing waiting for us, being led away by a policeman. Evidently he was a well known cigarette smuggler. However Duran was nonchalantly waiting for us outside the Dock Gates and happily joined us for a beer in the park alongside the anchorage.

An untidy nest on top of an old factory chimney with a stork in it caught our attention.

Our hundred million lira was sadly diminished and after some food shopping left us with only the equivalent of £9.72 from the £100. Back to the bank.

An untidy nest on top of an old factory chimney with a stork in it caught our attention. It looked just like the beginning of the film Dumbo. Although I had seen pictures of this Central European phenomenon, I'd never actually witnessed a stork on its nest before.

Keeping in touch with our family has been a major problem when voyaging, international telephone calls used to need the correct coins and was often difficult, but now thanks to modern technology, we were able to find an internet café and let them know we had arrived safely.

Peter winched up the anchor and we headed west for four miles to Limon Kalesi where a lone sandstone Crusader Castle stands on the headland. Nobody else disturbed the calm while we rested and swam. As the water darkened the silver moon rose over the mountains

The morning sun blazed down from a cloudless sky and glittered on the dancing water. The blue shallow sea was streaked with bars of vivid emerald, clear cerulean and a soft milky jade. The pungent smell of herbs heated by the sun wafted across the water, but no birds sang.

Peter winched up the anchor and we headed west for four miles to Limon Kalesi where a lone sandstone Crusader Castle stands on the headland. CLYPEUS from the castle.

Rowing ashore over water so crystal clear every rock, pebble and shell on the sea floor was clearly visible. We climbed over piles of yellow stone and some of the ramparts and towers are still standing strong after a thousand years, we wondered who built them? It's all very well to say "the Crusaders of course". But they were noblemen and soldiers not building workers. Who was the architect? There must have been an army who quarried the stone, found the water supply, chiselled the building stones, dug foundations and built the walls. Another army had to feed, water and keep the army of builders going and supply the Crusaders with

their wine and food. Where did these people come from? The castles are not near villages or fields of corn, vegetables or cattle?

I scrambled over walls and yellow rocks, climbing, climbing, to see as far as I could while Peter stayed below studying the layout and probability of an accident.

"Be careful," he called. At the top I surveyed the coastline and could see our little boat as though she was dreaming, floating still and safe on a blue glass plate, her shadow clearly outlined on the sand beneath her. No other boats, no people, I couldn't see a village or house.

A displaced slab of stone in the flooring looked odd. It had been pulled across a two by three foot dark hole beneath. I called to Peter

"Tread carefully. This floor is hollow. Come and see."

He warily, slowly approached up the slope. "You're so reckless," he again admonished me as he peered down. I dropped a stone down the hole and counted one, two, three, then splash.

"Wow, that's deep," he said and knelt down to peer into the black seemingly limitless space. "Hello," he called, "Hello, hello, hello," the echoes reverberated back from a vast cavern. "It must be a huge underground water cistern, not just a well. How did they dig so deep and wide with just shovels?" These Crusaders must have had faith just to establish themselves. The power of religion is incredible.

In the evening a couple wearing traditional baggy pantaloons (shalvars) sat on the rocks to fish for their supper. We waved and they waved back. Nobody else disturbed the peace, not even an aeroplane or sign of a vapour trail. We spent the evening trying to learn some more useful Turkish words:

Please – lutfen,
Thank you – tesek kirederim,
Hello – merhaba,
Stay happy – Hosca kalin.
Yes – evel, No - hayir,
How much? – Kaz para?,
Good – iyi, Bad – fenah, Beautiful – guzel.
Good morning – ginaydin,
Good afternoon – tunaydin,
My name is – Ismin Shirley,
What's your name? – isminiz ne?
Cheers! – sherefar!

A thin trickle of water was still coming into the boat from somewhere and during the night the automatic lower bilge pump still kept starting every four to five hours and running for 10-14 seconds until it eventually seized up. We sailed back to Tasucu in a misty, calm, early morning where Peter took the pump apart and freed the impeller. We still couldn't find the leak. Lifting a 35' eleven ton yacht out of the water and putting it back usually costs about £200, - if there is lifting equipment available. There wasn't in Tasucu.

Unfortunately our engine and accessories are beneath the main cabin floor, so we lose the use of the whole saloon area every time he works in the bilges. I have to climb over the seats, hanging on to the grab handles on the ceiling, to traverse the cabin, or get to the cooker, or wash up, or find a book, or a hair brush. The language on both sides gets heated. If I could fly over him, I would! We get on very well really although opposites. As soon as we arrive somewhere I like to get ashore, he prefers to stay on board and read. If I supply the ideas and momentum, he will back me up sensibly and cautiously.

He will seldom argue, just quietly not do anything he doesn't want to do. He says "there is no need to argue – the subject is either fact or fiction. If it is fact we can look up the answer. If it is fiction then we are only talking about different opinions! Everybody is entitled to their own opinions".

We have had plenty of time on night watches when crossing the Oceans just to sit and think about our compatibility; basically he is cautious and introvert and I'm much less cautious and extrovert, but have the ideas and get things going. However we do make a team. It is wonderful how nature has given us such different gifts. Our other male/female difference is that I fret and worry about our family and grandchildren - he doesn't.

We discovered we could travel by coach from Tasucu to Goreme for a four day trip to see the fairy towers of Kappadokia. Outside the bus station, sitting at a table, a Turkish man, with no English sold us tickets to Goreme. When we turned up at 7 p.m. with our bags to catch it, we found we had actually been booked on the next morning coach at 7 a.m. also there was some confusion about changing buses after Konya.

The morning drive was fascinating and we were pleased we got it wrong first time. It would have been criminal to have travelled in the dark. The air-conditioned Mercedes coach was luxurious. A young steward in black trousers, white shirt and black bow tie, poured cologne onto our hands and offered warm, white towels to wipe them. Coffee and biscuits were served. The cost for the journey of eleven hours, 300 miles each way, was about £10 each.

We journeyed through coastal orange groves, then north over the snow-capped Taurus mountains and across the steppes of Central Turkey where combines harvested the endless expanse of waving corn and wheat. We passed factories

The Flintstones' Cave Pansion, offered a room, with toilet and shower, carved out of the rock but with glass doors opening onto a balcony overlooking a swimming pool for the same price.

painted in rainbow colours which blended pleasantly into the countryside.

Suddenly, on a deserted strip of road making a 'Y' junction, the driver indicated we leave the coach, cross over the road and wait for the bus from Ankara to Goreme. We stood in the bright sunshine wondering what on earth we would do if the bus didn't come? Nobody else was around, no houses, few cars. However another coach arrived within twenty minutes and we carried on, now travelling South East.

On the bus, two charming young girls, 19 and 13, came and chatted. The nineteen year old was at Ankara University studying English and hoping to be employed in the Tourist Industry and travel the world. The younger girl had her little clipped, blonde, French poodle with her. They were going to surprise their grandparents and perhaps stay a week

At dusk we alighted in the car park between the extraordinary fairy chimneys and rock cone homes of Goreme. It's a magical place set amid towering tuff cones and honeycombed cliffs, surrounded by vineyards. Pantalooned families still live in the fantastic wind-eroded limestone cones. They have glass windows, wooden doors, and some have TV aerials and satellite dishes attached. Fords and Mitsubishis are parked outside.

The Tourist Office pointed us towards La Rosa, a recommended back- packers hostel, which had an excellent swimming pool, for $12 each a night. Young international tourists lounged on cushions and couches on the verandah dining room. As we hadn't booked ahead we were given a, not very satisfactory, back bedroom, but enjoyed an evening swim and the meal. Next morning at 6 a.m. I went off clutching our Lonely Planet Book to try and find a better bedroom, hopefully with an en suite. The Flintstones' Cave Pansion, offered a room, with

toilet and shower, carved out of the rock but with glass doors opening onto a balcony overlooking a swimming pool for the same price. Excellent! Other dormitories and bedrooms are carved out of solid rock.

The amazing open air World Heritage Museum of the, 'occupied until recent times', cut-out-of-the-rocks village and the Byzantine Monastery were within walking distance. Exciting hours were spent walking the paths, climbing stairways or passing through tunnels to reach the various monastery

churches with their wonderful, primitive 11th and 12th century frescoes. Sitting on the stone benches where the monks must have eaten made our imaginations soar. The utter improbability of the landscape flooded over us: the lovely, soft textures in the rock, the fairytale cave dwellings, the sparse vegetation growing vigorously from the stark but mineral-rich soil.

Goreme village itself is stunning. The restaurants in the main square are overlooked by the Roma-Kalesi, a tall volcanic column with the remains of a rock-cut Roman temple façade.

329 steps led down to Iilhara Gorge which was only opened up to visitors in 1980.

**Right:
At Kaymakli Underground city and followed our guide down narrow steps and passages into rooms carved into the solid rock four floors down.**

329 steps led down to Ilhara Gorge which has cave monasteries and churches, with well-preserved frescoes, alongside a tree-lined river. This Gorge was only opened up to visitors in 1980.

After a lunch of fresh trout from the river, we were taken to Kaymakli underground city and followed our guide down narrow steps and passages into rooms carved into the solid rock four floors down. I was afraid it was going to be claustrophobic and stuffy, but a fresh breeze wafted through and the temperature and ambience were pleasant.

Kaymakli is one of 35 troglodyte cities in this region, some inhabited as early as the 7th century BC. Derinkuyu is actually eight floors deep, the rooms fan out on alternate sides of a central staircase. Most were dug by early Christians to save their families and stock from the marauding hordes. They could live for up to six months underground hiding from Atilla the Hun, Alexander the Great, Genghis Khan, and Syrian, Greek, Arab and Roman armies. In Kaymakli twenty-six ventilation shafts reach down from the surface down, down, to an underground river. Drinking water was hauled from upstream shafts, effluent and waste was thrown in downstream. Cattle and fowl were kept

The tops of the columns are intact, but the bottoms are missing. Our meal was colourful and delicious, the tomatoes were carved like roses.

We took a mini-bus (dolmus) tour to more amazing rock formations where Star Wars opening scenes were filmed. I was enjoying the fantastic scenery but Peter has different interests. As we stood at the roadside he heard a familiar motorbike engine and went to investigate. He found a young English couple who had bought a new Royal Enfield motorcycle in India for $350 U.S. and were riding it home to England. They had already done 10,000 miles which they said was, hopefully, the worst bit!

in the first level and huge round stone discs are still ready to roll across entrances to stop invaders entering.

On the Old Silk Road Agzi Kara Han Caravanserai was built in 1231-1239 AD. A fortified, vaulted, resting stop for camel trains carrying the expensive cargoes of silks, gold, wines and spices to and from China, Europe and the Middle East. A small mosque dominated the central courtyard.

At Cavusin we were taken to a pottery where local red clay is used. Apple tea was distributed and drunk while watching volunteer, Carol, sit and pedal the wheel to turn a clay dish – amusingly it finished up with a big hole in its base. Evidently this town was still ruled by a 'Mukta' who looks after his people and collects his own taxes. The Authorities in Ankara let him get on with it rather than cause trouble.

In downtown Goreme there were few cars, horses drank at the village horse trough and elegant carts were parked outside houses. Ladies were dyeing and weaving wool into carpets in the back streets. An elderly lady, wearing pantaloons and a scarf around her head, cooked sweet corn mash in a large metal pan over a wooden fire outside her house. She wouldn't let me take a photo of her, but was OK about photographing the mash. Cheese and tomato-topped pitas were the lunch-time fast food snack.

On the way back to the boat the coach drove through Tarsus, of St Paul and Biblical fame, where Cleopatra met Mark Anthony – I'm not sure what I expected to see, but it wasn't the dirty, smoggy, industrial city we passed through where the superb Turkish cotton towelling is made. The rest of the drive was through sweet smelling, colourful orange groves along the coastal plain which brought us back to CLYPEUS serenely waiting as we had left her, the lower bilge pumps still working, every 15 minute or so.

That had been a tour to remember for the rest of our lives.

Top:
Huge round stone discs are still ready to roll across entrances to stop invaders entering.

Middle:
Ladies were dyeing and weaving wool into carpets in the back streets.

Bottom:
Kaymakli market.

CHAPTER FOUR | COAST HOPPING

Turkey 2001 Tasucu - Silifke - Ovacic - Bozyazi - Anamurium - Alanya - Kemer

TIED TO THE JETTY in Tacasu Harbour was a gulet, the first we had seen, a traditional wooden fishing boat, which was waiting for passengers to take them around the coast for a week or fortnight's holiday. The gulets are usually between 50' and 120' long with a high stern which gives them a slightly piratical air. They are rigged for sailing but we seldom saw any doing so.

The traditional craft have been widened to accommodate double cabins and en suites, a large deck space for dining, sun bathing and sleeping when it is too hot below, usually immaculately kept by their Turkish crew of three or four. However the gulet in Tasacu was owned and skippered by an ex RAF pilot who came and chatted, happily telling us that being based further east of the main tourist resorts his passengers enjoyed quieter remote anchorages and ancient harbours and ruins.

The gulets are usually between 50' and 120' long with a high stern which gives them a slightly piratical air.

Photo courtesy:
www.mizana.com

The next city we visited by local bus from Tacusu was Silifke, ancient Seleucia founded by Seleucus I Nicator in the 3rd century BC. He was one of Alexander the Great's most able generals. It is also the first landing place of St Paul on his first journey in 47-49 AD.

At a junction we were carefully handed over from the minibus to the coach driver of a new Mercedes air-conditioned coach to our reserved seats. The steward squirted our hands with cologne and distributed iced water. At 10.30 we were offered hot tea or coffee and salt cracker biscuits, all within the ticket price. We kept putting our hands in our pockets to pay but "No, No, hayir" and a huge grin.

Emperor Barbarossa (1125-90) drowned in the river here in Silifke while leading his troops on the Third Crusade. The striking castle on the hillside dominates the working, country town. The ruins of a Temple of Jupiter, which dates from the 2nd or 3rd Century AD is up by the fort. We began to learn that Turkey has so many fascinating ancient ruins there is never enough time to look at, or describe them. However the ghost story of Silifke Bridge is worth telling because once a year the citizens still throw the lungs of slaughtered animals (goats or camels) from the top of the stone bridge over the Goksu River. The ceremony is in remembrance of a bride who was buried alive in the masonry of the main pillar to appease the Gods who kept washing away the bridge foundations. Once a year the terrified scream of a woman is said to be heard in Silifke, which reminds the townspeople to keep sacrificing.

Next day, back on board CLYPEUS we headed for Ovacik in sunshine, but no wind, so the motor muttered away beneath our feet. Two dolphins passed by but didn't stop to play. Ovacik's pleasant bay had good fresh-water showers on the beach. It is a village of smart holiday homes but a couple of houses were burnt out. What had happened? – Gas explosions or ethnic problems? When shopping for tomatoes and grapes the shop owner actually gave me aubergines – I think they were getting a bit old, but it was a kind gesture.

At Sogusku Liman, after putting out two anchors and a line ashore, swimming in the warm sea was different with cool bubbles of fresh water swirling up from springs in the sea bed. It was like swimming in a gin and tonic. Underground fresh water streams run down from the cliffs to bubble up further from the shore. Some young boys climbing over the ancient ruins near the beach gave me a sea urchin shell. They seemed polite, curious and friendly. Their mothers would have been proud of them.

Bozyazi Liman was intriguing. Mooring up alongside in a huge empty harbour a pleasant policeman took our lines and inspected our cruising permit. We learned that Bozyazi is intended to be a new ferry port for Kyrenia in Northern Cyprus. On the far side two tugs were alongside and a vast expanse of thick, grey, neoprene rubber on the quayside was laid out with generators and pumps thumping away. What could it be? Talking to the English Skipper of one of the Norwegian tugs, it transpired they were filling large neoprene sausages with 30,000 tons of the abundant fresh water where it bubbles up in the sea, and towing it across to arid Northern Cyprus. As fresh water is less dense than sea water, it floats. It is a clever idea, but there were problems. Chris, the skipper, told us that towing was easy, but manoeuvring to the offshore loading buoys was difficult. It took fifteen hours to load and sixteen hours to cross to Cyprus at four mph, then twenty-four hours to unload. The unlit, huge black sausage, which floated with only 12" showing above water, was towed a mile behind the tug – a substantial hazard to shipping and yachts. Also the neoprene kept splitting and spilling all the precious cargo into the sea. Chris, was a British small boat sailor and pleased to come on board for a drink and talk

On the far side two tugs were alongside and a vast expanse of thick, grey, aneoprene rubber on the quayside was laid out with generators and pumps thumping away.

about yachts and amusing sailing experiences. After a cold Efes Pilsner in the Balloon Saloon at the end of the quay (they had used old bits of neoprene for tablecloths, the roof; anything and everything), he took us to his hotel for an alfresco dinner beside a romantically lit swimming pool.

The Balloon Saloon arranged a taxi to take us to spectacular Anamur Kalesi, guarding Anemurium ruined city. Evidently the English Naval Officer, Captain Beaufort, (of Beaufort Wind Scale) re-discovered the ruin and made it known. Since 1960 the Universities of Toronto and Columbia in Canada have been and are still excavating there. A lamp and pottery factory had flourished and 700 oil-lamps depicting a human face were found in one dig.

The city flourished in the 4th century B.C. under the Romans when they built. a theatre, odeon, three public baths, a water canal and a systematically organized necropolis, the ruins of which can all still be seen. A great number of coins were minted and in the 4th century it became a Christian city with its own bishopric until an earthquake in 580 AD destroyed much of it. Persian and Arab raids in the 6th and 7th centuries and then the invasion of the Seljuks completed the destruction. As there were no settlements within the city walls and no local villages, the building remains have stayed where they fell. The palaestra sports ground's whole floor 100m by 1,000m was covered with mosaics arranged in a geometrical design. The nearby public baths had hot water and central heating!

"Let's go to the excavated necropolis ruins." We wandered across, the taxi driver and son having disappeared, we were totally alone in the ancient site. Each tomb had an individual family garden courtyard where the living gave banquets for the dead, showing an amazing similarity to the customs that the Chinese followed in Taiwan where the old ways have been kept safe from Communism. In Taiwan on Grave Digging Day in April, a national holiday, families take out the ancestor's bones, clean them, put them back and lay out a meal on the little stone circular tables and stools for the ancestors to come and celebrate.

So much of Anamurium is still under two feet of earth and sand. The large site was overwhelming, it covers a whole hillside and valley. I had quick swim in bra and pants on the pebbly beach to cool my brain. (There were no other visitors.)

Next day as we waited for a bus into town, a family of about ten adults and children were picnicking on the grass verge beside their dolmus. They invited us to join them and generously insisted we shared their bread with butter, cheese and tomatoes. They were Muslims on their way to a family wedding in Silifke. They couldn't have been more friendly towards us. We enjoyed the Turkish people.

It was a full day's sail to Gazipasa the next good harbour so we let go the lines in a dark ominous dawn and headed for Cape Anamure but the sun, sea and wind picked up and CLYPEUS sailed in sparkling sunlight. We whizzed along the mountainous coast where bananas grow in tiny plots terraced into the cliff and every flat piece of land, with reasonable access, has plastic greenhouses built on it, glinting in the sunshine. Pink oleanders lined the river gulleys looking like little pink ribbons hanging down to the sea. Dramatic ruins topped the summits of three slender rock monoliths which rise out of the sea. 'Antiocelus'? There must have been defendable causeways or bridges once, but we couldn't see them. I would love to know more about this incredible ancient site but couldn't find anything on Google. No roads or village appeared on the cliff top.

Our anchorage in Gazipasa that night was in complete contrast to the other lonely anchorages we had been experiencing. It was a sophisticated holiday village with three swimming pools, but a wedding reception was being held in the restaurant so we couldn't have our dinner there. We wandered along the deserted road and found a Sports Club with many tennis courts. Nobody spoke English but they led us into the kitchen to choose from the pots of stews bubbling on the stove. We tried Raki for the first time – it's strong and clouds the half glass of water like Pernod (or Dettol!). We chose yufta, a big thin pancake filled with fried chopped onion and peppers which had been soaked in Soy sauce, then placed on the pancake with mixed Yoghurt and mint, folded into a parcel and fried on both sides. Good!

A brisk breeze bustled down the valley and over the harbour. We thought we would have a good sail, but once out on the blue, blue sea there was no wind, the jib leaned against the forestay like a dissolute rake, and we motored on again to Alanya, a thriving tourist city settled beneath an imposing castle high on the cliff which used to be called Coracesium (the Crows Nest) when the town was a pirate stronghold. The pirates preyed on shipping going to and from the Levant. Pompeii cleaned up this coast in 67BC during his campaign against piracy when he destroyed the combined pirate fleet here. (Kathleen McCulloch's *'Caesar's Women'* tells the story). We realized once again that pirates have been around for as long as vessels have put to sea. During our voyage we have been robbed three times and taken from our boat at gunpoint, so we have a healthy fear of 'pirates'.

The anchor rumbled out in the middle of the new harbour near the Red Tower (Kizil Kule) and the five stone vaulted galleries which open directly

Spectacular Anamur Kalesi, guarding Anemurium ruined city.

into the sea. They were built by the Romans to restore and repair their galleys and triremes (galleys with three banks of oars), within their shelter. The old Harbour was full of tourist boats, many of which were making their way out for a romantic evening of dinner and dancing on the calm dark blue sea.

Friends in Cyprus had given us a little wrapped present with 'not to be opened until Alanya' printed on it. Having a pre-dinner drink in the cockpit, with excitement we opened the wrapping to find a pair of ear plugs! We used them continuously, as when darkness descended, the fairground filling the wide promenade, burst into lights and loud sound. Pop music blared out as we went ashore to eat in one of the many tourist restaurants, watching harnessed children in a steel frame, bouncing up into the air like fleas, twenty times their own height.

Aladdin (Sultan Alaeddin Keytubud) took the town in 1221 renaming it after himself and building the naval dockyard and defences. Up on the promontory surrounding the castle an old village clings to the hillside. In the fortress is a cliff ledge called 'The Man Drop' where condemned criminals were pushed to plunge to their death on the rocks below. Sandy beaches flank either side of the promontory.

So much of Anamurium is still under two feet of earth and sand. The large site was overwhelming, it covers a whole hillside and valley.

The tourists seemed to be mainly German or Scandinavian.

The leak, which we still could not find on CLYPEUS was now being pumped every 10-12 minutes. Peter said he wasn't worried. (I was).

In bed, when all was quiet I said "Have you heard the bilge pump come on lately? It seems to have stopped."

"I'd better have a look straight away."

Peter got up, turned on the lights, lifted the saloon floor and said "Oh No! The small, lower, bilge pump must have failed."

After our wrecking on a South Pacific Reef in 1987 he had installed two pumps, one above the other, the lower one to be triggered as soon as a small amount of water was in the boat, and a larger capacity one above it to deal with real emergencies. Our near death wrecking had occurred when we were sailing between the Solomon Islands and New Caledonia and wanted to visit unspoiled, uninhabited, Chesterfield Reef where we could land and watch turtles come ashore to lay their eggs. The sea had been calm as we tried to solve the problem of how to enter Chesterfield Lagoon in daylight through the South West pass. Our chart had no details of a pass from the east; as it had never been surveyed, the area had just been left blank – a 'here be dragons area'. We decided caution was needed and hove-to to the north of the reef to wait and calculate. Our charts were very old as this area was last surveyed in the 1870s. Being of no strategic, commercial or military use, nobody had bothered to survey or print charts of the area in the 20th Century. The most up-to-date British Admiralty Pilot we had been able to buy was 1969. Now, of course, Google Earth could show you exactly where to go.

The Lagoon entrance was 40 miles south. It

would take at least eight hours, and when we got to the entrance needed another three of four hours of daylight to thread our way through the coral to the Anchorage Islands where whalers from New Zealand used to stop and rest. We couldn't do it all in daylight. Hopefully our Aussie friends would be there.

At 01.30 on a calm and balmy night with a full moon it was time to set sail again and carefully make our way down the reef keeping five miles off and be at the entrance at 10 a.m.. Peter was on watch trailing the fishing line. At 03.15 I suddenly woke up to the scream of the fishing reel running out, a shout from Peter, a twang, a bang and a crunch. Jumping out of my bunk I rushed up into the cockpit. White faced Peter was clenching the wheel. "Look behind," he whispered.

I looked behind and saw two slim coral towers almost meeting at their base.

"We went between those coral heads", he croaked.

"We did what? How on earth did we get through?"

"I don't know, but there wasn't time to take the sails down or even unrig the self-steering. We just ploughed straight between them. I thought there was a fish on the line but the hook must have snagged on coral. The line broke and when I looked up, there they were, dead ahead."Once through, which accounted for the bang and crunch, he had automatically turned right, away from the reef. He handed over the wheel to take the mainsail down. My teeth chattered as we slowly left the reef behind keeping a good lookout for any more uncharted coral. He took the wheel again and I put my arms around his shaking shoulders. "Well luckily we seem to be OK. I'll go and make us a hot drink and write our position and what happened in the log." As I stepped down into the cabin and turned on the light, I saw a cascade of white water tumbling down from the forward cabin. It bubbled over the cabin sill, ran along the floor and disappeared into the bilges.

"Peter, Peter" I shouted. "Come quickly. We're holed."

"Hang on while I set the self steering away from the reef."

I ran forward to try and see where the water was coming in.

"Oh my God! I didn't think we could possibly have got away with it." He groaned as he saw the water bubbling up under the bunk. "Quick start the engine, we must make sure the pumps work and the starter motor doesn't go under water." Immediately he pulled up the floorboards. The little 'Taiwan takeaway' automatic electric pump was doing its best, but it wasn't enough.

"Bucket" he shouted, "and start pumping in the cockpit."

In the cockpit I bent to the pump, the sea was calm beneath the unperturbed silver moon. Forward and back, forward and back I pumped as hard as I could. The noise of water tumbling into the cabin kept on. Peter was sloshing buckets of water out through the door where the cockpit drains funnelled it back into the sea.

He came up. "OK. I'll take over here. You go and pump the toilet bilge pump. I've changed the valves over. We're not keeping up with the inflow yet. The water's still rising."Pump, pump, forward and back, as I pumped sitting on the closed toilet seat I watched the water gurgling past in the passage-way and realised we were not succeeding. Nobody was mending the hole, nobody was steering or looking out, nobody was navigating. What the hell were we going to do?

A shout, "I think we're holding it. See if you can find the hole."

The main hole was obviously somewhere under the starboard 'V' berth which was piled high with books, sails, vegetables, letters, files, oilskins. Frantically I threw them all back onto our bed, pulled off the squab, lifted the lid and then started pulling everything out of the bin beneath: spare oilskins, blankets, sail material, sewing things, knitting gear, jars of shells, spare depth sounder, spare VHF.

Now I could see it. There it was. Not so big, only as big as a fist but with a star of cracks around it, through which the sea spurted each time the bow dipped.

"Found it. It isn't that big."

"OK. You take over here and pump and I'll come and look." We changed places.

"God I hope that Taiwanese electric pump doesn't give up, we've had it if it does," Peter muttered as he passed me. "I'll pump down here in the bathroom while I think what to do." As I stayed pumping in the cockpit he jammed rags into the hole but the outside pressure pushed them back. Then he lifted out the triple sealed the plastic bag of cement, and gallon can of Sika quick-setting-fluid. "Where are the rubber gloves? I'm going to try and fill the hole. Keep pumping."

The main hole was obviously somewhere under the starboard 'V' berth which was piled high with books, sails, vegetables, letters, files, and oilskins.

Ten minutes later he came back, "It's not working. The glove fingers split every time I put them on. I've slopped Sika everywhere and it seems very corrosive. Each time I mix a little in my hand and hold it over the hole the sea spurts through. What does stick on is OK and sets well. Let's inflate the Avon and try from the outside."

He took over to give my arms a rest while I undid the front half-inflated Avon and foot-pumped-up the back half. He launched it and disappeared over the side while I continued to pump.

Suddenly we were in rough water. The dinghy was alternately above or below CLYPEUS's deck, with a rise and fall of about six feet. I was so frightened and couldn't stop my chattering teeth. I didn't like him being out there, in the dark, on the ocean, without me. Why was it suddenly so rough? The minutes dragged on as I kept pumping: two thousand, eight hundred and one, eight hundred and two, eight hundred and three. Oh my back!

A hand and yellow cuff appeared over the rail. "It's no good I can't keep my hand with the cement in it over the hole because the dinghy and boat are going up and down against each other too far. Why is it so rough now? Help me aboard."

I helped him aboard and carried on pumping.

"OK. Where are the rags? I'm going to fill the hole with rags and put a board against it. I'll chisel the rags into the cracks. Seen anything?"

"Nothing, but my back is breaking and my arms aren't as strong now. The rags are under the bathroom basin,"

"OK. give me a turn pumping."

"No. You go and fill the hole or our situation won't get any better."

"I'm so sorry, sorry"

"Sorry, sorry too. Go on. Mend the hole and pray the electric pump keeps going." I listened to him banging away; find a piece of plywood; plug some fabric into the cracks with chisel and hammer. As I pumped I kept looking out but there was nothing to see except the moon shining on the water which was calm again.

Peter came up. "There must be other holes somewhere but I've stopped the main flow. OK. I'll take over. You make us a 'cup-a-soup'."

Back down in the cabin the throb of the engine and warm glow from the gas ring comforted me. Water still trickled down from under both forward bunks but we could cope with it.

"I'll drink mine first, and then I'll pump while you drink yours." I called to him.

"Thank goodness for that electric pump. It's done a wonderful job. Oh! my arms, will they ever recover?" He gasped.

"Here have your soup while I pump."

"Dawn's coming." He sat back and relaxed. I'll fix a larger outlet pipe that will get rid of the water quicker. We'll try and sail and keep the hole on the starboard side of the hull above the water. You know," he said conversationally, "if we were sinking, we'd never have gone down for the EPRIB (Emergency radio beacon). It's in the wrong place on the ceiling amidships isn't it?"

"I hadn't even thought about it. Just hoped, and knew you would think of something in time. I'm surprised we didn't even think of abandoning ship." I said. "Keeping the boat afloat took all our energies and thoughts didn't it?"

"Well, we still aren't OK if the pump stops. There should be a fix coming up soon. I'll go and find out our position and we'll decide on a course."

The sun rose. The water was calm. I looked over the side.

Oh my God! There it was! The bottom,

crowded with coral bommies only a few feet beneath us. I screeched in shock

"Peter. Come quickly. Come and look. We must be inside the lagoon."

"How can we be? How do you know?"

"Look over the side."

"Crumbs! Undo the self steering. Take the wheel. Look ahead. We've got to get CLYPEUS heeling to port and we've got to set a course to the islands so that we can beach her."

"No we can't. Somebody's got to keep pumping."

"You're right. OK, I'll reset the self steering and we will just have to hope no coral heads get in the way. I've no idea where we are, or what course to steer. Keep pumping and I'll be as quick as I can."

As I continued pushing the handle back and fore with a quick peep over the side every now and then, it seemed impossible that CLYPEUS could find her way through the coral heads, and I just waited for the scrape and bang. It never came. (Sometimes it seems quite obvious that our boat cares about survival just as much as we do, and is part of our team.)

Peter came up smiling grimly. "The uninhabited Anchorage Islands are to the south and the wind is from the same direction so we won't get any help in keeping the hole out of the water." That rough water must have been the tide rushing into the lagoon entrance. He hoisted the mainsail and we kept pumping alternately. Every time the bow dipped so the inflow of water increased. We still couldn't relax.

He found and fixed a fatter piece of tubing which emptied the bilge water directly over the side. At noon, by careful monitoring, we found that we could now stop pumping. Peter took the wheel. "Bring up the binoculars, it looks like low islands ahead. See if you can see a likely place to beach CLYPEUS."

I peered ahead. "I can see the islands and I can see six masts as well."

"What?"

"Six masts, they're here. NUAGES and TATTLER must be here."

"Give me the binoculars." He scanned the horizon. "I wonder if anyone has their VHF on? Go and call them."

I rushed below. "This is CLYPEUS, CLYPEUS, we have had some trouble and need to beach her. Is anybody there who can suggest a good place?"

"CLYPEUS CLYPEUS this is TARA II. G'day. Sorry about the trouble mate. Yes, we can find somewhere for you. Most of us have our dinghies in the water and handhelds, we'll scout around."

Peter came down and took over. "Great to hear you TARA II. We're holed just below the waterline on the starboard bow and have been pumping for eight hours. We would like a sandy beach where I can make repairs. We draw 5' 9". When is high tide?"

"High tide's now, at noon. No worries. I can see you. Keep heading towards us all and keep your VHF on. Cheers.

"Cheers. CLYPEUS standing by."

We went up into the cockpit and holding hands watched the red Zodiac and grey Avon inflatables zoom off to find our resting place. We were going to survive.

"CLYPEUS CLYPEUS" the VHF crackled

"Yes, TARA II"

"Head south east. I'll come and lead you in."

A few minutes later we greeted Jeff in his dinghy and slowly followed him between coral heads to a sandy beach on a scrub-covered sand bank. Willing hands took our anchor chain and pulled us into shallow water until our keel rested on the sand.

"I've got some polypropylene sugar sacks on board, shouted South African Jack as he zoomed off in his dinghy.

Sugar sacks? sugar sacks? what did he mean?

Our friends waded out, we bent to hold their hands and make contact and quickly tell what had happened. No time for stories now, somehow we must hold CLYPEUS upright so that she didn't fall over when the tide went out.

Jack returned. "OK. you guys come and help me fill these sacks with sand and we will make a wall under the hull so that she can lean on them."

They set to, filled the sacks with the soft white sand and as soon as CLYPEUS decided which way she would lean, banked them beneath her. She safely settled.

We climbed down, hugged and kissed our dear Australian friends and all crowded round to examine the hole. How insignificant it looked from the outside. How had so much water come in?

Peter set to work knocking out the loose concrete, he wanted to fill the hole and have it set before the tide came back in. As he worked waist deep, I emptied all the wet things onto the deck to dry in the sunshine. It was a perfect day in the fantastic blues of the lagoon

Willing hands took our anchor chain and pulled us into shallow water until our keel rested on the sand.

He managed to cement in the damaged area before dark when our friends called us to a barbecue on the beach. As dusk fell they plied us with consolation, food and drink. We sat around the glowing fire enjoying their companionship and hearing their stories while trying to stop little sand crabs committing suicide. The transparent crabs were fascinated by the flames and, unheeding of the heat, dashed into it to instant combustion. Pete of TATTLER, in true Australian humour, christened our sand cay: "Pyre Island".

Pam and John offered us a horizontal bed on NUAGE but we preferred to sleep together on dear CLYPEUS at an angle of 45°, just in case something went wrong as the tide came in.

All was well. Peter was waist deep at dawn putting an epoxy resin and a fibreglass patch over the new cement before the water rose again.

At noon when we refloated, they towed CLYPEUS to an anchorage alongside TARA II. The engine wouldn't start because water had entered the starter motor. Peter immediately dismantled it and dried it out.

Pam and John's offer of a peaceful night on dry, clean, sweet-smelling Nuage enabled us to have an untroubled sleep before leaving for Australia the next day. Fitting a new large bilge pump above the small one was top of Peter's 'To do' list when we got back to port.

While I was remembering that crisis, Peter raised the saloon floor and now the big upper bilge pump started. There was a substantial amount of water in our home.

"We must get going first thing and get to where we can be hauled out. Kemer Marina has lifting gear. He went to the chart table and measured with the dividers.

"It's 68 miles to the other side of Antalya Bay to Kemer." Neither of us slept.

At 6.30 next morning we set off, hand pumping to assist the large pump – I wrote in the Log '25 strokes every 15 minutes', - will we make it? What if the leak suddenly becomes more serious, will CLYPEUS sink in the middle of this seventy mile wide bay? Who would rescue us? The wind would probably blow our lifeboat to the shore, but, if the wind went further round to the North, it could miss. Where was the next land on the other side of the Med? Israel? Africa?

We scooted west across Antalya Bay, the self steering coping well. The floor was up while Peter examined the bilges. The sun was shining into the cabin through the open door. From the cockpit I could suddenly see where the water was coming in.

"I can see it! I can see where the water is coming in. Come up here, by the door and you will see the shining, silvery sheen slipping down the inner hull directly from the transducer seal."

Peter put his head close to mine. "Yes. OK. I can see it. It must be the block of wood I used as packing behind the new transducer in Cyprus. The wood must have swollen when we put her in the water and stretched the stem until it broke. Water must be seeping between the wood and the hull.

It was boisterous sailing all day until we were in the lee of the misty mountains ahead. As we entered the bay alongside Kemer Marina, hoping to save a night's marina fees, the heat hits us and, as Peter dropped the anchor, I tried to motor astern to make sure it had caught, there was a peculiar noise and nothing happened.

"She won't go astern," I shouted.

He rushed aft, and looked over the stern. "The propeller is still there. Thank God."

Launching the dinghy he found that the propeller shaft was loose. Back on board, under the floor he saw that the nuts had dropped off the coupling holding bolts and when we went astern the prop shaft had moved sternwards pulling the two halves of the coupling apart. With his ever-present magnet tied on a string, he retrieved the slimy nuts from the oily black bilge water and re-bolted the coupling. That magnet has been one his best 'essentials' – screws and nuts would leap eagerly towards it and land with a satisfying click. He also used in it chandleries or ironmongers when buying stainless steel screws and nails. If they attached themselves to the magnet, he knew they were not actually stainless.

While we were having our crisis on board, the Club Med ashore were beating drums to call their holiday guests to come and enjoy a feast and cabaret. They didn't sound like Tahitian rhythms which I had enjoyed so much, perhaps Whirling Dervishes or Belly Dancers?

As dusk fell a heavy swell began to roll into the bay.

"Look Peter, all the fishing boats are moving out. Something must be brewing. Let's get into the marina now. We have had enough for one day."

"OK. I'll call straight away." He picked up the VHF microphone and said, "Kemer Marina, Kemer Marina. This is sailing yacht CLYPEUS, CLYPEUS. We have a problem and wish to be hauled out immediately. Do you have room for us and can you help?"

"CLYPEUS, CLYPEUS, No problem. Come on in. A white RIB will lead you to the lifting bay."

"That's great. Thank you. CLYPEUS standing by on Channel 73"

At 8.45 p.m. we entered the calm marina and were piloted in by a white inflatable, crewed by two bronzed athletes in white shirts and shorts, straight to the lifting bay where slings were immediately put

beneath CLYPEUS to hold her up safely overnight.

Hassan, the Manager came to make sure that all was well. He indicated the elegant washrooms and said he would return at 9.30 to take us for a drink. After a delicious hot shower in pristine, marble surroundings, we sat down with him in the smart Marina's Navigator Restaurant and made plans before having an excellent meal.

During the night I still had to get up every three hours to pump the bilges, (Peter deserved a good sleep) but I will never forget the difference a kind and understanding Marina Manager can make to, not only the safety of a boat crew, but their egos as well. I felt I arrived at Kemer as a tired sea gypsy but five hours later, had gone to bed as a well-fed, slightly inebriated, princess.

At 8.45 p.m. we entered the calm marina and were piloted in by a white inflatable, crewed by two bronzed athletes.

We were led to the lifting bay where slings were immediately put beneath CLYPEUS to hold her up safely overnight.

CHAPTER FIVE | THE LYCIAN COAST OF TURKEY

2001 June, Kemer - Tekirova (ancient Phasaelis)- Chimaera - Cineviz - Finike - Kekova - Kas - Kemer

KEMER MARINA supplied everything we needed, including free internet and instant friends. Happy international crews, mainly couples from Holland, Germany, Norway, Sweden, Australia, America, were living on board, enjoying retirement and fulfilling their dreams. Like us, they found it easier to go down to the sea in a small ship than to remain on dry land. They were great company. Each evening at 6 p.m. the Navigator Bar bell was rung to summon the faithful to 'Happy Hour' when all the drinks were half price. By 7 p.m. many of us had had our aperitif and returned to our boats to prepare supper, dine at the Navigator or wander into town for a Turkish, French, Spanish or Italian meal.

The marina provided a spacious and comfortable Club Room with an extensive library: just swap books one for one. Green leather armchairs surrounded a log fireplace and a large satellite

television with VCR facilities. Also provided were free tennis courts, an on-board telephone if required, classes during the winter to improve your Turkish, a Bridge club, and a monthly Friday evening concert by a quartet from Antalya Orchestra. The marble showers and loos were

cleaned three times a day; the pleasant office staff were polite and helpful with reasonable English - and all for less than most British marinas.

On July 10th CLYPEUS was hauled out for four days while Peter tried to buy a new transducer fitting. None were available so he coated the old one liberally with epoxy resin and pushed it back through a wooden block into the hole. He also bought a new lower bilge pump from the Marina Chandlery: a Rule 1500 for about £77 and fitted it, grumbling as he was working, "West Marine catalogue price is £37 but we can't wait for delivery from the USA". With the floor up I lived like a monkey again, holding the ceiling grab rails to climb from one cabin to another.

Kemer is a tourist town full of bars, some with hookah pipes and bazaars selling rugs, ceramics, leather goods and designer knock-offs, all fronted by a throng of eager salesmen ready to barter: Let haggling commence.

The workshops for welding, specialist yacht repairs and wood yards necessary for do-it-yourself boat maintenance, were all a couple of miles inland. Our folding bicycle earned its stowage space on board. Peter accidently left his credit card in the nearby Bank machine. Next day he despondently returned to see if anyone had handed it in. While he was waiting for the Bank to open, the shop owner next door came and asked him if anything was wrong?

"Yes," said Peter, "I left my credit card in the slot yesterday."

"I saw you," said the shop owner, "and ran and called you, but you had cycled away too fast. I gave it in at the Bank."

He escorted Peter into the Bank and they were only too pleased to hand back his credit card with no problems.

Kemer town is well laid out and full of flowers, a pleasant place, but the tourist touts and shop owners are difficult to pass as they stand outside their establishments with constant hassles of "Come see," "Come Buy", "Come Eat."

Lying on a lounger beneath the umbrellas on the swimming pontoon attached to the sea side of the marina, I made friends with slightly built Rafika, whose husband was a Customs Officer. She

came on board for tea and then kindly invited us to her home. With her husband and sister they welcomed us with a table laid out with a variety of Turkish cakes. We ate on the balcony and had a

difficult couple of hours language-wise but managed to glean that their only son was away doing his National Service for two years. Their little apartment was spotlessly clean and sparsely

furnished with hand made lace doilies on tables and chair backs. It was obvious that Turkish Customs Officers were not overpaid. The little yellow Turkish/English dictionary had a busy time.

After being re-launched, we held our breath while we waited to see if any water was leaking into the hull. It wasn't. The new bilge pump was tested and appeared efficient. It was a huge relief to know that CLYPEUS was waterproof again.

Bottom left:
Kemer marina swimming area.

Right:
Rafika and her husband and sister welcomed us with a table laid out with a variety of Turkish cakes.

49

At last Peter's eyes sparkled as we motored westwards in a calm sea towards Phasaelis and anchored off the Necropolis. Phasaelis was a Lycian port founded around 334 BC by the Greeks for shipping: timber, rose oil and perfume and became rich enough to have its own mint. Shaded by soughing pines, the ruins are arranged around three small perfect bays in an idyllic setting. The car and coach tourists all left by 7 p.m. and we wandered quietly through the Theatre, Acropolis and Steam Baths and stepped beneath the aqueduct which had brought fresh water from the mountains to the centre of town.

In the morning the clear outlines of the old harbour walls could be seen under the water and it was uncanny to be snorkelling in the translucent warm sea discovering ancient stone carvings and breakwaters. Ashore the crumbling, eroding grey tombs of the Necropolis were sombrely slipping down into the sea. The exposed pine tree roots seemed to be doing their best to hold the tombs on land before their inevitable slide to eternity.

Next day we continued to Adrasan Beach to explore the scattered ruins of ancient Olympus, founded by the Lycians in the 2nd century BC which spread throughout a grove of pink oleanders surrounding a sparkling stream.

The ruins lie on a river which twists around the stone headland to the sea, protected from pirates and marauders by a grey rock fort, difficult to distinguish until close up. Small brightly coloured fishing boats gathered in the evening dusk all tied up together: four with their bows pointed inshore; four with bows pointed out to sea, each proudly flying their red flag with a white crescent moon and five pointed star: SISI, ULAS, and GULBAHAR sprouted four pronged anchors hooked over the bows, yellow floats and brown nets hung over the sides and drums of green fishing line were bolted on deck. Wives and daughters in pantaloons and head scarves appeared to have equal status to the men and chattered away to neighbours of either sex.

We were told that on the nearby hillside, alongside the Lycian Way, is the Chimaera where spontaneous fires flame directly out of small crevices on the cindery slope. Next afternoon we started off walking to see it, but gave up in the heat and returned downhill for a cooling swim and a cold beer. That night to the north, in the mountains, the fires of the Chimaera flickered red on the dark slopes.

Phasaelis was a Lycian port founded around 334 BC by the Greeks for shipping: timber, rose oil and perfume and became rich enough to have its own mint.

The Chimera where spontaneous fires flame directly out of small crevices in the cindery slope.

"I didn't realise there was a town or even a village around here." I mumbled to Peter. "I'll look in the Turkish Pilot," From the cabin I called, "It must be the Chimaera."

Peter read to me from Rod Heikell's Pilot Book. I extracted some of the information:

"Today it is not the spectacular phenomenon expected. It was described by Homer as a fire-breathing monster, part lion, part goat and part snake. It was slain by Bellerophon, a character very much like Heracles – a scene depicted on many early Greek vases. The fire burns a mixture of gases, including methane, produced underground, which ignites on contact with the atmosphere. 'Chimaera' later became a name for any fantastic beast."

Later, from the Internet, I gathered that the Chimaera consists of some two dozen vents in the ground, grouped in two patches on the hillside above the Temple of Hephaestus near ancient Olympos, in Lycia. The vents emit burning methane thought to be of metamorphic origin, which in ancient times sailors could navigate by, but on which today the custodian brews his tea.

It was difficult to see the entrance to the hidden fiord of Cineviz (Chineviz) Liman until we sailed dangerously close. Once inside, the towering pale grey cliffs, which are studded with green pines clinging to crevices, only allow the sun to shine into the gorge for four hours either side of high noon. While the sun shone the water blazed turquoise but at dusk turned into Homer's 'wine dark sea' until the moon and a million stars twinkled like flirting eyes. It was our favourite Turkish uninhabited sandy bay with its pale warm aquamarine water.

Although many yachts and gulets arrived during the day, most left by five o'clock to take their passengers back to their hotels in time for dinner. During the day we could hear the sounds of happy groups laughing, often sitting up to their necks in the warm water, and of goats' bells tinkling as they scrambled up the steep cliffs. Suddenly a roar of a fast motor boat would disturb the peace but later the chuff, chuff, of a single cylinder engine soothed.

An evening walk ashore through the whispering pines and pink oleanders, disclosed ruined cottages and a track leading up out of the valley. Over the col was a quiet bay with a fish farm. There didn't seem to be any mosquitoes so we slept on deck. The grey cliffs shimmered silver beneath the almost full moon. Silent at last, the cicadas had gone to sleep too. I slept so soundly that Peter had been up and changed the alternator before I woke next morning.

Another day was spent at anchor taking time to look down into the turquoise water, so calm and clear that every grain of sand and blade of sea grass was clearly visible from on deck. The water shimmered, yellow waves of light danced along the sandy bottom and bright, white, wandering scribble lit the shadowy under-bows of the gulets, their blue sunshades and red flags reflected bright on the surface.

On the way to Finike, 23 miles to the west, dolphins turned and joined us for a few minutes then continued their journey east. The afternoon haze rose into the white clouds gathering about the mountain tops. Our feet burned on the searing yellow decks as we stooped beneath improvised awnings.

Meandering around Finike early one evening, we looked in the window of a dilapidated jewellers, (our wedding anniversary was a few days away). The owner came out.
"Guneydin. You buy?" We shook our heads.
As he turned the key in the shop door grill he said, "Come. I show you my brother's new hotel. Come…Come…Come see." We couldn't think of an excuse quickly enough without appearing rude and meekly followed our new 'friend', 'The Harmonie', had well-appointed rooms, which as yet had had no occupants, and we agreed to have our dinner up on the flat, open, 5th floor, roof-top. It was romantic, eating by candlelight under the moon, but the poor owner/cook/waiter had to carry all the dishes for each course, up the stairs from the ground floor. Yes, we did pay for his leg work, but it was a good meal and memorable for the privilege of being his first roof-top guests. July in Finike was too hot even at 9 a.m. and we became sweaty and frustrated at being kept waiting for the marina office staff to arrive so that we could pay before leaving. When they added two noughts onto our Visa card and charge 3,200 million Turkish lire instead of 32 million Peter exploded and a correction was eventually made. He wrote in the log "Marina needs a large KICK behind it."

The next anchorage, Gokya Liman, restored our equilibrium. A small creek runs West South West from the main harbour opposite Ashil Adasi Island. There are many fresh water up-wellings along the north shore of the creek. It was a lovely anchorage and we had a good sleep in the cockpit with our mosquito net protecting us.

Rowing around next morning I was able to explore right into a cave as high as a cathedral. The water was incredibly clear but the coolness of the air inside the dark cave made it a bit scary.

Sailing on, time was taken to look at the

I was able to row into a cave as high as a cathedral. CLYPEUS is anchored in the background.

earthquake ridden sunken coast of Kekova Roads where steps rise up into semi-submerged rooms. Half a mile to the west are the remains of the sunken city of Tersane. Anchoring is prohibited but swimming isn't, so Peter slowly motored CLYPEUS nearby, while I snorkelled over ruined homes and warehouses and followed the stone block road until it emerged on the beach at the foot of a ruined church which is a haunting memorial to Christianity in the country of Islam. The floor plans of some

houses are only about three feet below the surface.

We anchored for the night behind Kalekoy peninsula and I climbed up through maquis and olive trees to the top of Kekova's small, but magnificent, Byzantine castle to watch the red orb sink below the darkening sea. The foundations of the old town are easy to distinguish beneath the water. They were the remains of the old city of Simena destroyed by an earthquake in 141 AD. It was an unbearably hot night and after breakfast we were pleased to climb up into the breeze wafting over the castle before descending on the other side between scattered Lycian Tombs down into the village. We walked through almost perpendicular lanes where the house balconies were spread with

Left: Kalekoy's magnificent Byzantine castle looked down on the sunken city

Top right: We rested beside a stone tomb high on the hillside. I looked inside 'Nothing in there'.

Bottom right: A workman sleeping having his siesta.

rich red carpets for sale. Persistent pantalooned ladies offering glass and shell necklaces or herbs were hard to discourage. I snorkelled over the sunken city with steps, rooms and tombs carved out of stone. We bought strong scented fresh oregano from an elderly lady who was sitting by the water side sorting it from basket to basket. After an excellent fish lunch at Hassan's on the water's edge we rested beneath an olive tree beside a stone tomb high on the hillside. I had a look inside and could see nothing, but one opened tomb had a workman sleeping in it having his siesta while his mate sat nearby reading the newspaper.

It was just too hot. Later in the afternoon we moved CLYPEUS nearer to the entrance of the Bay in the hope there would be more breeze. In the still of the following morning we motored out of Kekova Roads into a fresh, breezy and swelly sea. Sixteen miles later we prepared to tie up, stern to, in Kas. I jumped off the boat with the line in my hand into the arms of a fine Dutchman. I don't know why I hadn't seen him approach, but he was there, open-armed to catch me. After profuse apologies and laughter on both sides I secured CLYPEUS.

Kas is a lovely little town at the foot of steep slopes, a small green oasis beneath hills of sunburnt scrub. Cobbled streets climb up from the sea with pink and purple bougainvillea and colourful carpets hanging over balconies. An ice-cold beer in the leafy town square cost only 40p.

In Smiley's harbour-side restaurant, Peter almost fainted from the heat while having our evening meal. I asked the Maitre D' if there was somewhere Peter could cool off. He led us down steep stone steps into the cellar to sit on chairs placed on a wooden floor. The cool cellar proved to be a Roman water cistern (built about 500BC) but the ceiling didn't look too secure. After resting for an hour Peter felt well enough to walk home to CLYPEUS and we decided to fly home as soon as possible as it was too hot to enjoy this delightful coastline. There was no reason why we shouldn't return next year and continue west then.

We were still full of hope and sure of our abilities.

Kemer seemed the obvious place to leave CLYPEUS for the winter. On our way back we

Kas was a delightful little town on a steep slope but we were too hot!

stopped at Kalaroz, a well hidden, uninhabited little inlet between white chalk cliffs with incredibly clear water. Peter dropped the anchor and I swam a stern line ashore to tie to a tree and chatted to an Israeli charter crew who insisted we come on CHAPPI for drinks and then supper. They were charming and we enjoyed a very convivial evening. They were intensely interested in our voyage around the world.

We left this beautiful place in early morning pink sunlight and motored back to Cavus Liman's wide bay. An English boat was anchored nearby, ASHANTI. Liz and David and their two boys swam over to talk and sat in our dinghy for an hour. They are nearly home from their three year round the world voyage and invited us over for drink and for dinner too. Liz quickly prepared a light and tasty curried eggs supper. It showed the resourcefulness of many sailing wives, producing an improvised dinner for unexpected guests with whatever

was on board that would stretch to six people. It was good to talk again about oceans, what weather? What damage? What sail or mechanical problems experienced? Fish caught, beaches seen, shells collected? Which people had been friendliest and which most officious?

The following day was our wedding anniversary so we invited ASHANTI'S crew for a celebration dinner. After a swim and refreshing fresh water shower on the beach we sat and read and had a real holiday day. It was lovely to share it with a happy family and made me long to be with our own children and grandchildren. The boys made excellent contributions to our Visitors' Book.

We discussed how cruising changes us irretrievably in many ways. At home even now a part of you still belongs on the ocean. High winds

Peter was led down into the Roman Cistern to cool off.

ASHANTI were nearly home from their three year voyage around the world and invited us over for a drink and dinner

make you think and pray for the boats at sea. So many news items are about places you know as are many novels. We still can't run a tap to clean our teeth without feeling wasteful and decadent. Cruising made us become more self reliant, less tolerant of superficialities, pretensions and trivialities. So much to do, so much to see. Life seems so short. There is a sense of urgency to cram as much into our days as possible.

Their boys talked of what they had seen, the harshness of deserts, the poor fishermen of the Red Sea. They had also learned that being poor doesn't mean being unhappy and how little you need to make a contented life if you are healthy. They had seen the wonders of Galapagos and watched marine iguanas and stroked dolphins and giant tortoises, been embraced by Polynesian and Australian families.

In the morning ASHANTI sailed west as we returned to the east to get our home-going sorted. Peter was patient enough to gill around while I rowed into more caves. One had many underwater entrances – Exciting exploring for scuba divers. There are no roads in this area so a description of the natural surroundings from the sea may help future visitors. The earth above the caves was conglomerate, like rock cakes, and full of holes. That night was spent continuously rolling while anchored in Tekarova, but it was a lovely place to be for an early morning snorkel over the submerged Harbour.

A good sail took us back to Kemer Marina and we dodged between about thirty gulets motoring out full of tourists, for a splendid day excursion. A restful week followed while we booked our flights

A good sail took us back to Kemer Marina and we dodged between about thirty gulets motoring out full of tourists, for a splendid day excursion.

from Anatalya, cleared the boat and arranged to be hauled out on the 1st of August. The costs for over-wintering were reasonable: 9 months for £898 and 12 months for £957, which with our 10% Cruising Association discount, was a very good deal, much cheaper than any British Marina.

Before the flight home there was time to visit Antalya's world class museum and the old port dominated by its 13th Century Fluted Minaret with its clusters of slim, brickwork pilasters. The crowded labyrinth of the huge covered Bazaar was intimidating and I didn't venture far into the dark interior in case I couldn't find my way out again.

Having the winters at home in Wales gave us the opportunity to enter into local village and town life and gradually become part of the community and make friends. Peter wanted to rest and not have any responsibilities for a while, but I couldn't wait to get going and make friends.(later, when he was ready, he volunteered to deliver Meals on Wheels every Tuesday which he has done without fail every week we are at home.) I joined the village Women's Institute and Tangent and volunteered to serve in the Oxfam Shop (which I enjoy enormously. It is well run, clean and didn't smell of old clothes) and I started a Keep Fit Class for 'the Gracious Years'.

Then undreamed of opportunities opened up for me: In October 2000 I joined Pembroke Dock Writers' Group. They are a friendly, encouraging and inspirational crowd. Trinity College Carmarthen was looking to expand the University of Wales Courses and decided our Group would benefit from a tutor to instruct a B.A. Course in Creative Writing. We all responded enthusiastically and for two years enjoyed a structured syllabus with our work being marked and critiqued. The BA turned out to be a Higher Certificate of Education, but later some of us were offered a chance to apply

for a Master's Degree in Creative Writing at Trinity College, Carmarthen. I started the Course in October 2002, one afternoon a week, which was completed in 2004 just after my 70th birthday. I really wanted to do my very best to write about our life and experiences sailing around the world, to tell the world about the kindness of strangers, the beauty of our planet and observe that you don't have to be rich to adventure and travel.

There was time to visit Antalya's world class museum.

CHAPTER SIX | ANCIENT RUINS, OPERAS and BALLETS

2002 Kemer – Chimaera – Phasaelis - Salagossus – Perge – Selge – Kopoulu Kanyon – Sillyon – Aspendos – Cineviz – Kemer

ON THE 28TH APRIL 2002 we flew from Birmingham to Antalya. The marina staff had organized a very good deal at the five star Turkis Hotel and I thought a little luxury would do us good before getting back on the boat. CLYPEUS seemed fine, only the usual minor problems: a rain leak above the navigation desk, a gouge out of the concrete keel, and some rust showing through on the white hull near the bow. Basically all was well and after lunch on board and a bottle of EFES, the Turkish Beer, it seemed as though the world was ours again. Hooray! Off came the covers to be washed and carefully folded under Peter's tight instructions before being packed away in the cockpit lockers.

April in Kemer.

In the marina Bar we met up with old friends and enjoyed their happy faces and good health. It affirms that this is a good way of life although Peter is now 70. We could see there were many sailors older than him still enjoying the lifestyle. We are all much of an age: well past the point where life seems infinite. What unites us is a compulsive itch to escape to a simple life and our common discovery that Europe still has a last frontier in the sea. We discussed the claustrophobia of living in a country that has grown too small, too smoky, too intimate, too man–made and civilised for comfort. Most of our European countries are overloaded, sinking ships, and we were taking to the lifeboats.

In thunder and rain Peter started working on the boat. The motor wouldn't start and he was despondent. Had the water pump failed? No. The injector pump failed? No. The starter battery kaput? No. Fuel pump failed? No. Fuel lines blocked? No. Exhaust full of water? Yes, the swan neck was full. No problem to empty it. Now all was well and it was up the ladder, down the ladder, twenty times a day.

He connected the batteries and the tape recorder sprang into life playing recorded memories of Tahiti Radio's melodic ukulele bands and gentle rhythmic singing. It brought back wonderful lagoon-side nights when the wahines swayed beneath the palm trees. The drums, the drums frequently called us to watch the beautiful girls sway and undulate wearing a coron of flowers or high head dresses, and coconut shell bras, above long grass skirts slung low on a flower or shell band around their hips. Flowers around their ankles and

Peter servicing
the engine.

Sail repairs.

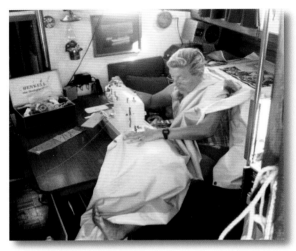

bare feet made it easy to appreciate the whole body movements of the strong athletic girls whose bottoms gyrated at incredible speed beneath their romantic exterior. In the moonlight I would sit on the grass with the warm breeze sighing through the palm tree fronds admiring the godlike young men whacking their knees together.

We moved back on board and prepared the hull for its annual coat of anti-fouling paint. As I swam from the Marina bathing platform I noticed that snow still sparkled on the mountain tops. Bronzed seamen in their white uniforms put up the beach umbrellas and zoomed around in their RIBs placing marking floats to define the protected swimming area. 'Summer was a'comin'.

On the 9th of May, CLYPEUS was lowered into the water. The stern gland was leaking slightly and the water pump seals needed replacing. The next three weeks were spent sanding and painting, buying bits, and a disgruntled Peter put in the new seals saying,

"These new seals cost more than a whole new pump would have done in Cyprus!"

The singing of cicadas awakened us and while breakfasting in the cockpit, swallows chirped and chattered as they swooped beneath the pontoons to tend their well-hidden nestlings.

While we were working, a knock on the hull heralded a great reunion with Americans, Tom and Lee, with whom we had sailed in company from Tonga to New Zealand in 1985. We had rented a car together and toured North and South Islands for a brilliant month. We were all amazed at the variety of scenery in that small country: majestic snow covered mountain peaks, deep fiords, barely extinct volcanoes, hot sulphur springs and bubbling mud pools with steam vents and geysers; beautiful sandy beaches and bays, untamed forests and bush and 30 million sheep grazing on green, green grass. The hospitality and friendliness of the New Zealanders is legendary. One example was at a hot springs campsite where, outside each cabin, was a stainless steel lid opening into a natural steam oven. As we booked in the proprietress said:

"Do you like trout?"

"Yes, we do."

She handed us a beautiful five pound glistening, bright-eyed rainbow trout. "Have this then. Wrap it in aluminium foil and put it in the steam oven for half an hour. I'm sure you will find it delicious."

We did and it was.

Now Lee and Tom were accompanied by Kate, their seven year old daughter, who charmed us. I asked her to read one of the children's sailing adventure stories I had written and give me her opinion. She said she had enjoyed it and then advised me to "keep writing. One day someone will publish it!" We took photos to send to our mutual sailing friends Rose and Bob who were also in our little fleet through Tonga. (*Seize The Day* pages 126-140)

Kate and I had a fun day together swimming and playing cards, while her worried parents attended Kemer Life Hospital for a mammogram, scan and tests. We all had quiet dinner together on board CLYPEUS and the following day Lee was given the all clear, her tests proved non-malignant. They were both very happy with the efficient medical treatment and costs and the evening meal on Voyager was a real celebration. Few ocean voyagers carry health insurance, it is usually too expensive as we are an incalculable risk.

I think it is worth recounting an incident which may be of interest to travellers to Australia where I needed surgery. We were worried about the cost, having no health insurance, except for our National Insurance contributions which we were keeping up to date. Peter left me with the hospital admissions clerk to fill in the admittance forms. One question was: "Who is responsible for payment?"

I asked her, "Who shall I put? Me or my husband? After all, I may kick the bucket."

She said "But you're British aren't you?"

"Yes."

"And you are here on a current tourist visa?"

"Yes."

"Then with the reciprocal arrangement that visiting Australians get free treatment in the UK, you will receive free treatment here. Just enter your tourist visa number."

"That's great. Thank you. What a relief!"

When Peter phoned that evening I said "It's all right about payment, they only asked for my visa number."

"What! They took your Barclay Card Visa Number?" he asked in horror.

"No, no, only my tourist visa number."

"Phew! That's good news. Everything OK?"

"Yes," I replied. "Everything is wonderful. Everybody is so friendly and it's all very informal."

In Kemer, the Cruising Associations' East Mediterranean Rally boats started arriving. Competitions were organized for the participating crews. An exciting tug-of-war almost gave some of the older members apoplexy as they dug their heels in and pulled hard.

A coach tour to Chimeara and Phaesalis included lunch up in the mountains - on a camel farm of all things. In Phaeselis I thought I knew my way, and wanted to get off the easy tourist route we had explored last year, so peeled away on my own out onto the peninsula in the hope of finding house ruins, somewhere real people had lived, but after about an hour I panicked in the dense bushes when I couldn't find a path leading back to the crowded centre. I was afraid the coach would leave without me. Barging my way through the thorny scrub, it seemed to be trying to hold me back and thorns dug deep scratches on my legs and arms – serves me right! I should have acted my age and stayed with the crowd, but I did manage to be at the coach assembly point in time. The evening cocktail party, dinner and good dancing restored my spirits.

I organized a writing competition for crews to submit scripts about the Rally: the prize to be a copy of my just published 'Red Sea Peril' but also a promise to send the winner's manuscript to the yachting magazines who publish my sailing articles, which I did, but I never heard whether the winner's article ever actually got into print.

A smart Turkish Customs Launch, which was one end of the start line for the Rally departure, invited non-competing boat owners on board. It was an exhilarating and raucous scene as the 40 or so boats sailed in a strong breeze towards us, with

We drove up the high mountains to the amphitheatre of Salagossos (City in the Clouds).

the backdrop of the sun reflecting on the snow mountain tops. Each yacht received a blast on the horn to acknowledge their start, which they returned tenfold. Flags and balloons soared through the air as we shouted "Bon voyage" to our departing friends.

Sitting under the sun umbrella on deck in the marina writing Seize The Day, I noticed the lady on the next boat was scribbling away in a notebook. We smiled but didn't talk. After an hour or so we both looked up at the same time.

"What are you writing?" I asked.

"A book. And you?"

"A book too."

We swapped names and the contents of our books. French Canadian Marie Andre was a doctor who has specialised in gynaecology, menopause and andropause problems. Her books are published in French and although she gave me "The desire hormone" my French isn't good enough to take full advantage of it. Her husband Emilien was energetic and full of testosterone - Marie Andre prescribes the doses! He was a strong, romantic figure, with a shock of white hair, who quoted French, Quebec and English poetry, drove like a Frenchman and had an excellent grasp of history and told us much about the ancient sites we visited together. They were videoing Turkey for Quebec TV and Marie was writing a book of their voyage. The conversation of our new friends from ANDANTE MA NON TROPPO, over dinner on CLYPEUS that night, made our eyes pop out like organ stops. Never had intimate details of the sex issues of human beings been so thoroughly discussed on our boat, or anywhere else in our lives. Marie Andre is still studying music and had an electric keyboard fitted in the cabin, beneath the side deck

The charming couple had sailed their 38' yacht

from Quebec to the Mediterranean. We were fortunate to find such a compatible pair to share a car and together visited some of the many ancient sites inland.

The first day we visited deep caves which

contain brilliant blue underground lakes… Up in the mountains Salagossos (City in the Clouds) was a fascinating Pisidian settlement, then Roman, which was written about in 1224 BC. It lay in a pass through the snowy mountain tops, 1,400 feet above sea level. The Nympheum water trough was

legs and sandaled feet. What excitement these new finds must have engendered.)

When filling our water bottles at the village well we talked to the village school children who had crowded to the fence to talk to us. They were

interested and had some English and looked so neat and well cared for. Each white lace collar was hand embroidered and their blue uniforms and pinafores smocked and embroidered. Their mothers, or grandmothers, obviously still had time, if not money, to spend on their children.

On to Perge, founded in 1000 BC and formerly a Pamphylian trading city. Alexander the Great, and

particularly well restored together with the library. Niches were intricately carved into the cliff face where the cremated ashes of loved ones had rested in covered jars. Dig areas were cordoned off by blue plastic sheeting. (In 2007 the huge marble head of Hadrian was found and is now the centre piece of an exhibition at the British Museum. Then in August 2008 great news was heralded on the BBC that a head of Marcus Aurelius had been found in the Roman Baths and a portrait head of Empress Faustina AD 138-161 together with marble arms,

Left:
Niches carved for ashes of loved ones.

Top right:
We talked to the village school children who had crowded to the fence to talk to us.

Bottom:
Perge founded in 1000 BC. Alexander the Great came here in 333BC.

Apollonius, visited Perge in 333BC. The ruins are extensive with an enormous Theatre which we couldn't see as it was boarded up and under reconstruction. At the top of the town were the remains of a fountain and nympheum with a

The Nympheum water trough was particularly well restored.

waist-high stone channel running down the centre of the main street. It evidently carried fresh water through the town into which anybody could dip a jug. It seems such a sensible idea. If the Ancients could have a fresh water feature running through their town 3000 years ago, why can't we?

The weather was so good Peter made a cockpit table so that we could have our lunch al fresco. CLYPEUS has a very small cockpit, which is ideal for ocean sailing but makes a very cramped dining area.

On another car tour Marie Andre and Emillien drove us through fantastic mountain scenery, to snow-fed bright blue rivers and canyons and across fertile plains. Selge was another big sprawling site with a well restored nympheum and library. At Kopoulu Kanyon white water rafters challenged the breathtakingly blue tumbling water. We sat on soft pine needles beside the river for our picnic. Central Turkey is amazingly green and verdant. The main mountain ranges run east to west so that rain water is trapped in the centre of the fertile country before it finds its way to the sea.

Sillyon's historic site is large and interesting but village ladies were a persistent pain. We didn't want to buy their necklaces or embroidery. In fact Emilien refused to go on to the site ruins as he can't stand being bothered by the hawkers. Earthquakes had struck this area many time but the stone seats of the large theatre were mostly intact.

On another trip we visited Finike, Lymra, Kumulka, Termossus and Arykanda, all splendid. There are so many fantastic ancient Greek and Roman archaeological sites in Turkey, it is mind-boggling.

Kemer Tourist Board offered a trip to Aspendos for the opening night of their Music Festival to be held in the ancient hill-top Amphitheatre. A wall 30m high encircles the theatre of 40 rows of marble benches in a grand horseshoe looking down to the Arena. It was built in 167 AD in the time of Marcus Aurelius and dedicated to the Gods. Evidently the Seljuks renovated it in the 13th Century which helps to explain why it is so well preserved. Unfortunately due to a language misunderstanding we missed the coach to the opening ceremony and had to enjoy our picnic and wine on the romantic Marina swimming pontoon. However a few days later we saw a superb performance of AIDA. It is one of the highlights of our whole voyage. I wrote in my journal:

"From the overflowing coach park we made our

way through a costumed and theatrically made-up chorus of hundreds of local people, all awaiting their part in the performance. An audience of 14,000 people crammed onto the stone tiers to see Aida. The Plough constellation sparkled immediately overhead as it did for Roman citizens 2000 years ago. I felt an affinity with the Roman ladies in their robes who must have sat on this seat. There were no hawkers: no programs to buy, no water or ice creams on sale, no vending machines. It is, as it was.

An arc light suddenly illuminated the high arches as the orchestra entered, young attractive girls in sophisticated black evening gowns, the men in black open neck long sleeved shirts and trousers. The Conductor takes the rostrum in his white tuxedo and bows. The scene is set.

It is a special performance with dignitaries who make a few speeches which drag. First in Turkish and then in French translation, and a slow handclap starts. The audience is impatient. The Minister of Tourism brings his speech to a quick close, shrugs,   wishes us all 'bien venue' and sits down. The lady next to me whispers and I feel her trembling with excitement which she just can't hide. She points to the second violinist "My daughter." She and her husband are Turkish Cypriots from Kyrenia who had flown over for this performance and were overflowing with happiness and pride.

The conductor raises his baton. The overture begins and young dancers grace the music, their slim bodies silhouetted by the breeze wafting their vaporous dresses around them.

As the music strengthens, soldiers, guards, village folk and children amble onto the stage in a relaxed manner and eventually take positions for the singing to commence. The International cast does more than justice to the one night's magnificent performance.

The Grand March is splendid with horses

cantering across the stage ridden by soldiers with their pennants flying, each led by a fast running slave. The dances are superbly choreographed and executed – Oh for a video of the performance!

Finding our coach at the end was difficult. Armed with our coach number and a few noted bearings we searched through the hundreds of coaches and eventually 'homed in' to take our seats. It was now 2.30 am but we eat our picnic with relish. It had been too crowded within the arena to do anything but sit and stand up during intervals between acts to alleviate the numbness derived from solid stone seating.

Snoozing all the way home, we are woken at 4 a.m. by the hiss of brakes and are back in Kemer – a walk to the boat – "Guneydin" (good morning) to the sleepy guard. As we snuggle into bed I look at my watch. 4.30am . What an evening!"

When there was no urgent scraping or painting, shopping, cooking or cleaning to be done I wrote *Seize The Day*, researched information for the Appendices and painted in water colours. When shopping one day I fell off my bike and hurt my elbow – no big deal but it relieved me of scraping and varnishing for a few days. Boats arrived, boats left.

Swallows were swooping and flitting to their nests beneath the pontoons – there were some very bossy and nagging wives. A tragedy almost occurred when a fledgling fell into the water and was drowning. Peter managed to save it by lifting it out with the deck broom head. He gently placed the gasping chick on the wooden pontoon and when we looked for it half an hour later, it had disappeared.

"Let's go to Cineviz for a couple of days and meet up with our Quebequoise friends."

"Great!"

After a good hot shower and shampoo I cycled

Stocking up in the market.

into the market for more vegetables and fresh bread.

On the 12th June on the VHF Channel Peter said "Kemer Harbour Control. This is CLYPEUS. We would like to leave almost immediately."

"OK CLYPEUS. A seaman will be with you."

A few moments later a white RIB zoomed up crewed by a bronzed young man resplendent in his white uniform. He let go the stern chain while I slipped the forward lines.

Peter reversed us out of our slot. The RIB pushed our bow round in the restricted space.

We appreciated the care and help yachtsmen are given in Turkey – not like the UK where "it's up to you mate!"

Out of the harbour entrance and into the blue calm sparkling Med. Sails up, clothes off as we rounded the headland to the west. White pearly tongues licked down the chin of wavelets, the wind was on the nose of course. It's wonderful, we can go where we want – today it's just sixteen miles into an aquamarine high-sided bay to meet up with friends, to swim, read, write, sunbathe and have a BBQ together this evening. Our boat owes us nothing. We have sailed about 60,000 miles in her

and lived on board for twelve years. For just over £1,000 we can keep the boat here and enjoy three, four, five or six months in the sun in a five star marina in Turkey. When the maintenance is done (and she does need it after 30 years), we can take off where, when, and for however long, to suit ourselves.

Even Peter's eyes twinkled and we both enjoyed a great exhilaration of freedom and life. The engine performed smoothly after his various ministrations but the wind was against the current and we ploughed through two foot high waves spreading a bow wave of sparkling white water. I sat on the bowsprit with my legs dangling and was sometimes surprised by a thump and splash of water hitting me from behind as our flared bow threw the water up and away from the hull in curling white arcs. How different from the olden days when British sailors called the bowsprit 'the old widow-maker.'

First stop was to be Cineviz but we couldn't see the entrance until we saw a blue yacht with white sails ahead so we just followed her in.

We cautiously crept into the fiord, tucked beneath twin peaks in a valley where pines cascade down the slopes taking root on every niche down the ravine. The anchor plunged to the bottom with a clatter, the hum of the engine ceased and we found ourselves surrounded by the deafening song of the cicadas and the scent of the pine trees that filled the sunlit air.

A cup of tea, swim and snorkel and we were back in the cruising life-style. The sandy bottom was strewn with *conus mediterraneas,* hermit crabs and *ocenebra evinacea* seaweed. Underwater caves emit cold streams and the, mostly white, well rounded pebbles have no weed furring them.

A three-masted schooner 'GRAND MAGIC'

came in and spread across two thirds of the Bay. We would all be in trouble if her anchor dragged in the sudden thundery squalls which came up in the afternoon when waves rose steeply to crash on the shore.

We dined below on ANDANTE MA NON TROPPO but Peter couldn't relax. It is a yacht with portholes where you can't see outside whilst eating. He was apprehensive about the weather. We are lucky that in CLYPEUS our saloon windows give a good view of what is happening outside. (We carried storm boards and nuts and bolts to cover them if caught in a cyclone, but they were never needed, so dumped in Cyprus). All boats had lines ashore as well as one or two anchors laid. The expected storm didn't arrive and as we rowed home some Germans on a gulet started singing to a piano accordion. It sounded like a WWII film set.

The next afternoon SEA GLASS came to chat, Cruising Association friends Jean and Bill Anderson on OKYLYPTUS and the crew of FAFIN all raised their glasses. The sun sank below the mountain crags by 6 p.m. so it was early drinks in Cineviz.

While we sat in the cockpit nursing our Turkish gin and tonic we listened to goats bleating, people snorkelling and splashing, the anchor chain gently rumbling across the sand and cicadas zinging and chirruping. The air was warm and soporiphic. It was perfect.

We awoke to the early morning scent of pines. A cockerel crowed, and hens chuck, chuck, chucked around him. Sounds of bleating goats, mingled with the bubbles and rhythmic splash of swimmers.

A fishing boat chugged out in the sleepy dawn. A few yachts purred away, not hoisting sails until outside the Bay. The smell of coffee floated in the air and breakfast gongs on the gulets called the swimmers. Soon the beautiful schooner and gulets departed with their guests to another gorgeous turquoise bay leaving only us, one fishing boat and a single villager already sitting beneath a striped awning awaiting the day's customers. There is only one ruined stone house with an awning where a family provides a temporary summer café. A small boy stood screaming at the water's edge – did he want to go in or come out? The mother lost patience, grabbed him up squealing and kicking and took him indoors. Sudden hush, just the cicadas zinging.

Gulets began to arrive. As they took visitors ashore one of the crew passed in his dinghy while I was swimming and called "Where you from?"

"England"

"I love England."

"I love Turkey" I replied. He zoomed off.

Later, as his Gulet leaves he is pulling up the anchor. "I love you English" he shouts and waves as they motor off across the turquoise sea.

Another gulet crew called to me from his dinghy as I was sitting on the foredeck trying out an evening Raki. (It is less expensive to drink local drinks.)

"Cheers English" he shouted – our ensign hangs from our stern.

"Cheers" I shouted back and raise my glass.

Next morning, yesterday's friendly gulet arrived and at lunchtime, the crew zoomed up in the dinghy and handed us each a plate of the lunch his passengers are having: grilled fresh herring, lettuce and various salads. We offer money but "No, no. Plenty more."

At 5.30 the sun sank below the mountain top. The bay is in shade and Peter is ready for a swim. On board after a hot shower from the solar bag hanging from the boom, we return to our books. We slept on deck. Under a ceiling of a million stars

**A dramatic
monolith guards
the bay where
rings of floats
indicate a fish
farm.**

we noticed two satellites, one very bright, following each other across the sky. I wanted to watch the stars but my eyes kept closing. They seemed so far away, quietly shooting, tumbling and disappearing, silently falling and being extinguished, lost utterly silent in space, falling from nowhere to nowhere into an unimaginable nothing. How many of them there are. How insignificant are we.

We moved around to the next, less frequented bay – Hidden Bay. The sea depth was 50 fathoms off the entrance – as deep as the cliffs are high. It makes us realize once again what a grain of sand we are in the universe. Sleeping on deck the boat lifts and rocks as though it was resting on the breathing, heaving chest of some undersea giant. Dark hills slope up from the bay, their outline silhouetted against the star filled dark blue sky. The sea glistens like well-polished silver.

Another day includes a walk beneath the pines up to the col to look down into the next bay. Our pilot book says 'foul ground' so we cannot enter there. The aquamarine water is so clear we can see the large rocks and stones under the surface. A dramatic monolith guards the bay where rings of floats indicate a fish farm.

Following the high path, banked by oleanders, sweet smelling green/grey herbs and flowers catch our attention. In particular, a type of star thistle with violet purple leaves and stems which give the whole area a soft haze of violet, rather like a prickly, dry, bluebell wood – it makes me realize how soft and lush our English copses and forests are. Pine martins have picked the pine cones clean and the cores of nibbled cones lie around where they have been 'tossed aside like used teabags'.

Not everyone is happy, Rob, a spare 45/50 year old precise English Accountant with thin lips, beak nose and glasses, confessed it is his first year in the

Med with his new boat. He zoomed to Andante and asked him to turn the engine off saying "This is supposed to be a quiet harbour". Everybody would like it to be quiet, but those boats with fridges and freezers who have anchored or stayed in the bay all day have to run their engines in the evening to keep their batteries charged – we didn't suffer this problem not having those luxuries.

Another evening of Germans making music on a gulet. They sang, played instruments, discoed, dived and splashed around until 4.30 a.m. which is a little over the top. But hey! They were on holiday.

Some large motor cruisers had generators running all night to keep owners and guests in air conditioned comfort which did stop the rest of us enjoying the peace of the moonlight. Often a fisherman woke us as he put putted out at dawn. Cicadas started their deafening chorus at 5.30 and goat bells start tinkling and the odd kid bleats when it has stranded itself on a shelf on the high cliff face. But that is the boating life – this heaven must have some little annoyances!

Leaving the harbour early next day we turned into the blood red path of the rising sun. As the orange glow rose higher it tinged the red with gold and the dark sea began to glow and sparkle beneath a duck egg blue sky until we headed west. Then white foam hissed all around us. Sunshine, a salty tang of iodine in the air and a caressing warmth turned the world into paradise for we Northern Europeans.

There didn't seem to be a steady wind pattern on this Southern Turkish coast. It was difficult to decide whether to leave early to take advantage of the morning southerlies and arrive at a destination in the blistering mid-day heat, or to leave later to sail during the heat but perhaps fight westerly's and only just make it.

At Kalekoy we radioed Hassans Restaurant to book dinner then enjoyed a swim, a nap and a walk. An old lady lay asleep on the wooden slatted floor outside her house. As we walked back she was crying and keening and seemed almost in agony as she rocked back and forth. What to do? We couldn't help so quietly walked away feeling guilty.

After an early swim to explore around the semi-submerged sarcophagus standing solitary in the water we left for Kas. Whose tomb is it? There doesn't appear to be any carving in the stone. Further out are the fascinating Roman ruins with

After an early swim to explore around the semi-submerged sarcophagus standing solitary in the water we left for Kas,

steps rising up from house foundations lost beneath the waves in the second century.

In the calm sea on our way to Kas we passed a Turkish Giant's causeway, a larger outcrop than in Ireland but with less regular stones.

On to Kas Bay, where a pushy gulet beat us into anchoring in a tiny bay beneath a pleasant new house and flowered terraces. Anchoring further south we were joined by a Dive Boat from which a French father encouraged his little ones to swim. Their confident high pitched laughter and exclamations as they bicycled through the water,

Boats around us dragged their anchors and the rain sheeted down as white horses raced across the bay.

held up by arm floats, made us laugh. The water here was clear and deep. Large smooth rocks led down to a yellow sandy bottom where the sea grass was streaked with bald patches caused by anchors and chains dragging.

Peter was worrying about re-entering Europe next year. We had left England before VAT on boats was introduced. Would we have to pay it as soon as we entered the EU again? How much would it be? 17%on the value of CLYPEUS?

Ferries run from Marmaris to Rhodes, the port of entry into Europe. 'Let's take the ferry and ask?' I suggested. We arrived in the supposedly sheltered Marmaris Bay in time to pick up a Sunsail permanent mooring before a squall swept down

from the mountains. Boats around us dragged their anchors and the rain sheeted down as white horses raced across the bay. When all was calm we entered the new Marina which is still under construction. The pool had a little fountain playing into the deep end.

Next morning it took fifty minutes for the catamaran ferry to speed to Rhodes and then another fifty minutes to pass through Greek passport control. At the Harbour Office in Mandraki, a white uniformed lady officer assured us that no demand would be made for VAT, just 60 euros for a visa for Greece and 29 euros for a cruising permit. Happy that 100 euros would see us back into the EU we explored Rhodes.

Windmills with their sails furled, and a splendid castle, shimmered in the noonday sun. We walked through touristy but charming alleys within the Knights of St John Castle. No shop keepers touted for custom, we were allowed to look and choose without being harassed and the firm price is shown on the display ticket – what a change from Turkish tourist areas.

The Archaeological Museum within the Hospitalier Area showed a fine display of pieces including stone dolphins dating from 600 BC. We walked through burning streets to a supermarket to buy some of the things we'd missed in Turkey: bacon and some 'porco choppos' ("dos porco choppos" and "dos gin and tonics" was the extent of my Father's Spanish when they lived on Teneriffe), Martinis and Retsina, then back through the castle's old town streets and squares. A girl in a red blouse leaned out of a window like a geranium in a window box. Attractive young Italian girls were having their portraits drawn in pastels by street artists.

We lost our way back to the Harbour through twisting castle alleys not having noticed that there were two sets of windmills. Arriving hot and agitated at the ferry terminal just in time to get on board before they removed the gang plank and we climbed upstairs in the catamaran for a welcome long drink.

As the ferry approached Marmaris vertical streaks of lightning spat and thunder roared and an almighty deluge hit the boat. On reaching port heavy rain had flooded the quay and we had to paddle to Passport Control. The dolmus bus took us home exhausted, but happy, after a fulfilling day.

Then, after two rest days we left early and passed Fethiye Bay to sail directly to Karacaoren Buku where we picked up a mooring.

From the Log.....

Wed 17th July. Left 7.30 to pass the Seven Capes. CLYPEUS bounced out of the harbour into the strong hot breeze and lumpy sea but it is going with us. The wind came round so, letting out the mainsheet, we flew along with the wind on the beam. Flying fish rise from our bow wave and fly close to the surface until they land 'splat' into a wave.

We have our usual argument about sailing closer inshore so that I can see scenery. Peter likes to sail so far out to sea we don't see much detail. We came close enough to shore to recognise Nine Mile Beach and Patara.

At 3pm Anchored in Kas Bay at Bayfinder Liman. Huge private yacht comes and anchors - CEDAR SEA 2 – Enormous! At night it was lit to look like Las Vegas. A large motor boat is hidden inside one of the side compartments. The yacht seems absolutely over the top with three high domed satellite antennae. A seaplane flew in and landed beside it, then took off again three hours later. As a private yacht it was definitely "beyond the dreams of avarice".

We left Kas for Kekova next morning in a strong following wind and chickened out of sailing through Akar Boyazi, a narrow quick-way channel between two islands. Anchored in good solid mud at Polemos Buku we later watched Cedar Sea 2 come in to rumble and glow all night in the middle of the Bay.

Anchored as we were, right at the western end of the bay, there was a restaurant but no village. A path was indicated so we walked across the isthmus to some Lycian ruins. The scenery was dry but colourful with red earth, green scrub, and grey/green olive trees between pale grey rocks. It is a splendid archaeological site with nobody around. Ruined palaces, temples, houses and sarcophagi are scattered in the fields where goats graze. I had carried my snorkelling gear all the way as I wanted to swim over more Lycian ruins but the sea was too rough to look tempting.

No road reaches this area now and it surprised us there was no archaeological interest. There were wells and the fields looked fertile as though they could raise crops but now goats nibbled every fresh blade of grass. We found out that it was formerly Aperlore, a Lycian town. There were four cities in league Simena, Apollonia, Aperlore and Isinda and together they were called "Aperlites". A hand painted sign showed us the way back to the Restaurant.

Back to Kemer and the Marina social life to enjoy the wide variety of "yachts' people" enjoying this laid-back life style. The convenient thing about being on a boat is, of course, that if you don't like the present company you can just move away!

Some of the other voyagers were so interesting:

Haroon, one of the few Turkish yachtsmen who stayed to socialize with visitors was thirty plus, the son of a senior politician, he was recovering from a brain tumour. He had already divorced three wives but was still good friends with them all – he said! He spent an amusing evening telling us of his Housekeeper's problems looking after his new retriever puppy which enjoyed chewing a good Turkish rug.

Stewart, was a handsome, broken-nosed, quietly spoken public school, ex sky diving instructor. For twenty years he had a home in Turkish Cyprus. His boat was built in Formosa (Taiwan) and he sailed it to Hong Kong and then to the Med. When he divorced his wife she had their house, he had his boat.

Dorit, a 55ish archaeologist who had spent six years in Turkey studying Hittites. Pretty and charming and devoted to her almost blind husband, an ex RAF Air Commodore who was an inveterate name dropper.

Hal and Wendy, Americans, who flew to Europe for the summers. He was a dynamic, knowledgeable Banker, a fast talker and thinker. His eyes were always on the move even when his ears were not. He didn't always listen but was a generous man. He sold Peter his spare anchor for very little. Wendy was quiet and dignified, soft voiced but strong. I thought her personality was probably too fastidious to really enjoy the boating life.

Swedish Carl, was tall, blonde, 70ish. His long muscular tanned legs covered with a blonde fuzz looked like those of a 17 year old beneath his tennis shorts. He was quietly spoken and seemed solitary.

A German yacht owner, 65 year old, small, brusque with short grey hair and a moustache, a very Kaiser like character, just had to dominate the conversation but fortunately he and his patient wife only stayed a few days.

Hassan, the sociable Turkish Marina Manager was handsome, intelligent and enthusiastic, a natural and positive leader and the marina ran like clockwork with happy employees and customers. His English, German and French were excellent and he just exuded encouragement and well being.

The office girls were all charming and gentle but their English wasn't very good and a few hiccups occurred – of course their German and French may have been better. They always seemed squeaky clean, soft spoken with huge brown eyes and clear complexions.

We didn't want to leave this idyllic lifestyle but promised ourselves that next year we really would make an effort to move on towards home.

CHAPTER SEVEN | WESTERING HOME

2003 Kemer – Cineviz –Kekova – Kastellorizo - GREECE – Pigadhia on Karpathos – Khalatros Bay – Sitia – Spinalonga – Heraklion – Chania – Kithera - Methoni.

THREE SUMMERS of idyllic sailing from Cyprus to Eastern Turkey and then meandering along the historic southern Turkish Coast softened us and we lost the stern disciplines we had acquired ocean sailing. We began to realise we were getting old and our time for serious sailing was running out.

In May 2003 we were determined to sail all the way home and leave the 'lotus eating' lifestyle. A cheapie flight from Gatwick landed us at Antalya Airport at three a.m. The taxi to the Otem Hotel in Kemer charged us 70 million lire when it should have been 35m but four o'clock in the morning isn't a good time to argue.

We stayed in the hotel for seven nights while during the days we worked on CLYPEUS preparing her for, what we then thought was going to be the last lap to Ibiza where we would cross our outward track of 1983.

To give those who may follow in our wake an idea of the boat jobs that needed to be done to make CLYPEUS ready for sea, the following list may be helpful, and those who are not interested can just ignore the boring necessities.

1.   Peter repaired the keel with cement,
2.   Cleaned the hull, and tidied up the bow paintwork where the wooden dolphins, which Bruce had fashioned and fixed in New Zealand, had suffered. One had been knocked off and lost at sea in bad weather, so Peter removed the other dolphin and just painted a prosaic blue arrow on both sides.
3.   The wooden cockpit locker lids were rotting and needed repairs.
4.   He serviced the engine and it started without problems.
5.   The GPS, radios and all the movable electronic gear which had been hidden away for the winter had to be re-installed.
6.   The starboard side fuel gauge transmitter needed repair and re-fitting.
7.   Both bilge pumps were serviced.
8.   Bow rollers were replaced to ease hauling up the anchor
10.   The stern gland needed tightening.
11.   The broken hose connector to the swan neck exhaust needed repairing.
12.   Made a new elliptical steering seat

While he was busy with those maintenance items:

1.   I scrubbed the decks,
2.   Scrubbed the sail covers,
3.   Prepared and painted the bathroom white,
4.   Prepared and painted the saloon bulkhead.
5.   Made a maroon Rexine cover for the rusting heater and table leg
6.   Varnished all the teak.
7.   e-mailed family and friends from Owners email room.
8.   Shopped, cleaned, kept house and enjoyed swimming each afternoon and generally being in the sunshine and making friends with like-minded free spirits.

On the 26th of May 2003 we moved on board and were launched two days later.

Insurance is a problem when ocean sailing as it is difficult for companies to assess the dangers and they therefore charge high premiums. In the first couple of years we were insured by Lloyds but by the time we got to Tahiti the premium quoted was over half our income. From then, 1985, until now 2003, we had no insurance for the boat or ourselves. However Third Party boat insurance is now compulsory in the EU. Peter organized a new policy through Pantenaeus who have a good reputation and also supply Cover Notes translated into many European languages which is particularly convenient. No harbour authority did ever check our insurance papers but some yachts have needed to produce them.

We enjoyed one more fun trip to Cineviz before starting for Spain. It was great to be at sea again. Sitting on the bowsprit singing my head off in the hope that dolphins would come and join me – *The Ash Grove, My Bonnie, Westering Home, Blow the Winds Southerly* – but no dolphins came this time. I watched the dissolving clots of froth in the bow wave, they look like clusters of tadpoles before disappearing. I thank God or who/whatever caused our existence for the happiness of being here, where I want to be. Yes, religion is a crutch. I need it. In times of disaster when we can do no more to save ourselves, I need someone to pray to. In times of delight, like now, I need some being to thank (as well as Peter).

The Lycian Coast beckons: Phasaelis, Olympia, the Chimera; exciting caves with dark recesses penetrating into the rock strewn cliffs; the sparkling calm sea with white froth creaming away from our hull and our wake curling dark circles behind us. A single cotton wool puff of cloud hovers over the pale bare mountain tops. Snow still lingers in the gullies near the top. Gulets are tucked into bays and creeks. Sunbathers spread themselves on the rocks, exploring caves or snorkeling - the silhouette of their flippers suddenly rising as they dive, like the fluke of a whale. We putter along – Peter always

taking the safest, seemingly longest, route to our destination.

This time there were already ten boats moored in Cineviz so we motored round to Hidden Bay. I sit at dusk in the silent bay – thrice blessed – my husband, my family, my life. The dark water sucks and laps the secret crevices between the rounded boulders. Goat's bells tinkle, but I can't see them as they scramble beneath the cliff side pines. The pungent scent of the trees drifts across the water. Two yacht groups have fires on the beach, the smell of their steaks combines with the woodsmoke. A local group of men gather at the rear of a red truck and pass drinks around with laughter. A fishing boat chugs past the entrance to the bay. White cliffs reflect in the dark water. Cicadas make their last shrill statement of the day. The boat swings in the slight chill of a breeze.

On that day I found an unusual empty perfect Mediterannean cowrie shell; smooth and shiny, brown spotted with a fawn underside and strong teeth. It's about an inch long and ½" inch high and doesn't conform to any of the illustrations in Hamlyn's *Mediterranean Sea Life Book*. Snorkelling was perfect in clear aquamarine water with swirling currents of cold fresh water springs rising from the sea floor combining like gin and tonic again.

High granite cliffs, brown stained with pine trees clinging in each cleft. Rock falls tumbled into the sea – I wonder how long ago they fell? Our awnings droop in the stillness, the reflection of the moon in the water beside me catches my eye. Peter tests the lights and asks for confirmation: "Stern OK?" "Yes", "Bow?" "Yes", "Masthead?" "Yes," "Port and Starboard?" "Yes, Yes."

It had been a typical Turkish day of glorious sailing, swimming and after dinner an amusing cut-throat game of Trivial Pursuits – picked up from the swop table in Larnaca Marina. Most Continental marinas have a swop table where 'not needed' items are left – every crew wishes to constantly lighten their boat and tries to get rid of inessential stuff. However, as you know, other people's trash can be your treasure. Trivial Pursuits Australian Version includes questions like 'Which horse won the Melbourne Cup in 1979?' 'How many players are there in an Australian Rules Football Game?' and various Australian History, Literature, Pop, TV, and film celebrity questions. "Tough." or "My turn then" are the only replies for pleas of "Mercy," or "it's a ridiculous question."

We slept on deck under the stars. All was magical peace and calm as the moon rose over the granite cliff tops.

The following day we headed back to Kemer to fill up with fuel, pick up our new European Third Party Insurance Policy, check out of Turkey in the Customs and Immigration Offices conveniently situated in the marina compound, answer last minute emails and shop for fresh fruit and vegetables in the market.

At last, on the 10th of June we were finally on our way home at 05.45. Looking back towards the shore, Kemer, snuggled beneath the high mountains, took on a brilliant pink hue in the rising sun. We were sorry to say goodbye but pleased to be on our way.

In the late afternoon when anchored off

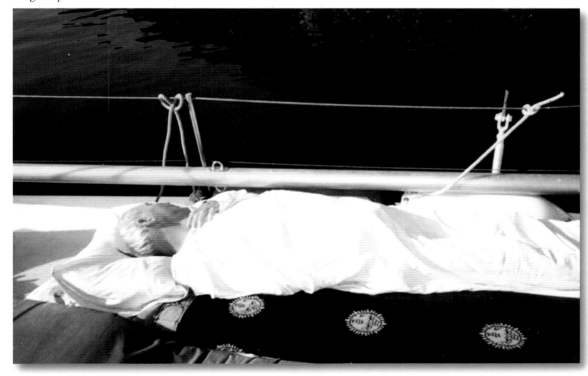

We slept on deck under the stars.

Healthy looking cats sat around patiently waiting for any tidbits.

Kalekoy Peter radioed Ibraham to pick us up at 7 p.m. for dinner. We were joined by 'ANDANTE', and new friends on 'CLAIRE DE LUNE' and 'SHARPEN UP'. During the meal there was a power cut but one of our group produced a small accordion from under the table and serenaded us with Cajun music in the candlelight.

Evidently he had mangled his left hand in an anchor winch and learning to play a music box was helping restore the muscles. It was a memorable night for our last evening with Marie Andre and Emilien. A strong friendship had developed which we hope will be lifelong.

After Ibraham had delivered his generous free bread at 8 am we left for Kastellorizon to book into Greece.

Travelling west we threaded our way through Akar Boyazi Strait, a narrow channel between a harsh sun-baked peninsula and a steep-sided treeless island. It looked dangerous, but our echo sounder showed the channel to be deep and there were no problems.

At 11a.m., only three miles off the Turkish coast, we moored stern-to in Greek Kastellorizon Harbour with help of a local Restauranteur. He took our lines efficiently calling out: "Complimentary cold beers in my Taverna over there", he pointed. "When you are ready."

What a great welcome back into the EU. We walked to the Customs Post to book in and the officer sent us to the Police Office where we were given permission to stay for 24 hours "Then go to Crete to book in."

However, when we met the Officer next morning he had found the right forms and all was settled very quickly with no VAT charges. We were now definitely in the European Union.

It was an excellent lunch with cold beers, Greek

salad, grilled fresh herrings, creamy moussaka, a jug of Retsina, all for €17.50 (£11 for two). A group of Israeli men from the Israeli yacht 'YAM' were having a hilarious lunch and invited us to join them. All spoke excellent English and we put the world to rights over more coffee and ouzo. There are many Israeli yachts around the Turkish coast.

Kastellorizo, is the smallest inhabited Greek Island in the Dodecanese group, (6km by 3 km) only two miles from the Turkish coast, 72 miles east of Rhodes and 150 miles from Cyprus – we hadn't got very far in three years had we? It is a mountainous and rocky island with its small colourful capital in the centre of an aquamarine bay. It is the southernmost Greek Island, often left off the maps of Greece. From the 5th to 19th Century it had been an important trading post between Europe and the Middle East. The town was virtually destroyed during the First World War and then when Mussolini's flying boats used the town's north facing horse-shoe bay of sparkling blue as their base, it became a target to be bombed in 1942.

The history of the island is long. Originally named Megiste, Neolithic tombs and a gold crown from the Mycenaean period, and Lycian and Doric inscriptions, have been found. The Knights of

Rhodes had the castle built (1377-1396) to be one of the strongest fortresses in the Aegean Sea to protect its 'wondrous' port from pirates, despots, an Egyptian Armada, Spanish, Franks, Venetians and of course, Turks, until the Greeks conquered it and encouraged a flourishing port. Magnificent churches were built with sumptuous icons; famous schools were founded. Then the French took it, abolished the Greek authorities and in 1920 handed it over to the Italians when it had a population of around 15,000. From then on the people started leaving for safer homes. When the friendly British Army landed in 1941 there were only 2,000 inhabitants. Two days later the Italians bombed the island so heavily the British left and the Fascists took over. Later it was bombed again by the Germans completing the destruction of the palatial houses, schools and churches.

Now Kastelorizo has a population of only 275 but it is rising like a Phoenix from the ashes. Many Islanders emigrated to Australia after both World Wars. These now affluent "Kassies", (Kastellorizo Aussies) are returning to find their family homes and restore them on their former glorious Athenian lines. We noticed 'lucky eyes' built into the front

doorstep of one harbour-side house. It is becoming a beautiful resort for the rich and famous but for us it was still a village of friendly, hard working people, speaking a mixture of Greek and Australian. 'Gooday Mate' was often the greeting.

There are many routes to choose to get to Spain, island hopping via the Cyclades Islands and southern Greece but we decided to head west via Crete.

After collecting 500 euros from the bank we booked out at the Harbour Office, the Officer raised an eyebrow when we said we were sailing directly to Crete but didn't say anything. We still don't understand why he didn't warn us.

After the disastrous night on The Angry Sea, told in Chapter One, we lost our nerve. So here we were in Pigadia on Karpathos, chastened, unsure of our ability to carry on, very aware that time had taken its toll and we weren't the strong young things we thought we were. This wasn't the place to try and sell a concrete yacht. We must carry on, but with greater care. The new plan was to sail from Crete to Sicily, Sardinia, Menorca, cross our outward track at Ibiza then make our way to nearby Denia Marina in Spain; where our son, Noel, has a villa. If we couldn't sell CLYPEUS there, perhaps we could use her as a floating holiday home? It meant we wouldn't have to go out into the Atlantic again, at least, not this year

Pigadia seemed a clean and friendly town with few tourists. Rod Heikell's *Greek Waters Pilot* describes our next landfalls of Karpathos and nearby Kasos as:

'Two sea-swept islands which are the most southerly of the Dodecanese. Lying between Crete and Rhodes in a stretch of angry sea, the islands seem to have been bypassed by history.'

If only we had appreciated what that 'stretch of

Lucky eyes' built into the front doorstep of one harbour-side house.

angry sea' involved before we set out.

In the morning a Pigadian Harbour official informed us we could move to a more convenient place so that we could climb ashore. After spreading the wet books, carpets and cushions out to dry we walked into town. Prices were reasonable in euros and nobody hassled us to buy or eat in their restaurant. A restaurant terrace festooned with vines and purple and pink bougainvillea beckoned us. The white marble-topped round tables and blue wooden chairs with woven straw seats looked perfect.

The plump owner introduced herself in excellent English and told us, "I married a Yank after the War and lived in Milwaukee for many years. He died ten years ago, so I decided to come home and bought this restaurant. It's going well and I feel useful. I didn't really know what to do with myself in America after Jim died. I'm happy and busy here."

We knew Milwaukee as the headquarters of Peter's Company is based there and we had lived there in an apartment in 1998, so we had plenty to talk about.

A carafe of retsina with spinach pie and calamari was eaten while looking out over the sparkling harbour to our dear boat. We did say a little 'Thank you God' grace before we ate.

Next day we gave ourselves a treat and hired a car stopping for coffee on a steep cliff side overlooking the underwater remains of an old Roman Harbour. There was no real road to the village at the base of the cliff so donkeys carried provisions down in panniers slung either side of the saddles.

A taverna beside a sandy beach provided a fresh sardine lunch and a rest on the sand. A perfect relaxing day exploring the mountainous island restored our equilibrium.

With great trepidation we nosed out of relatively safe Pigadia Harbour into calm seas. There was no wind and our confidence gradually returned as we motored for twenty miles to Helatros Bay on the south of Kasos Island. After lunch at anchor, a swim, and reading, I rowed into a spooky cave as high as an aircraft hangar. Ashore there were ruins but no habitable houses, just goats nibbling the dry grass. Heikell says:

"In 1824 the Egyptians ravaged the islands and Kasos never recovered. (The Kasiots remember it as the Holocaust.)"

Ominous mist and driving cloud greeted us next morning. The forecast on the laptop was "S. Aegean - W 4-5 all week". We decide to go, go, go. Pulled up the dinghy and boarding ladder, sealed the hatches, took a Dramamine pill each to hold back sea sickness, reefed the mainsail and hoped for the best.

We started out, ready to turn back if necessary. The engine performed perfectly and eventually the sky cleared and the wind freshened, so up jib and staysail. Our landfall in Crete was Sitia Marina where, as soon as we arrived, we made friends with a New Zealand family on ESSENCE, a spacious Bavarian 47' moored alongside. We'd been asked to look out for them by our American friends on FAIR ROSE and VOYAGER. Their yacht seemed huge, but lightly built, compared to CLYPEUS. They were circumnavigating with 14 year old Sven and 12 year old Belinda who were enjoying their school correspondence courses and sailing lifestyle, although often lonely for other teenagers.

After a couple of days we motored on through an uncomfortable swell towards Spinalonga Lagoon. It was getting very rough and windy and we happily pulled in to shelter behind the old Leper Colony upon which Victoria Hislop based her

popular novel *"The Island."*

In the wind I rowed to the island to explore the old leper village and hospital which had only been abandoned in 1957. A sad history as once the lepers arrived they were destined never to leave. The old fort ruins and dilapidated hospital, houses, laundry, graveyard and the still functioning little church, made it easy to imagine the pleasant caring community which eventually evolved. The lepers were remarkably resourceful producing their own newspaper, choirs, theatre productions and of course a school. Some of the village houses are now being restored.

Next day the wind was still blowing hard, so we weren't going anywhere. Peter took the opportunity to make new lids for the cockpit lockers.

Trying to leave next morning it was still too rough outside the Lagoon so we changed our minds and turned back, re-anchored and caught the bus into Aya Nikolas. There we found an internet café to email our family and visit the Marina which seemed modern, well sheltered and inexpensive. When we arrived back at the boat it was calm enough to swim to scrub weed and dirt from CLYPEUS's waterline. Another day was spent waiting nervously for the wind to die down.

Crete has a long and interesting history, the Minoans being only one of the ancient civilizations. One gruesome story recounts the island being retaken for Byzantium by Emperor Nikephoros who catapulted the heads of captured prisoners into the stronghold of Heraklion and so demoralized the defenders that they capitulated. (I wouldn't have given much for their chances of long and happy life!)

At last on the 25th we burst out of the lagoon heading into white horses with the reefed main and staysail up. We were going so well Peter added the Yankee jib and we headed for Heraklion. The rugged coast is topped by many wind farms with propeller blades spinning around with a great whirring and whistling. Ravines in the cliff were crowded with pink oleander blossoms looking like pink waterfalls flowing down to the sea. CLYPEUS was scooting along towards Heracklion so we by-passed Khersonison.

It was exciting to sail into the narrow gap behind the Venetian Fortress guarding the end of the harbour wall and see huge cruise liners docked on the inland side, close to town. The view from the marina was spectacular towards the ancient vaulted workshops where Roman galleys had been built and

After a couple of days we motored on through an uncomfortable swell towards Spinalonga Lagoon.

The view from the marina was spectacular towards the ancient vaulted workshops where Roman galleys had been built.

repaired. How had the Town Planners allowed a large modern angular khaki building to be erected above the ancient vaults? It looked so out of place.

Friendly Pam of ESSENCE took our lines to moor near them. After dinner, with Pam and the children, we walked along the Harbour Wall and enjoyed an iced coffee. Sven loaned me the second Harry Potter book so I crawled in beside a sleeping Peter and read until midnight. We stayed with Sven and Belinda the following evening while their parents enjoyed a meal on their own. Monopoly was suggested and we were soundly thrashed at the game we have been playing for fifty years by these two youngsters. They bought and sold houses and hotels, redeeming Mortgages and playing a much more sophisticated game than we had ever seen.

For three days there was plenty to explore. We went to the Historical Museum first where displays were limited to Heraklion town. It contained icons and models of the town's development from Byzantine times with its ancient city walls, gates and bastions, up to the present day. More interesting, for us, was the Archeological Museum, full of fascinating artifacts which gave us some idea of the Minoan civilization but we noted that Antalya Museum which we had visited last year had better Roman artifacts and there is no doubt that Cairo Museum is a winner with the solid gold funerary mask of Tutankhamen being more beautiful than I had imagined, with a softness that was palpable. Of course Taiwan's fabulous "largest collection of stolen goods in the world" beats them all. We had spent many hours in the Chang Kai Shek Museum when living in Taipei. Chang Kai Shek and his followers denuded the Palaces and Museums of mainland China to prevent the Communists breaking up and destroying the collections of fabulous jewelry and artifacts. The

Generals and War Lords escaped to Taiwan with their cargoes of beautiful and historic pieces dating back to 5,000 BC and took them to Taipei where a magnificent Museum displays less than a quarter of the total spoils. (The rest are stored in caves in the mountainside behind the Museum.)

Next day Peter had had enough of museums, so I pushed off on my own to Zachros and the following day to Knossus.

I took the local bus to the low, grey-walled Greek ruins at Zachros which looked boring so I decided to spoil myself with a typical lunch which included a small carafe of Retsina at the beach-side Taverna with straw-seated chairs and blue and white check-clothed tables. Contented, I staggered to the bus stop to wait for the local bus to take me home. It passed the entrance to the extraordinary rift valley of palms which, we were later told, we should have hiked down.

Knossus was fascinating. I appreciated the painted walls of the Minoan ruins and the restored frescos. It made it much easier to imagine how the ancients lived.

As soon as the Harbour Officials come on duty we paid our dues and headed twenty miles to

Knossus was fascinating. I appreciated the painted walls of the Minoan ruins and the restored frescos. It made it much easier to imagine how the ancients lived.

Osmos Bali in a flat calm, eventually mooring stern-to in a protected little spot but with a dozen hotels overlooking the small cove. We made full use of the free water hoses on the jetty for, washing the decks, showers and shampoos. Peter walked up to the village three times for various boat bits and the easy, happy day ended with a good dinner ashore.

Sixteen miles later we tied up alongside the huge quay in Rethimon. It was the 1st July and it was HOT! To refuel, the tanker drove onto the Quay and put aboard 131 litres of diesel. I watched young boys squealing with delight as they jumped from the high roof of the boat in front then scrambled back up the hull and superstructure like marauding pirates.

The Cretan capital, Khania (Chania) looked quaint and romantic as we entered between the red towers of the Venetian Harbour and moored immediately in front of the Customs and Harbour Master's Office. Visiting officials was never easier.

Horse-drawn tourist carriages clip-clopped past the cockpit and along the crowded cobbled alleys. Most of the tourists seemed to be attractive blonde Scandinavians. After a few pleasant days exploring the town we booked out of Crete with the Authorities and decide to follow our new Plan C:

MILES TO	DESTINATION
32	Anti-Kithera
20	Kapsali Bay
30	Cape Matapan on the Greek mainland
41	Sapientza and on through the Ionian Sea
20	Proti Channel
38	Katakolon
25	Glarenza
25	Akra Aspro
28	Levkas East Coast
16	Preveza where CLYPEUS could be hauled out

275 miles

After a strong wind weather forecast we decided to make straight for Kapsali Bay, on Kithera, where we dropped anchor and motored astern to the quay and tied up in the calm and peaceful evening. After seeing the Harbour Police and supper we fell into bed only to be up at 4 a.m. in the rising wind when Peter rowed out and dropped the additional fisherman's anchor.

We moored immediately in front of the Customs and Harbour Master's Office. Visiting officials was never easier.

In the morning when I returned with fresh bread he was anxious because more wind was forecast. We hauled up both anchors and tied up alongside the quay with the help of a friendly young Greek crew. It was blowing hard but we felt safer and could step ashore.

Kithera and Anti-Kithera were important stepping stones between Crete and the mainland. From 3000 BC Kithera has been regularly fought over because of its strategic location. Minoans, Phoenicians, Romans, Greeks, pirates, Ottomans, Venetians, French, English and Germans have all occupied the island at various times and it shows in the architecture. The Athenians and Spartans fought over it and the population has varied between less than 50, after being sacked by Barbarossa and the survivors being sold as slaves by the Algerian pirate Kemel Reis, and 7,500 during the prosperous Venetian years.

During the economic downturn after WWII many Kitheranians emigrated to Australia and have now returned bringing prosperity and nicknamed it 'Kangaroo Island'.

The wind moderated during the night and in the morning we walked up through vineyards to Chora, the small capital and enjoyed ice creams in the shaded central square of Venetian and English looking houses. There is still an English Cemetery but we climbed up to the exciting old castle above the bay.

After a Sunday lunch 'small beer plate' at a beach restaurant, Peter returned to CLYPEUS for a good sleep. Thank goodness, as at 5 p.m. PRINCE came in and wished to tie up to the quay and needed more space. They didn't offer to help as Peter rowed out and moved both our anchors in the heavy swell sweeping into the harbour. Marcus, a new Greek friend, swam out to help but it was stressful and Peter looked exhausted when all was secure.

Our new young Greeks friends on the adjoining large, smart and modern GRP yacht came for coffee and extolled the virtues of our humble craft. They were part of a team researching dolphins in Greek waters and said:

"CLYPEUS is a proper yacht, with character, not a soul-less plastic hull like ours. It makes our boat seem like a modern machine, not a comfortable home in which to travel the world."

I offered them extra cake!

The Marine Police supplied correct weather forecasts daily and on Tuesday 8th July they, and the fishermen, said it would be perfect to sail for Cape Matapan the south western corner of mainland Greece. Hooray! We felt we were almost back in real mainland Europe.

North of Kithera there were many merchant vessels and we held back each time to let them pass. With the main and staysail up and the motor going we were averaging more than five knots. Anchoring in Port Kaio in 15 to 20 feet of water in the early evening it suddenly seemed much cooler and we needed a blanket for the first time for years.

The sea was calm to Cape Matapan (Akritas) until nearing Venetico Island where the shallow water became rough and we were pleased to find an anchorage in Longos Bay on Sapientza Island.

After another rest day we headed towards Methoni, which turned out to be a pretty town renowned for its wine and bacon. Mid morning our feet landed on the sand of mainland Greece and we headed into town to celebrate.

CHAPTER EIGHT | BACK IN MAINLAND EUROPE | 2003 GREEK MAINLAND

2003 Greek Mainland: Methoni – Proti Island – Katakolon – Olympus - Zakynthos – Ithaca –
Parapagidi Island - Frikes - Levkas – Nidri Lagoon – Preveza

IT WAS THE 11TH OF JULY when we finally anchored beneath Methoni's Venetian and Turkish Fort on the Greek mainland. Methoni was mentioned by Homer as being 'rich in vines'. A fisherman's lunch of fresh grilled sardines and Greek salad was exactly what we wanted. The Moorish Fort and Castle were well worth exploring.

That evening I washed my hair in the sea and then showered on the beach to rinse it properly. It

seems a long time since our ocean voyages when I had to wash my hair in sea water and then, with conditioner in just a pint of water, rinse it through my hair time and time again to get rid all the salt. It's amazing now to look back on those thirty day long voyages across the Pacific and Atlantic. (The Indian Ocean has convenient ten day long steps from Thailand: Sri Lanka and The Maldives before you reach Oman). Now we were anchored close to modern, bigger boats with so many facilities – but could they keep them all working long term without huge fuel tanks and help from freezer and electronic mechanics?

Peter topped up the engine oil as he calculated it was 90 hours since the last time. I just mention these little maintenance details as while I gaily row ashore and explore, he keeps the boat and equipment in good order. He just doesn't seem to want to come with me. He enjoys being on the boat and looking forward to any emergencies so that he can prove he was ready for them! He has successfully done that and I do appreciate his devotion to keeping everything running well.

Left:
A fisherman's lunch of fresh grilled sardines and Greek salad was exactly what we wanted.

Right:
We finally anchored beneath Methoni's Venetian and Turkish Fort on the Greek mainland. Methoni was mentioned by Homer as being 'rich in vines'.

I stood on a plinth for a funny photo but jumped off when shouted at by a guard. It sounded like the Greek equivalent of "Gerrroff".

A couple of days later we anchored further northwest on the east side of Proti Island. An interesting wreck lay submerged in the bay identified by a single sloping spar sticking up about a metre above the water. Snorkelling over it was a bit scary out there on my own: would the arm of a giant octopus reach out and grab me? Of course it wouldn't, but I can't help these thoughts flashing through my mind as I swim alone. (Peter doesn't like getting wet. He says that is why he bought a boat.) After a lovely day, a full, bright, white moon rose, so we slept on deck and in the morning were surprised by the heavy dew. As we crossed the bay of Arcadia for once the smell wasn't fishy or industrial but the agricultural sweet acrid scent of wood smoke rising from fires on the misty shore. The flat white clouds strung towards us in parallel lines across the water. They were burning vine prunings to give more nutrition to the bunches of grapes that hung white and hard like clusters of olives. This is currant country.

The background of mountains gradually receded and gave way to flat marshland – so the book says! We still haven't seen a charter Flotilla. Last night we slept on deck, lying directly in the moon's silver path. CLYPEUS 'sushed' and gently slapped the water as though telling it to keep quiet and rest.

A few days later we had trouble tying up at Katakolon as the bollards were spaced for Ocean Liners. Two huge white sparkling vessels came in next morning and disgorged their passengers into coaches to visit Olympia about 25 miles away. When the tourist shops opened, I was astounded at the excellent quality and variety of 'goodies' available and bought pleasing birthday and Christmas gifts.

We had a local visitor which we appreciated.

There are so many yachts in the Mediterranean that now hardly any locals come to chat, so we enjoyed Dr. Alexander Diamondopoulis coming to talk to us and offering an invitation to his boat for drinks and slices of juicy red water melon so that Peter could explain how our self-steering gear worked. The next day, with a promise that he would join us for dinner on board, he drove us into Pirgos where we caught the bus to Olympia.

There were many workmen and archaeologists working on the site preparing it for the 2004 Olympic Games to be held there the following year. I stood on a plinth for a funny photo but jumped off when shouted at by a guard. It sounded like the Greek equivalent of "Gerrroff".

Back on the quay at 4 p.m. a little sign pinned to the wall in the Port Office offered showers in a holiday cottage. Collecting soap and towel I started uphill through a vineyard to shower in an outbuilding (probably an old goat shed) looking out over the hills and harbour. CLYPEUS looked like a tiny toy boat surrounded by bathtub size cruise liners. Then back down to prepare dinner. It turned out to be a good evening. Dr. Diamondopoulis had had a fascinating career.

Off we motor-sailed towards Zante and anchored somewhere – we were not quite sure, but decided it must have been Porta Roma. The swell rolled in and we had to re-anchor twice.

Sailing up the coast of Zakynthos to Zante town presented a green and pleasant island. However for some reason I had chest pains and stayed in bed all the following day. It is essential that with limited access to doctors and no private health insurance we take all obvious steps to prevent any illness. Next day I was perfectly all right.

On Sunday a coach tour around Zakynthos was

supposed to include a boat trip to the Blue Caves. Unfortunately it was too rough so we had to make do with a post card! However Shipwreck Bay was spectacular. The earthquake of 1953 hasn't left many ancient ruins on Zakynthos, but two ancient olive trees have survived for over 2,000 years. The

Venetians called Zakynthos 'the flower of the Levant', the fertile interior, planted with vines, figs, olives, orange and lemon groves, is surrounded by mountains.

We chatted to two French couples on a charter yacht who enjoyed coming on board for drinks and a chat to find out about sailing the world. Zante is a big tourist town with good hotels. The Manager of the nearest Hotel allowed us to spend an afternoon swimming and sunning ourselves in their roof top pool and take the opportunity for shampoo and showers.

We tried to leave early on the 22nd but the anchor chain of an Italian yacht had fouled our anchor and Peter didn't want to wake them. He struggled, heaving chains from the dinghy and eventually managed to extricate the CQR and we headed for Cephalonia only 35 miles away on a windless morning. We were going so well that he

**Left:
Shipwreck Bay
on Zakynthos
was spectacular.**

**Right:
Two ancient
olive trees have
survived for over
2,000 years.**

insisted we carried straight on to Ithaca in spite of my having read *Captain Corelli's Mandolin* in readiness for exploring Cephalonia.

Ithaca's high dragon back was covered with silvery grey shrubs and the anchor clattered out in an uninhabited cove near Arethusa's Stream. The rippling sea, was now as smooth as glass, as the sun pierced the clear depths. After a swim, and barbecue on a drift-wood fire on the beach, we prepared for sleep, but a big swell began to roll. At 21.30 we fired up the engine and carefully motored to the channel between Pera Pigadhi Island (Rat island) and Ithaca. The Greek Pilot Book told us to beware of rats on Pera Pigadhi, so instead of tying up to the jetty in the dark, we anchored in a deep 45' of calm water. We were sorry for a charter yacht which did unknowingly tie to the jetty. We could hear the crew shouting and banging pans all night to fight off the rats. In the morning it was a long job retrieving our anchor, but worth it.

On to Sarkiniko Bay for another perfect day and another beach barbecue. We watched a fisherman's wife bait seemingly hundreds of hooks on a line and lay it in neat circles ready to pop over the side later. The swell from passing ships rolled CLYPEUS from gunwale to gunwale. However it wasn't as bad as the previous bay as we were further inside the cove and in less danger from breaking waves.

After exchanging anniversary gifts and an egg and bacon celebration breakfast, we motored through a mist- shrouded heaving sea into Frikes Harbour just in time to meet a flotilla of Sunsail charter boats leaving to continue their holiday. They looked as thought they were doomed to sail on for ever like the Flying Dutchman, as they disappeared into the haze.

The mist rolled in again and then rolled away. I loved Ithaca and want to return. It seemed criminal to only stay for twenty-four hours but Peter was adamant that we must push on. I knew he was right but remembered

Cavafy's poem:

To ITHACA
by Constantine Peter Cavafy
1863 born in Alexandria

Setting out on the voyage to Ithaca
You must pray that the way be long;
Many be the summer mornings
When with what pleasure, with what delight
You enter harbours never seen before….
You must always have Ithaca in your mind
Arrival there is your predestination.
But do not hurry the journey at all
Better that it lasts many years;
Be quite old when you anchor at the island,
Rich with all you have gained on the way…

Well, our 'way' had certainly been long and we are more than 'quite old' but there is no reason why we can't fly back one day.

In the morning the water was as calm and full of mercurial colour as a pool of motor oil. When the fog cleared we made for Sivota Harbour on Levkas. Peter did allow us to divert to look at the caves on Meganisi Island before trying to anchor in Rouda Bay. The wind was blowing directly into the Bay and untenable so we carried on to Sivota where again, the anchor refused to hold.

It looked such a pretty island but we couldn't find a bay which was shallow, or sheltered enough to anchor. We gave up and continued on to anchor in over-populated Nidri Lagoon in the middle of a host of boats, happy and safe. The sounds from the town were incredible after our days of quiet sailing into small coves. A wedding fleet of guests followed the bride and groom's car, their blaring car horns filled the air for many minutes.

We were trying to decide where to leave CLYPEUS for the winter. A local bus took us into Levkas where we explored the Marina and questioned other yachtsmen moored up against the pavement quay near the town centre. Everyone was very helpful and gave us information and many choices of good wintering places. Yacht Chandlers abounded with a vast array of spare parts.

On 29th July we motored through the Canal from Nidri to Levkas Town. A new friend Mark, to whom we had chatted the day before on LORNA, helped us to tie up. Moored stern-to the low pavement promenade it was only possible to get on and off CLYPEUS by standing on the Aries self-steering gear and, carefully, hoicking a leg over the pushpit.

Levkas town was charming: pretty flowered alleyways, most of them too narrow for cars. The people were friendly and many spoke some English. It had an air of a family town enjoying itself. From nine to midnight each weekend evening the main pedestrian streets were crowded with ambulating families: smartly dressed mothers holding hands with husbands in short-sleeved shirts and long pants; little girls in fashionable outfits clutching handbags; babies in strollers; toddlers at tables ploughing through plates of chips.

At 11.30 p.m. in the squares, tables were still full of diners and drinkers but no drunks. Many shops were still open. Levkas was rebuilt after the 1953 earthquake following the higgledy-piggledy lanes where the old houses had been. I felt able to

walk down alleys and mingle with the crowds without feeling threatened in any way. There seem to be no rough youths or leery men – if there are some, they are not obvious.

The following day we took the local bus to inspect the recommended marinas at Preveza on the mainland. Three marinas front the southern shore of the entrance to The Inland Sea. After inspecting the Yards and talking to the different office staff, Peter decided on Aktio Marina, a Greek business run by two brothers, rather than an international marina. We always like to support local firms if possible.

Aktio had unusual hydraulic boat lifting gear and Peter was worried that the rectangular pads on the hydraulic trolley might punch through our ferro-cement hull. On land, all the yachts, nestling on their cradles and props, were chained upright for extra stability in case of an earthquake. We left, asking for time to think about it.

While Peter was thinking and working out ways and means, I took the local bus over the mountains to Vassiliki Harbour on the south coast. It was an exciting scenic ride and my lunch beside the water was delicious. We have come to the stage in our marriage where we both do our own thing, I like to explore the land, Peter likes to stay on the boat. I guiltily 'Seize the Day' at every opportunity.

Levkas Festival was about to start and I was desperate to see some of the Greek Dance displays. Years of teaching Keep Fit and folk dancing had given me a passion for Greek Dancing which had been nourished by a six week voyage back from Australia in 1968 on the Greek Liner ELLENIS when I had been able to join in the cabarets and spend two hours each day practising Greek traditional dances.

Peter thought we should leave before the

Festival officially started. However one dance group kindly let me watch their rehearsals led by handsome Spiros Patapoupolis. A Sangria Evening at the Marina Restaurant looked fun but we didn't find anyone who wished to talk to us, so left early and slowly wandered home in the warm evening air.

On Sunday Peter decided he could afford the time for a day out and we both took the local bus to Kalisthisma. The bus chugged up mountain roads and around hair pin bends. Twenty miles for 1.30 euros through olive groves pierced with pencil pines reaching up dark green between the grey green olive trees. The pepper and salt sand beach had blue, clear clean water with no rubbish at the water's edge. Many of the beaches at the eastern end of the Mediterranean particularly in Israel, have a thick soup of plastic mush at the edge of the tide where the prevailing westerly winds have driven plastic bottles and bags from all the other upwind countries and islands.

For my birthday treat we enjoyed 'Tango Argentine,' one of the first items in the International Festival. At 11.30 p.m. when the show ended, we walked to the Romantica Restaurant where six local men were sitting around a table harmonising on guitars and bouzoukis. It was a pleasant authentic sound until at one o'clock when they decided it was time to go home.

On August 5th at 08.30, we let go from Levkas and waited for the canal swing bridge to open. No problems and the sea was calm as we motored across the bay to Aktio Boatyard opposite Preveza Town. We did visit the other two marinas again before Peter made his final decision. At Atkio, Yannis, the proprietor, reassured him and the lift out, although traumatic, was successful. Yannis proved to be master of his hydraulic launching trolley - he wore it rather than drove it. The friendly and efficient girls in the Office organized our charter air tickets home for 110euros (£66.00) each. The day after we arrived home to our lovely, but overgrown, Pembrokeshire garden, we heard that an earthquake of 6.5 on the Richter Scale had been recorded in Levkas. The Canal gates had been damaged and would be closed for at least six months. Houses and shops had collapsed and the promenade where we had moored was now a tumbled mess of paving stones. Many yachts stored in other yards had been knocked over and damaged by the domino effect. Fortunately our chained-down boat had survived, as had all the others in the Aktio Yard.

We had cruised 660 miles and thoroughly frightened ourselves in the three months of 2003 and decided to have the following year off, to collect our wits, and enjoy our Golden Wedding celebrations when all the family from America and Australia were travelling to Wales to be with us.

CHAPTER NINE | A CELEBRATION YEAR then GREEK MONASTRIES and ITALIAN ISLANDS

2004 Golden Wedding Anniversary Year. 2005 GREECE – SICILY. Aktio – Meteora – Vikos Gorge - Preveza – Riposto – Messina – Calabria – Volcano – Porto di Levane – Mandello Bay– Palermo – San Nicola de L'Arena – medical problem – Flight for MA.

IN 2004 WE DECIDED to have a rest and enjoy our Golden Wedding year and make the most of our first full year together for 24 years, in our very own house and garden alongside Milford

Haven. My sister Sheila and I had a double wedding in 1954 when our father escorted us up the aisle with a daughter on each arm. When he had been approached by Tony and Peter for our 'hands in marriage' (as was usual in those days) Father said "Well, you can have two small weddings or one big double one." We all opted for the double day and it has been a joyful cause of celebrating together whenever possible. I wonder if in the future families will be able to celebrate as we did at our Silver Wedding, when Peter's, and our parents, celebrated their Golden Weddings in the same year and we had a line up of 150 years of marriage. This was also my 70th birthday party year, and I had to finish the dissertation for my MA in Creative Writing.

In May 2005, after an anniversary cruise from Mombassa to the Seychelles, we set off from Wales

refreshed and encouraged, looking forward to sailing CLYPEUS home and completing our quest. Peter had now decided that we would voyage all the way home without going to Spain, or out into the Atlantic, but up through the French Rivers and Canals. He was slowing down appreciably and had occasional pains in his chest for which he carried a small bottle of glyceryl trinitrate to squirt under his tongue if he felt ill.

At Preveza Airport on the 8th May, Yannis, one of the brothers who owned Aktio Marina, was waiting for us with his Land Rover. Although we came off the plane first, the new bobstay wire which Peter had had made up by commercial riggers in the UK, was the very last item to appear on the luggage belt. Yannis quietly waited for us for over an hour with no word of complaint.

There was a small apartment for boat owners at the boat yard which we occupied while we worked on CLYPEUS. Within a few minutes of arriving, new 'instant friends' from Liverpool with yachts up on the hard, offered tea bags and fresh milk to see us over until we went into town next morning in the marina bus. It was great to be back in this relaxed life-style with new and old friends and the cruising philosophy of 'help and appreciate your fellow yachtsmen and leave a clean wake."

For a month we worked on the boat. The first job was to clear a wasps' nest from inside the air vents, then we knuckled down. In the workshop provided for boat owners, Peter made a new bowsprit platform and re-welded the pulpit, repaired the hull and topsides, while I painted the decks, made courtesy ensigns for Italy, France,

Celebrating our Golden Wedding together.

Peter made a new bowsprit platform.

Malta and Spain.(I still wasn't really sure where we were going). He anti-fouled the port side of the hull, I did the starboard. Many evenings we strolled along the sandy waterfront to Ponni's Restaurant, where the waitress, Caliope, led us to the pots in the kitchen to choose our tasty supper. Making telephone calls from public boxes required punching in 38 digits.

A warning – even plants can bite. A pretty red-flowered bush bloomed in the grassy clothes-drying area. I tried to break off a sprig to see if it would sprout roots and grow in our garden as a reminder of a happy time. The prickly spines bit into my hand and hurt. Within two days my hand and arm became swollen and very painful and a visit to the hospital was necessary. It was a pomegranate bush. After waiting for hours in the packed Emergency Room of the local hospital I was kindly given a soothing cream and anti-biotics to cure my 'bush-bite'.

On Monday June 8th CLYPEUS was launched; always a heart-stopping event. Will they drop the boat? Everything was ready, provisions stowed, Yard paid, and the Greek Launching Certificate in order. The boat was lifted, trundled, then lowered towards the water. We climbed aboard and watched with our hearts in our mouths until that magic moment when the bowsprit dipped and we felt that wonderful soft movement - the inexpressible sensation of floating. We drifted slowly backwards as the trolley rolled back to the beach, while CLYPEUS curtseyed to her friends ashore. We motored a mile across the entrance to the Inland Sea to Preveza and anchored.

My hand was still swollen and painful, so after another visit to the crowded A & E department of the local hospital where they accepted the numbers on my E 111 as payment, and as the weather forecast was poor, we rented a little Fiat to visit Meteora ('in the air') and Vikos Gorge. Our new friends offered to keep an eye on CLYPEUS so we enjoyed a wonderful week driving through the Pindus Mountains, over the legendary Styx. Every corner opened up another magnificent snow-capped mountain view. Halfway lunch was enjoyed beside Ioannina Lake with its island monastery, then on to Kastraki (Kalembaka) in the middle of Thessalonika. It nestled beneath the towering grey monoliths topped with Monasteries, many of which

We walked around the high Churches, Sacristies, Libraries, store houses, cellars and scanned the incredible scenery from balconies across to the Plain of Thessaly. As I stumbled up the stairs to high monasteries I tried to imagine how they were first built when there were no steps or bridges. Even now food and goods are hauled up in a net by rope and pulley, which is how the monks used to arrive too.

Half-collapsed wooden ladders stick out from clefts in the rock where penitents existed in the caves for months on end without coming down; to punish their bodies for some act of disobedience or for allowing their thoughts to take flight back to the sinful world. I wonder what happened in a storm when the wind whirls and screams around the monoliths and thunder and lightning strikes those closest to heaven. What must have it been like when cold, cold winds and snow crept into every crevice? What wimpy creatures we have become!

Nearby were Neolithic cave dwellings only recently abandoned and now given over to goats and sheep. Spiros, our Greek Australian host, who owned the Hotel Sydney, told of an old man who still lived in the cave village and only came out on

encouraged visitors. Dopey from antibiotics I stumbled and bumbled up the stairs to high monasteries with my arm in a sling.

The Monasteries were established in the 11th Century on this 'stone forest' where contemplation, spiritual training and self-discipline could be pursued in peace. It is where the first great doctor, Asclepius was born. It is a place of silence and solitude where even I sat quietly to think about the thousands of ascetic Orthodox monks who had learned to be "wise in thought and humble in will".

Perfect sailng,
our passport to
adventure.

Fridays for shopping.

Most clichéd Greek images still exist up country where there are few tourists. Women in black shawls, laden donkeys, cats sprawled on whitewashed ledges, pots of red geraniums, old men playing cards and drinking ouzo.

Vikos Gorge was also mind boggling. We drove up a white pebbled track through towers and cliffs of pancake stones, to what we assumed was as far as we could go, then walked on a path through pleasant dappled woodland following a sign to 'LOOK OUT'. Suddenly we came to the cliff edge which was unguarded and about 1,000 feet below, a deep tree-lined gorge, which divided, both valley arms disappearing into the far distance. A million, million trees lined the gorge. It reminded us of the Australian Three Sisters Lookout in the Blue Mountains west of Sydney where gum tree tops also disappear into the distance.

On the way home, as we neared Preveza, we paused at ancient Nicopolis and were astonished again at magnificent ruins of the old city founded by the Roman emperor Octavian (Augustus) after he had defeated the combined fleets of Mark Anthony and Cleopatra in the naval Battle of Actium in 31 BC. Apostle Paul preached here in AD63. The city declined after an earthquake in 373, then was raided by the Goths and Vandals but then eventually abandoned in the 11th Century.

At last on the 15th June we left, bound for Sicily. We had decided not to visit mainland Italy as we had been told of Mafia problems in some harbours. The church clocks of Preveza struck eight o'clock as we glided past. The water was smooth with mist shrouding the mountains astern and Levkas Island on our left. The sun strengthened as we passed through the shipping lanes, dodging ferries, hydrofoils and merchant vessels. Peter

hoisted the mainsail, staysail and Yankee but there wasn't enough wind, so we motor-sailed west for three days and two nights with the mainsail up to keep us steady. When we started our voyage in 1983 the engine was a treasure, a luxury to be used only in emergencies and certainly never on ocean crossings, so all available diesel was kept for any possible emergency. Now, we are less purist, if we want to get somewhere, let's go for it. Sails up and if necessary to make a port in daylight, engine on as well. If the wind heads us from our course, tough! Sails down and we point where we want to go with all the power of our Perkins 4108. (BUT only at under1500 revs of course!)

Peter did it all as I watched him with my arm still in a sling as he carefully thought ahead before each action. – now, more than ever, my hero after fifty years together. (It was difficult to appreciate him when 'The Company' took all his energy and thoughts). He stands and thinks, chewing his cheek before he makes a move. Tall, fair, gentle and quiet; he is a patient man who copes with the boat and all practicalities with ingenious devices, usually using a piece of raw material carefully stored 'just in case'. A major project is a challenge but a decorative need - a chore. Mid-ocean, or on any boat, anywhere, he really comes into his own solving all practical problems with patient, ingenious engineering skills gathered over a lifetime of interest in all things mechanical. He has kept a 30 year old ferro-cement ketch ocean-worthy and used every skill he ever acquired: plumbing, engine repairs, making a new rudder, installing a new engine, rope splicing, maintaining GPS, electronics, wind vane steering, Auto Helm, Calor gas supply, cool box, plastering, painting and carpentry. He even welded a steel cradle together to hold CLYPEUS safely in Cyprus while we flew off to Shanghai.

His infinite patience reading and studying service manuals is extraordinary. He almost enjoys reading a good service manual as much as he does reading a John Grisham or a Frederick Forsythe novel. He likes rules. If we dance, which he does well and precisely, (but not often) it has to be to known and identifiable steps. Not for him a disco dance of varied undulations and timing. Not for him either an incautious act or laugh. Pleasures and acknowledged happiness are almost regarded as a sin! We are such opposites with my 'enjoy today, now,' attitude, it's amazing we have managed to stay together. But I appreciate his stability and ingenuity and he lives vicariously through me

without have to expend energy in exploring, making friends, dancing or swimming. He prefers me to try things out then he picks out the bits he wants to share – it works for us! For him things are simple, people are unpredictable and he is singularly self sufficient.

My swollen hand didn't prevent me from taking my three hour watches through the night as we crossed the southern limit of the Adriatic Sea. A misty moon peered down. Through the gloom I saw the ghostly lights of two merchant ships glimmering on the leaden surface, but they passed by safely. I love the night watches when I can sit and sing my way through all the songs I know without embarrassment, or play audio tapes I want to enjoy on the cockpit speakers: Dvorjak's New World soaring up to the stars; the Beatles and pop songs to exercise to while hanging on to the boom. Peter hates the long night watches – he resents having to be awake when his body says he should be asleep

The next night, sailing along in the dark I wondered: where is the moon? Where are the stars? Silence.

I sat in the cockpit at 2 a.m. halfway between here and there. Sicily was somewhere ahead. Our boat slid through the dark sea, the curling phosphorescent lips of the bow waves grinning their way across the black water.

Alone, alone, but not alone. Our children, 2,000 miles away, dance in my mind: baby days, funny sayings, school years and a mother's proud memories of their efforts. I sing the lullabies I used to sing to them: *Golden slumbers, Oh No John, No John, No John, No* – the boys liked that. *In Dublin's Fair City, My Bonny Lies over the ocean, The Sky Boat Song.* Then I launch into the songs we used to sing when I was a girl at home while we were washing up, particularly after

Sunday lunch. My mother harmonised naturally and sometimes even my father would join us in the kitchen with his strong baritone voice for *"The Bells of St. Mary."*

In 1998, in Australia when I was looking after him when he was 89 years old and failing, I sat beside his bed and held his hand. "Would you like me to sing to you, Daddy?"

"Must you?" he replied.

Not the reply I expected!

I had been fortunate to be able to fly from Singapore to be with my mother when she was dying and for the last three days in the hospital sang our family songs to her as she tried to squeeze my hand or move her fingers in time to the music. It was a major reason for our voyage, to spend more time with my parents who emigrated to Australia in 1981, when they were 75 years old to enjoy the sun and be near my sister Hilary. As they became older they had found it difficult to receive correct medical attention in Spanish Teneriffe where they had had a winter home for over twenty years. After spending some Christmases with Hilary in Rockingham, West Australia, they had made the decision to end their days there.

The compass glowed. No star to steer her by tonight. 'Poof'! A dolphin blows.

On the 17th June we could just see the toe of Italy through the mist as we approached Sicily. The peak of Mt Etna rose above the fog, and as the sun strengthened, we watched light trails of smoke blow in the wind from the summit. We were met at Riposto Marina entrance by white-shirted, short-shorted, tanned young Italians in a white RIB and led to a pontoon where they efficiently tied CLYPEUS up and asked us to report to marina office within the hour. Pleasant, smart receptionists welcomed us for 45e's a night (the most we had

ever paid) and showed us how to use the remote control for opening the security gate and showers.

We walked ashore and up towards Etna looking for a Clinic in the hope of a prescription for my still painful hand. The streets were paved with diamond shaped slabs of shiny black volcanic rock. Crumbling walls were made of grey stones and pebbles encased in grey volcanic ash with cement plastered over to smooth the surface. There was a good covered market with large and luscious vegetables but no supermarkets, only small family shops where our Italian dictionary earned its keep.

The ice cream parlours were un-passable and we enjoyed huge gelatos. Once we sat licking our cornets in a park watching a joyous fountain. It spewed plum-sized globs of water to varying heights where they paused, suspended, before they fell. They looked as though they were randomly jumping for joy.

Riposto was a good place, worth the marina fee. The shower was wonderful, I stood underneath the warm downpour, opening and closing my mouth like a fish.

A short lumpy sea breaking over our bows, discouraged us as we headed north to Taormina, so turned back, then tried again by sailing east, but gave up again and returned to Riposto. Next day, we set off again for Taormina, which looked very appealing terraced up to the summit of the hillside; if that was too difficult, we would carry on to Messina direct. Again we headed straight into rough steep seas. CLYPEUS turned into a bucking bronco. 'This can't be usual' we thought. 'Let's go back and try again tomorrow - another 45e's but worth it to lie still.' In Riposto outer basin we found a place to tie up against the wall alongside a stack of 3m x 2m concrete blocks. The view wasn't great but watching the Italians zooming around in sophisticated motor boats, mainly macho men, was exciting. The Marina was full of mega yachts and small sleek motorboats. Apprehensively we tried to sleep, sub consciously dreaming of stories of the whirlpools and dangers of Messina Strait which lies between Sicily and Italy :

From Homer's Oddyssey Book 12,
translated by R. Fitzgerald:
"Sobbing, gaining on the current, we rowed into the Strait - dire gorge of the Salt Sea Tide. By heavens! When she vomited, all the sea was like a cauldron seething over intense fire, when the mixture suddenly heaves and rises."

The Whirlpools: "Scylla to port, on our starboard beam Charybdis the giant whirlpool which swallowed ships which strayed too close. Salla was said to dwell in a cave atop a sheer cliff on the east side of the Strait. She had twelve feet which dangled down and six long necks with horrible hands which reached down to pluck dolphins and swordfish or sailors from passing ships. At the bottom of the cliff a whirlpool sucked down unwary ships".

However, it seems an earthquake in 1873 altered the local underwater typography and now the whirlpools are not quite so impressive but still strike fear in the hearts of those in small boats.

Rod Heikell's Pilot Books are a must for anyone sailing in the Mediterranean, not only for weather and coastal information, but also for snippets of geography, history and personal experiences.

'Whirlpools and eddies are caused by the less dense (salty) and warmer Tyrrhenian Sea mixing with the Ionian Sea and the submarine shape of the Strait. In the narrow part of the Strait the resulting eddies and whirlpools can bother small yachts. With wind against tide there are short high breaking seas and with eddies and whirlpools it is no place for a yacht to be. The eddies are termed 'bastardi'. The whirlpools are caused by denser water sinking and are accompanied by smooth oily patches and up-wellings of the less dense water rising up.'

On the 19th June we left Riposto again at 0600. The seas were not actually breaking but still lumpy. Over fifty fishermen were out in small boats. If they could do it, so could we. We headed well offshore to escape the swell. Taormino looked inviting descending towards the sea. Ever onward – the seas were not so bad, but it was still very windy.

With the wind on the beam, flying up through Messina Strait the mainsail blew out, one whole seam of stitching came undone. Hastily Peter rushed forward and pulled it down while I held the wheel and turned our bows into the wind. Under Yankee jib and staysail we diverted to Calabria where we tried to shelter, but the marina was full and we were told to 'go away'. The Main Harbour was lumpy and confused but we managed to tie up with difficulty, we were so tired.

However Peter reluctantly decided it wasn't safe to moor against the harbour wall with so much water movement, so we let go again and headed off to Messina. In the middle of all this he decided we should stop mid-channel so that he could change over the fuel tanks to make sure we would have plenty of diesel ready for whatever might befall.

Italy, on our right, was shrouded in mist. We just glimpsed the occasional dark skyline against the sun until we passed Cape Andrea and Cape Allessio on Sicily.

The rain ceased but Messina was murky in the dusk as we dodged ferries and cruise liners. Eventually, after waiting in line behind other yachts, were allowed in to find a berth beneath the view of evening promenaders who rested their elbows on the sea front wall and watched every movement.

The space to manoeuvre was tight, especially under critical eyes, but eventually we were tied up and safe again and we didn't care how much it cost. At 8 p.m. our Martinis tasted extra good that night.

Messina Marina has no protecting walls from the sea, just pontoons floating and rocking with every passing ship. Within the Marina a multitude of jelly fish undulated in the wakes of passing ships. The shower here was a contrast to Riposto and entailed a steep learning curve in the curtainless single cubicle. It was one metre square, windowless, with one clothes' hook. No electric light switch. I fumbled to find the tap and achieved a warm dribble. "Best to leave your shoes outside" I advised the next lady. Although it cost 40€s a night there was only one toilet and shower for each sex, although there must have been over fifty boats in the Marina..

Messina is a vibrant, happy, city. A variety of clocks chimed the hours, one after the other. High on the front face of the Cathedral clock at mid-day, golden images moved: a lion roared, a cockerel crowed, Father Time with a boy, slowly revolved. Multi-coloured Disciples rose up behind a white cloud then descended. All the while *Ave Maria* was playing. Sitting in the tree-lined square it was a 15 minute show. When I told Peter, he was interested in the mechanism and next day climbed the tower and was able to see the intricate workings: fascinating for any clock fancier.

In 1908 an earthquake caused the shores to subside by 0.6m and in Messina alone the tidal wave caused the death of some 64,000 souls. Another historic tragedy about which we knew nothing!

We took the mainsail to a sail maker for repair. There were so many small cars and scooters zipping around, you felt you could swat them and send them back to where they came from. The more difficult the terrain, be it mountainous hairpin bends, or busy city traffic, it stimulates Italians to ever greater recklessness. With the accelerator jammed down and the exuberant engines singing a poem of freedom, one small car after another comes rushing towards you at curves and tunnels, or on pedestrian crossings. On the water they zoom around the blue-water boats, engines roaring. Italians love a dangerous sport more than an arduous one.

One day as I left the patisserie the elegant male owner opened the door for me. "From where? Ah! England. Ah! Shakespeare, Marlow, Shelley, Byron, Keats, Wordsworth!"

The only European author I could think of that the spur of the moment was French: Voltaire, so I just nodded graciously with a full smile and 'grazi, grazi' to acknowledge his erudition.

A pavement café beckoned with delicious coffee and an opportunity to sit and people-watch. An obvious retiree from the Music Academy was being feted by her peers and students. She was given a huge bunch of deep red roses and I was shown a cake that had been made for her evening party covered in red rose petals made of icing sugar.

I lost my way through the streets while trying to find an Internet Café and asked an elderly gentleman with a stick if he could point me in the right direction. He laughed, faced me and pointed to his eyes. Both pupils were completely covered in cataracts. I hadn't notice his stick was white. We laughed together and shook hands.

He reminded me of the 'in' blind-person joke, told the other evening on a yacht whose owner taught blind people to sail.

"During a calm, when everyone was sitting in the cockpit waiting for the wind. One of my blind students, David, was asked by a sighted guest, "Isn't it dangerous for blind people to try and sail?"

"Not really," said David. "The wind on your cheek tells you its strength and direction. Some of my mates go parachuting." He said proudly.

The guest thought for a moment than asked, "But how do they know when they are nearing the ground?"

"Oh! The lead goes slack" David grinned.

I wished my Italian was good enough to share the joke with my blind friend – he would appreciate it.

I walked on and approached two 30/40 year old men leaning on the wall to ask the way to an Internet Cafe. After much discussion about routes, (and how you could tell the wealth and technological advance of a nation by how many internet cafes there were - the fewer cafes the higher the GDP). They offered to drive me to an email facility. Should I get into a car with two strangers? I decided to trust my judgment. It was an exciting ride, zooming in and out of the traffic. They were really kind and, after making sure I knew how to get back to CLYPEUS, they dropped me off opposite an internet café and didn't leave until I had safely crossed the road, opened the door and turned to wave a grateful goodbye.

It was the end of term for the Music Academy with concert performances by the students. Two excellent evenings were spent at classical concerts. All the ladies in the audience carried posies of flowers. Why? Was it a pretty tradition? Perhaps to avoid the smell of a hot neighbour?

Air tickets from Palermo to Stanstead were booked for two weeks hence to attend my Masters Degree Ceremony at Trinity College, Carmarthen, in July.

Morning sun and calm seas greeted us as we nervously headed north to pass by the whirlpools – there would never be a better day. The swirling pools could be distinguished but they didn't look deep or vigorous, still,

"Better not go too close," I shouted to Peter as CLYPEUS skirted the edges of a shallow spiraling Charybdis 'the sucker down'.

In the Odyssey Odysseus is warned by the Goddess Circe that he would have to steer a course between two rocks which were inhabited by two menacing monsters. On one side lived Scilla, a terrible beast with six heads who snatched anyone that dared to come near and tore them apart, while on the other was Charybdis, who swallowed the sea and then vomited it out creating sudden storms and whirlpools. Odysseus managed to overcome these obstacles, though he lost another six of his companions.

The peculiar sword-fishing boats were out with bowsprits as long as their hulls and a high cab fifty feet above the deck to scout for the swordfish. Evidently the fishermen's technique has been practised here for hundreds of years. The skipper, sitting in the cab on top of a tower set in the middle of the boat, controls it with a duplicate rudder. As the fish swim lazily along the surface, they splash about happily. When the skipper sees the movement, he turns the boat to approach the fish from behind. One of the crew takes a harpoon and walks out along the walkway projecting from the bows. As the tip of the bowsprit arrives overhead the unsuspecting fish is harpooned and pulled aboard. The boats didn't look seamanlike with their out-of-proportion appurtenances. The many smaller heavy fishing dinghies did though, as patient fishermen sat and waited for a bite.

The mainsail looked good after its repair and we decided it would 'see us out' as we made for

Porto di Levante on the Aeolian Island of Volcano. The strong smell of sulphur and anchoring over black sand was a reminder of Vanuatu in the Western Pacific. No sharks here though. In Vanuatu after I'd swum from the boat a couple of times, a local man ashore casually mentioned that three people had been 'taken' last year!

I wrote in my journal:
'Small island. Huge ice creams.'

The beach was of pumice, shingle and sand. I rowed ashore to spend a day under our beach umbrella. There were signs to a First Aid Tent. My hand was still swollen and painful. Brandishing my E111 I was allowed yet another free consultation and given a prescription for more anti-biotics. A German patient with severe jellyfish (medusa) stings on his enormously swollen arm helped me at the pharmacy. He had been in pain for days – so beware!

On shore, two feet above the sea, surrounded by flat rock is a pale warm mud pool. Sun-hatted heads, of rotund tourists sit and wallow, their heads resembled periscopes in sunglasses peering around or hippos in the Okavango swamp.

In the western corner of the Bay hot springs bubble up clouding the water. I sat, neck-deep on a stone deciding with my feet which under-water bubbles were the most comfortable heat and tried to float above them to feel them burst into my back.

However, a hazard was the wakes of the multitudinous ferries which zoom into the adjoining landing stage - nothing chugs in Italy, everything zooms on finely engineered machinery.

The Aoelian Islands are named after Aeolus, God of the Winds. In the Odyssey he gives Odysseus the contrary winds tied up in a bag, but

his curious crew open it and the ship is blown off course to further delay Odysseus' return to Ithaca. We decided to move to the west facing bay out of the ferry traffic. It was sheltered, deep and clear. We could see Stromboli smoking nearby. Lipari island sounded fascinating but we had to carry on west-wards.

One of the disadvantages of getting old was the increasing difficulty in climbing back on board from swimming in the sea. The lower rungs of our swimming ladder sloped in towards the hull. Peter put a fender behind the ladder to make it more upright but it was still difficult. Formerly I could heave myself into the Avon rubber dinghy, but now, even kicking as strongly as I could, my arms were hardly strong enough to pull me up and over the flotation chambers. I eventually flopped into it, to lie panting like a beached whale.

At seven o'clock one morning, before it became too hot, we rowed ashore to climb the Gran Cratere

Volcano on Volcano. It was a steep climb up the grey dust and shingle track to the ridge, where a sign warned us not to breathe the sulphurous air. It was exciting to look down into the crater and see

It was exciting to look down into the crater and see the steaming bubbling mud pool below.

the steaming bubbling mud pool below.

We thought Palermo Marina was the obvious place to leave CLYPEUS while we flew home, but on arrival found that :

a) they didn't want us,
b) it was incredibly expensive at 60 euros a night, and
c) the showers and toilets were disgusting – no seats and no paper, dirty and smelly.

I made a fuss and when we left next morning the Amaggiore (manager) tried to recompense by giving Peter a colourful print of the harbour for me.

Palermo itself was hot and dusty with magnificent buildings. Unfortunately there were no performances of opera, concerts or ballets at the grand Opera House. The waiter at our lunchtime restaurant warned us that a tourist had been shot in town the previous week. We couldn't wait to move on.

While in Messina, with the help of the Marina Receptionist, by email we had provisionally booked into San Nicola d'Arena Marina and now confirmed it again from Palermo, but when we arrived at the little Harbour, the Amaggiore insisted there was no room for us. We persisted that we had pre-booked and they eventually squeezed us into a berth for two weeks. We must pay 320€s now and 320 more when we returned. Here there were no toilets or showers, but water and electricity were included. Peter discovered that the Marina Pontoons are rented to various Mafia groups but nobody was responsible for shore facilities.

San Nicola d'Arena was a pleasant one street village where the Church clock played *Amazing Grace* before striking 8 a.m. and 8 p.m. On the

waterfront LOUD pop music was played on Wednesday, Friday, Saturday and Sunday evenings.

Swinging my leg over the bow rail to get aboard one morning I pulled a muscle in my groin and couldn't move. I couldn't even sit up to see what was going on or go out to dinner. Peter had made friends with the baker and his brother when he went for croissants each morning. They had lived in Chicago and spoke English. When Peter told them on Monday that I couldn't walk and we had tickets to fly to England on Thursday, the Baker sent his brother with Peter to get a Dottore and Nurse. I managed to get into my bathing costume before the three climbed down into the cabin. The Doctor examined me and said I had 'Footballer's Disease'- when footballers kick across sideways awkwardly they sometimes do the same damage I had incurred by swinging my leg over the pulpit. Anyway, he stuck an injection into my bottom and arranged for more.

The plump baker's brother, in true Italian style, in his floury singlet, shorts and thongs, kissed my hand so gently and gallantly offering words of encouragement before he left, that he made me feel better already as, lying flat on my back, I sucked my coffee through a straw and tried to eat my buttery, crispy, croissant.

The Doctor came again that evening, gave an injection and showed Peter how to do it. From then on Peter gave me injections morning and evening. He was brilliant, gentle and patient but firm: 'if I couldn't walk around the deck by Wednesday, I couldn't go to the UK for my Degree ceremony. On Wednesday he took a dummy run on the train to Palermo to make sure I would be able to manage the journey to the airport.

The marina secretary arranged for the night watchman to drive us to the train station at 5.30

Gentle Peter gave me injections morning and evening.

I was able to fly home to receive my M.A. Degree.

a.m. The train was very new and computerised with a mid-carriage display screen showing stations and times. Unfortunately it was too new and kept stopping. Each time it stopped, the screen had to re-boot from 'Start' and go through all the computer menus before it got going again. We only just made it to the airport in time. In the Concourse Peter found an Alitalia wheelchair and dumped me in it before the attendants realized we were Ryan Air passengers. The Ryan Air departure lounges were miles away from the main entrance.

However all was well and I was able to receive my MA Degree at Carmarthen Trinity College with an enormous sense of achievement with my husband, sister, daughter and grandson in the audience. (I write this to encourage others. I never took A levels and had a poor opinion of my academic ability, but knew I wanted to do my best to write our story and am a persistent person).

After nine happy family days we arrived back in Palermo Airport by 10 a.m. and took the now working-well train back to CLYPEUS and were on board by mid-day.

Peter settled our accounts and next day we set off to Sardinia.

CHAPTER TEN | ISLANDS IN THE SUN

2005 Sicily – Sardinia. Arbatax – La Calletta – calla Cavello – Olbia – Pt Nuraghe – Port Cerva – Isola Maddalena – Corsica - Bonifacio – Ajaccio – Isles Sanguinaires - Calvi – Bay de Crevani – Les Porquerelles

DURING TWO DAYS AND TWO NIGHTS of good sailing when the wind self-steering did all the work, we headed for Arbatax on the South East coast of Sardinia.

This is the life, I spend long moments on deck watching the flecks of foam and the water that chase along the hull. I couldn't ask for more; I have it all. Peter says he enjoys it, but can't give the moment his full attention as he is looking for the next problem which might, or might not, occur. Then came a problem we hadn't thought about for twenty years.

When day dawned we were surrounded by FOG and couldn't see the island or harbour entrance. Our world was suddenly grey and cold. Moisture gathered on the mainsail and dripped from the boom. Gradually, cautiously, straining our eyes and constantly referring to the GPS, a headland surfaced lazily out of the sea, and we followed its vague looming shape around to the entrance of the huge harbour, our hearts in our mouths. The Pilot Book showed no rocks or dangers and CLYPEUS entered safely between mist-licked harbour walls where clammy dribbles found their way down to the sea.

Once inside the marina the skies immediately cleared and a warm greeting of "Good morning" was called by Alan from Barrow-In-Furness. He and his wife set sail three years ago to meet up with friends in Corfu, but enjoyed Sardinia so much, Abertax in particular, they decided to stay. He was now the Marina Harbour Master, living on board comfortably in a Nicholson 35 and leading a leisurely, very sociable, life. They kindly let me use their email to let the family know all was well, and came on board for spaghetti bolognese that first evening.

A three hour tourist train tour up to Sidali in the mountains sounded interesting. At 8.30 a.m. we boarded the wheezing train, and listened to the familiar diddlee dee, diddle da, diddlee dee, diddlee da, up the slopes, round the curves, over wooded valleys to pastel coloured houses and apartment blocks with magnificent views down to the shimmering sea.

At Sidali passengers transferred to a coach to visit ancient religious Philia Grotto - a remarkable cavern of stalagmites, stalactites and underwater lakes. On to Su Stori Restaurant for a spit-roasted suckling pig which had been cooked in the regional style. First on the menu were slivers of Parma ham with fat green olives and crusty bread. Followed by a creamy pasta, made by the wife of the owner - the best, lightest, I have ever tasted. The suckling pig was paraded at shoulder height by the aproned proprietor.

The roast suckling pig was paraded at shoulder height.

The historic village and Folk Museum of farm buildings and open houses were still furnished the old way. Then it was diddle dee dee, diddle dee dum, back down the mountains with a screech screech of brakes to give a warning for road crossings in towns. Yellow waist-coated ladies with red and green-sided paddles held up traffic until the train passed. However it had slowed to avoid black pigs snuffling along the track edges until they scampered up the bank to let the engine steam by. The landscape was of scrub, olives, walnut and fig trees. Cows on the line delayed the train again. Handsome young cowboys in leather chaps rode fine horses – evidently it is still a preferred open air, independent way of life giving a reasonable income and young men still want to do it. The train was 15 minutes late and queues of stationery cars at the crossings were formidable. A great day out for us though!

A fantastic sail with the wind behind us brought CLYPEUS to La Calletta. As we sailed along the Sardinian coast we could see smoke and bush fires. Small planes zoomed close to the sea, scooped up water then flew through the smoke to drop it. A mushroom of steam replaced the smoke. We saw eight flights and discussed what a dangerous occupation it must be. What forces hit the plane as it scooped the water on board? How did the pilot adjust to an extra heavy weight so quickly? Actually the following morning, in the newspaper, we saw that a water pilot had been killed when his plane crashed into the sea the previous day.

On the free pontoon at La Calletta, while I mended a small tear in the Yankee, we chatted to Trish and Peter on JENNY WREN, an 80 year old gaffer from England, and had drinks on board.

There are many reasons for yachtsmen's passion, apart from the freedom and taking advantage of natural winds: the exhilaration of fast sailing and the satisfaction of arriving at a new destination due to our own efforts, in spite of the risks and tribulations to be overcome, but high on the list is also the enjoyment of other yachtsmen. The instant friendships, the common interests, problems and dreams, the help and comradeship offered and accepted.

Early next morning before the wind rose, we set off to have a 51st anniversary lazy holiday day. Anchored in a delightful bay I couldn't wait to swim, the water looked gorgeous: an aquamarine marbled iridescence over golden sand. But suddenly the wind changed and we had to up anchor and move on to Calo Cavello. While I rowed ashore and swam from the beach Peter fixed the boarding ladder for me, putting a strut between the ladder and the receding stern to make a more vertical climb (my arms were losing the will to hold me on the less than perpendicular ladder). The joint owners of CRYSTAL SPIRIT chatted as I rowed back to CLYPEUS and invited us for evening drinks.

Arriving in Olbia we sent emails and shopped for bread, but it was hot, humid and grimy up the river in the town. Acres of mussel beds lined the banks and huge ferries plied from mainland Italy.

We anchored in an estuary bay for a quiet, fresh night. A few scattered old rowboats lay like worn out shoes on the shore.

Next morning Peter added engine oil and when he put the engine into gear it stopped. Mussel bags and ropes were wound round the propeller and shaft so I had to dive down and unwind the tangled mass from around prop.

Further up the Sardinian coast near Rotondo we gawped at huge five storey private yachts powering along causing a heavy swell. The pink sand beaches were beautiful with sparkling specks of mica mixed in the sand and made swimming under water seem like fairyland.

At Palau we posted letters and bought bread before continuing on to NW Maddelena Island where I sat with my back against a warm pink granite boulder to watch large happy extended Italian families play on the beach and in the clear emerald, cooler, water.

On the 27th of July CLYPEUS headed towards Corsica in poor visibility. A pale sun was just rising through parting mist and scudding cloud in a strong wind but the sea was calm. Sweeping

Top left:
At La Calletta I mended a small tear in the Yankee.

Right:
Olbia's mussel nets were wound around the propeller shaft.

through Bonifacio Strait the cream cliffs of Corsica looked smooth and warm. Although French it is closer to Italy, is fiercely independent yet utterly reliant upon economic support from the mainland. The main body of the island is a little larger than Devon, yet it retains its own language and customs.

At 10.30, in a howling wind, we entered Bonifacio's dramatic narrow gorge. It is tucked within the striated folds of limestone cliff and curves around beneath The Citadel. The Calanque forms one of the most memorable harbours in the Med and is probably where the Laestrygonians in the Odyssey killed three of Odysseus's sailors. One was ripped apart and eaten on the spot. The other two were chased to the boats where boulders rained down to crush their ships and the sailors were speared in the water. Odysseus escaped to sea having sheltered in the little creek where we eventually anchored.

As we sped further into the harbour there was no room to manoeuvre especially in the strong wind. Turning around we nosed into Calangue de la Catena and tried to anchor, but it wouldn't hold. Peter raised the Bruce anchor and found a round boulder had fitted itself exactly into the metal curve. We tried again further up the inlet in the shallows and at 3 p.m. finally felt safe.

In the evening dressed for dinner, we pumped up the dinghy, fitted the outboard and puttered into town. It was romantic, fashionable and exciting with many big motor yachts tied up around the basin. After a harbour-side meal we strolled the promenade before rowing home.

During the night, squalls battered the boats. CLYPEUS seemed stable but our elderly neighbours were worried about their lines. In the strong wind which funnelled up the gorge Peter climbed the cliff at midnight to add extra ropes for them while I held the torch to show him foot and hand holds. At daylight we laid our big CQR anchor and with help from other crews re-set the Bruce as well. We didn't dare leave CLYPEUS and spent an interesting afternoon warding off other boats and watching them bang about trying to get settled. Many gave up. Thank goodness! In the melee we made friends with a French couple who invited us on board for Pastis before going ashore for dinner. (He was a helicopter pilot and of great interest to Peter.)

Walking along the waterside trying to decide in which attractive restaurant we would eat, we couldn't help noticing how many of the multi-million pound motor yachts flew the red ensign and were registered in London, Southampton, Jersey or the Isle of Man. Is our country really so rich? Do red ensigns really dominate the super-yacht scene or do we just give more advantageous rates for registration and insurance?

At 7 a.m. after a shower ashore and a look at the Weather Forecast at the Capitanerie, we should have taken time to climb up to Bonifacio town which sits on the cliff top and is entered through a still working drawbridge. The houses are four or five storeys high, crammed within the City walls shutting out the light from narrow cobbled streets. Why do I stupidly wait to read the tourist brochures until after we have left an interesting harbour?

Back on board I stowed shopping while Peter started undoing lines and getting anchors up with the help of a kind Frenchman who was trying to disentangle various anchor chains.

We set off motor-sailing north in bright sunshine and strengthening wind. As usual we were trailing a fishing line. A Marine Park motor boat appeared to be chasing us. We slowed down to see what he wanted and were severely chastised for fishing within the Marine Park – we didn't know we were in one.

Peter decided to anchor in the lee of Pt de la Parata in 15m over sand and rocks for a peaceful but roly night. The stars were spectacular and at 4 a.m. a sliver of moon rose up behind the mountain peaks. Dawn seemed as though the whole world was just sleepily waking up as a pale sun appeared through misty clouds. The anchor came up with no problem as Peter racked the anchor winch pole forward and back, forward and back. We could see it suspended in the clear water as it rose.

It was a bumpy ride around a headland where granite needles pierced up through the sea with a gurgle of white water around them. The sea seemed angry, thudding against the rocks and spitting

spray. Roly poly with a clatter of jars and bottles in the cupboards as we breasted the swell to Ajaccio the capital of Corsica, a city bustling and zooming with energy and traffic jams. Fashionable Parisian boutiques and shops in the main streets, but washing still hung out on poles from balconies over narrow cobbled side streets. Napoleon was born and raised here, but never returned.

The overflowing marina re-berthed us three times. Peter made friends with Luke, a ten year old French boy from the next boat. They spent two days chatting together and working on the boat while I shopped. It was sale time and the bargains were unmissable.

The Publishers emailed that they had forwarded the first print copy of my book *Seize The Day*. Where was it? Not here, perhaps at the other marina? We walked a couple of miles along the front to no avail, but did enjoy a delicious lunch in their five star restaurant with crisp yellow linen, flowers, iced water and tasty little complimentary starters. Peter had been very reluctant to enter the restaurant in case it was out of our price bracket, but actually our lunch cost less than many of the harbour side pavement cafes.

My birthday dinner was special. Peter ordered a huge plat de fruit de mer, just for me at La Palette. Usually I'm still fighting with the little shells while my 'friends'? have tucked in directly to the lobsters, crabs, prawns and oysters. This time I ate until satiated. My fruit de mer looked so appetizing that the young couple on the next table chatted and ordered the same. He was a Brazilian footballer now playing for Ajaccio and she was English, tall, tanned and charming. They told us of the Corsican Mafia who do not tolerate outsiders setting up new businesses in the town, somehow their premises always catch fire or are bombed.

Top:
Granite needles pierced up through the sea in a gurgle of white water.

Ajaccio, the capital of Corsica – a favourite place.

My birthday Plat de fruit de mer.

Ajaccio has a splendid market with good, fresh, local produce. CLYPEUS' tanks were refilled with diesel, water and petrol mix for the outboard motor. The post came, but still no book.

At noon we left for Calvi. and stopped for lunch at Baie D'argent, (Bay of Silver) sheltered from the forecast NW wind. It looked like Switzerland with high mountains but gently curving meadows down to the sand and aquamarine sea. We read there was silver mica here in a large lagoon behind the beach. It looked an interesting place to walk ashore. However before finishing our lunch an uncomfortable swell was beginning to roll in and a SW wind was getting stronger by the minute.

Hastily eating up and dumping the dishes in the sink I started the engine while Peter cranked in the 60' of anchor chain. It jagged and tugged in every rolling swell. At last it clanked against the bow roller and we were away bucking into the oncoming waves, fighting against the wind and tide from a lee shore. Once out of the bay with only the Yankee up, we whizzed along the coast over the crested swell. The anchor was dropped in another sheltered bay but we weren't happy. We have learned not to trust the Mediterranean, so hauled it up again and motored into the relative quiet of Calvi Bay.

I called Harbour Control – no answer. We assumed there was no room in the Marina. On the VHF we could hear other yachts asking for 'postes' but we couldn't see any posts, then realized they were talking about the mooring buoys curving along the bay. Eventually helpful Marina employees in a RIB secured us to a buoy in line with 50 other boats. Peter doubled up the ropes and we relaxed. Calvi looked an exciting, warm, pastel-coloured town snuggled beneath the dominant Citadel. A little train chuffed around the beaches of the bay. We looked forward to exploring in the morning.

A lad came around in a wooden dinghy to ask what bread, croissants or fruit juice we would like delivered at 8 a.m.? We just had time to enjoy them and decided it probably wasn't a good idea to leave the boat to go ashore as the breeze had changed to NE directly into Calvi Bay. Quickly the wind rose to slam waves and boats around. A Mistral? It seemed wise to evacuate without even going ashore and for the next two hours we fought to get out of the Bay. It took all our energy and concentration to get north of the island so that we could scoot back to yesterday's anchorage sheltered from the north.

It was our last night under Corsican stars. We had enjoyed the people, a complete contrast to their harsh history. They seemed happy affectionate and gentle, family orientated, kindly and soft spoken.

That night I wrote in my journal:

In the middle of cooking dinner I came into the cockpit and stopped, stared at the glorious pink mountains shielding the bay from the blustering NE wind. The sun was setting over the surf at the entrance of the bay its rosy glow was dazzlingly reflected from the rocks and cosily absorbed by the trees. Even the sea sparkled pink twinkles.

That night we slept in the cockpit. The slender moon lay on her back, she too gazing up at a million stars, each a pinprick in the Milky Way visible through the binoculars. How infinite the Universe. How finite our lives. What a privilege to be here, away from industrial pollution, rocking to the gentle Mediterranean night. If this is the last night of my life (which I hope it isn't) I feel I have witnessed the enormity of the Universe and my little life is of importance to no one but me and my immediate family.

Heading for France in the morning Peter nonchalantly measured the distance on the chart on his knee. Fleets of French motor boats roared towards us to start their holiday. All day and night

we sailed towards The Poquerelle Islands.

From the saloon bunk, which we often used in turn when on night watch, I could look up through the open hatch and see Peter's face, pale and disembodied in the compass light. His hands are on the wheel, his eyes on the sails, or searching the dark horizon for the lights of ships or buoys. He is a still and lonely figure – and yet not lonely, for below him is the warmth and glow of dimmed light from the navigation desk and a partner waiting to take the helm on the hour. Those last few minutes off watch lying warm and cosy with a background noise of wind in the sails and rigging and the hiss of water along the outer skin of the boat, close beside your ear, the gentle roll and lift of the hull … travelling … fills me with the joy of going somewhere, independent of any mechanical aid. Three o'clock, time to put the kettle on for some hot chocolate to sip together in the open cockpit under the stars.

On my watch, sitting in the dark behind the wheel, a pair of trawlers with a white light above green appeared to be chasing us. Every time I steered to get out of their way they followed. As I tacked and zigzagged, they followed. Were they trying to catch us in the wide maw of their net? I woke Peter and after assessing the situation he decided to head back south out of their way. They wouldn't be able to turn the trawl nets on a reciprocal course quickly. After a while their lights faded in the distance and we resumed our course towards Poquerolles. (43.00N, 6.12E). Cars are not used on the island so cycling is the norm and we were looking forward to exploring. In a fresh clear morning we joyfully dropped our anchor amongst other yachts in a corner sheltered from the NE. But within two hours again the wind backed and tried to push us towards the lee shore, so it was up anchor again and on towards La Ciotat Marina (43.10N 5.36E) on the French Mainland to shelter from another Mistral.

Peter nonchalantly measured the distance on the chart.

CHAPTER ELEVEN | LA BELLE FRANCE

2005 FRANCE - La Ciotat – Port St Louis – Rhone – Arles – Avignon – St Etienne – Viviers – La Roche de Glun – Roches de Condrieu – Lyons – Montmerle Sur Soane – Tournos – St Jean de Losne.

Map of the French waterways, showing our route.

went to the office to plead that we only wanted shelter for the duration of the storm. They agreed we could stay for a few days and we thoroughly enjoyed this ancient and modern town. It was interesting to see how they coped with the enormous number of runabout motor boats; a modified fork lift truck lifted them from their racks and gently lowered them into the sea when needed – "stack-a-boat".

The people were gracious, friendly and unfailingly polite and the take-away food fantastic. Stalls in the narrow cobbled pedestrian precinct displayed huge shallow pans of delicious smelling, tasty, paellas of saffron-yellow rice adorned with prawns; mussels a la crème; and shrimps, were oh! so tempting! Fat stuffed tomatoes; still-bubbling cheese-topped plump, purple, aubergines; spaghetti bolognaise and 'musselaine' simmered away. We decided this was the best take-away food since the Muslim Night Market in Langkawi, Malaysia, where 'murtabak', spicy chicken legs and various meats in a creamy, coconut curry sauce had been offered. La Ciotat was the first place in the world where the Lumiere brothers showed their motion picture. The old town still looked like a film set.

In the Bouches-du-Rhone area (mouth of the Rhone) les anciens (pensioners) can travel anywhere by long distance coach within the region for just one euro. We bussed to Marseilles, to see if the first copy of Seize the Day had arrived at the Harbour Master's Office. It hadn't. The ancient, crowded Vieux Port is entered between dramatic massive walls of the old fortifications leaving a narrow gap between two forts of St Jean and St. Nicolas. The reception dock is immediately to starboard on entering and, even if there isn't a

LA CIOTAT IS A TOURIST TOWN with a picturesque fishing harbour housing a large fleet of small boats and a clean and splendid looking, yellow and white, modern steel works. Both marina and boat harbours were crammed full. Yachts were not allowed in the fishing harbour. As the Mistral was gaining in strength we returned to the marina and squeezed into a vacant slot then

berth in the Marina, the Port Captain will allow one night on the visitors' pontoon. The ancient Greek port of Lacydon, in the heart of Marseilles, has been turned over to pleasure craft with 3,200 slips but is always crowded. A good Internet Café with thirty plus computers let us receive and send off emails.

Aix en Provence sounded historic and scenic. The tourist brochure says:

"A stunningly beautiful place. Originally a spa town founded by the Romans, Today, it is a labyrinth of tiny alleyways and squares and is known as the 'city of a thousand fountains.' This is provincial France at its best. Paul Cezanne was a favourite son and he painted 300 of his works here with his workshop preserved exactly how it was when he died in 1906."

On Sunday Peter as usual wanted to sit on board and read his book in peace, so he was only too happy for me to push off on my own. The sleek bus powered up the motorway through mountains and vineyards and arrived at Aix at 12 20 where, unfortunately, everything was closed, even the bus station buffet. The Park gates nearby were bolted and chained. I had forgotten that everything closes on Sundays in France, especially in August. The provincial French people don't change their traditional customs just for a few tourists.

"Oui", said the Bus Driver, "C'est Dimanche. Toutes sont ferme."

If I didn't return on the bus I had travelled in, I would have to wait six hours for a bus back to La Ciotat. I decided I would rather be on the beach close to Peter and have a swim. Perhaps we could come back another day.

As I stepped down from the bus back in La Ciotat I was surrounded by a throng of people many wearing traditional dress. It was the annual 'Blessing of the Fleet'. A special service was to be held in the enormous harbour-side church, with the Clergy, Mayor and choir also in traditional robes. A pipe and drum band led the way to the church where an immense organ throbbed beneath the stained glass windows and vaulted ceiling. It was an up-beat relaxed service with modern tuneful hymns.

At the end of the service the Town Band led the Bearers carrying the painted plaster model of the Virgin shoulder high in procession, to be carefully placed on the 50' Police Launch. Many boats gathered in the offing, doing their best to keep in the lee of the land and ignoring the Mistral which blew from the North. A priest on the deck of the launch sprinkled holy water and blessed each craft as it passed beneath the bows. Crews made the sign of the cross and threw grey/green leafed olive branches into the water. The choir led a large crowd on the quayside singing Ave Maria. It was a happy, grateful and forward, as well as backward, looking ceremony. It seemed full of hope although the major shipyard, which built 300,000 ton tankers, closed three years ago when all the workers were laid off as it was not financially viable against Chinese imports. We had been told it was a sad town with many unemployed, but it didn't seem so in the middle of the holiday season.

The only drawback to this idyllic stop-over was a funfair at the end of our pontoon. At 1.30 a.m. there was still shouting and screaming on the Boomer and Stargate. Are the forty people screaming, hanging upside down strapped into a rolling suspended bench, actually enjoying themselves? I guess so. The Antalya earplugs were brought back into circulation.

Sun-blessed holiday makers crowded beaches which were not of sand, but creamy gravel. Lovely bronzed bodies lazed and children were busy on the

Sun blessed holiday makers crowded the beaches.

'sand' as only toddlers can be with a bucket and spade at the seaside. The Life Guards' blackboard showed that the water temperature was 28 degrees on Saturday, 24 on Sunday and a cold 18 on Monday – the Mistral does more than just blow air, it blows the warm coastal surface water out to sea which is replaced by cold water welling up to take its place.

An astronomy Night with the Stars was publicised. A colourful slide presentation was followed by an invitation to look at the constellations through local enthusiasts' telescopes which were set up in the surrounding park. Unfortunately the astronomers didn't appear to have focused on anything significant and it was difficult to distinguish what I was supposed to be seeing as I peered through eyepieces. Peter had a few conversations in fractured French as he has a six inch reflecting telescope at home.

At last, the text forecast was: 'WF 08.05 for W. Provence, E. Provence, W. Corse, Riviera, SW 2-3. It turned out to be SE 3-4! CLYPEUS sped along towards Marseilles, past the Chateau d'If, made famous by the Count of Monte Cristo's legendary *Man in the Iron Mask*, and on to the Gulf du Fos

to enter the French Canal system via the River Rhone The sea was as dull and grey as luke-warm porridge, but as the sun rose higher so did it become a shiny bright blue. It was a pity there wasn't time to explore into the Calanquets, which we were passing. They are narrow limestone coastal gorges which can be entered by small boats, but Peter wanted to get to Port St Louis. He was fretting about booking-in to have our masts taken down before entering the Rhone.

The Gulf du Fos, was wide and grey, blighted by the industrial haze from surrounding refineries and factories. Entering a small canal which led to Port St. Louis we started our voyage through France. Moored to a pontoon alongside British and Swedish yachts, it was a social time with instant friends on board for supper. Friendly Julian and Paul swopped two 'Navicartes' (an essential series of charts depicting the French canal system) for Heikell's *'Greek Waters Pilot'*. Julian wasn't feeling well. He had been to the local doctor who diagnosed low blood pressure and prescribed pills. Two days later he was in intensive care with DVT in his legs and lungs. With the excellent free medical care he was out of danger and recovering well when we left ten days later. He is going to have his E111 framed!

Late August, when the French are returning from holidays, is the busiest time for the Naval Services Boatyard which hauls out boats and lifts out their masts for winter storage. We had to wait six days until Monday for our turn, which gave us time to look around the propped–up boats to see if there were any we recognized from our years in the Pacific or Asia. Yes, there was TIMSHELL looking in good condition on her props. We sent an email off to Wendy and Geoff in Queensland to assure them that their beloved boat was looking good. We had sailed with them and their daughters Deborah and Kathy, and our buddy-boat, SUTAMON, (with their children Tao and Monique) around the Louisiade Archipelago which lies at the southern tip of Papua New Guinea. Wendy and family had had to fly back to Oz to look after her ailing parents. (SUTAMON-completed their circumnavigation in 2005 and TIMSHELL in 2008)

Another Mistral was blowing up to Force 10/11 in the bright sunshine. Peter used the days to prepare the engine for the long hours of motoring

ahead and to construct strong cross-members on which to rest our masts. All the mast lights and electronic wires needed disconnecting and all the rigging prepared for easy disassembling. The haul out charge would be 70 euros for the first half hour in the crane bay, then 35 euros for each further 15 minutes. (Our masts were down and laid in their cradle in 20 minutes thanks to Peter's careful preparations. Is that a record for a ketch?) Now we were ready to voyage through France. In Guernsey in 1983 he managed a similar feat when replacing the old Perkins engine with the new. With a block and tackle he had lifted the old engine off its mounting and slid a thick plank beneath it which rested on the door sill. Pulling it further into the cockpit with the block and tackle it was ready for the crane driver to lift out onto his lorry and then lower the new one down. It took less than fifteen minutes and the crane driver never asked for

Left top:
Port St Louis
Peter constructed
strong cross-
members
on which to
rest our masts.

Left bottom:
Our masts were
down and laid on
their cradle in 20
minutes.

Right:
Now we were
ready to voyage
through France.

money or sent a bill.

I took the bus to Marseilles to collect post and enjoyed some retail therapy and a Vietnamese lunch. On my return I found a very pale and upset Peter. When cycling around the harbour side to help Lucy and Jay of SEAJAY with their hauling-out lines at The Navy Yard, a fisherman had cast his line, flicking it just in front of Peter's face. He fell off his bike, severely grazing his knee, elbow and confidence. Instead of lying down and recovering from shock he took the bus to Arles to buy a sixteen day VNF canal license. It took many days before he felt really well again. The Seine and canals are administered by Voies Navigables de France – VNF. It is necessary to buy a licence for 16 or 30 days, three months or a year.

We were apprehensive about setting off although this voyage was hardly likely to be life-threatening. Shipwreck wasn't likely but damaging ourselves, or our boat, in the locks was on the cards – our deep keel was bound to cause huge stresses as it had done in the Panama Canal and our ferro-cement shell didn't take kindly to stone and sturdy concrete walls. It isn't feasible to continue voyaging through the canals in winter, not just because it is cold and uncomfortable but the water often freezes solid and many stretches are closed for maintenance. Also most of the umbrella shaded canal-side shops and restaurants open only during the summer months. We would return home in September and, like sensible French sailors, snuggle up before a log fire with a glass or two of warm red sunshine.

On Wednesday the 24th August 2005 we entered the Rhone – not very efficiently I'm afraid. Every lock is a potential crisis and this first one was no exception. The lock provided just one short rope to cling to that I could actually reach, no mooring cleats or bollards. As the water rushed in from the Rhone so it carried our bow right around so that CLYPEUS finished up facing the way we had just come in – what a blessing the lock was more than 35' wide, and no other boats were in it. A cold wind greeted us as we started up the lumpy, wide, and treacherous Rhone, which has been partly tamed. Floods, only two years previously, had devastated large areas and destroyed many river craft.

On arriving in Arles, Peter rested, his knees and elbows were still sore. I explored. It is a charming, historic town and I wandered the warm streets in delight. As I passed the Roman Amphitheatre crowds were lining up to buy tickets for the Course Camarguaise.

"What is it?" I asked some people in the queue who were speaking English.

"We think it's bulls chasing men – not a bullfight – nothing gets killed."

The seven euro ticket gave us all an exciting two hours watching fourteen agile young men, divided into two teams. All wore white shirts and trousers and the aim of the game was to pluck away two tassels tied between the horns of aggressive, wiry, young bulls. The horns are wide apart in the shape of a lyre. Each bull displayed different attitudes to the men who, in ballet like sequence, ran across its line of vision. As they passed each other at top speed the men touched the bull's head to try and snatch the tassels. They teased the bulls, rushing around them like mosquitoes. The bulls snorted and pawed the ground and charged at random while the 'mosquitoes' ran, jumped and flew over the balustrade to clutch the spectator rails. Sometimes the bulls followed, jumping the balustrade too and charging around inside the narrow gap between arena and audience and 'wannabee' mosquitoes, who had hidden behind

The seven euro ticket gave us all an exciting two hours watching fourteen agile young men, divided into two teams.

Top right: Tarascon Castle heralded our first Rhone Lock.

the protection boards. Every so often after an unrewarding charge, the bull would push his horn into a wooden arena side panel and flip it up and out of the surround. I started watching from the top seats but gradually worked my way down over the 2,000 year old stone benches to where I could see the mosquitoes' faces and the gleam in the eyes of the bull as he spotted a likely target. Injuries and frustrations were about equal. If a bull seemed too strong or feisty, two cows were brought in and the three encouraged out of the ring. The bull always followed the cows.

CLYPEUS thrust her way up against the strongly flowing river. A numbered post marked every kilometre starting at PK332, which makes it easy to tell exactly where you are. Tarascon Castle heralded our first Rhone Lock, Beaucaire, where it was necessary to moor alongside posts in the fast flowing river to await the lock opening. Obeying the instructions we donned life-jackets. Evidently a pleasure boater had been drowned in a lock recently and this requirement was now enforced in all officially manned locks. This was all new stuff to us and we were scared. Commercial traffic has right of way. The steel lock gates opened and a huge

barge, known as a peniche in France, and a smaller barge came out, but another enormous peniche coming up behind us entered and filled the lock, so we had to wait another thirty minutes. When we eventually entered the intimidating cavern with its high, grey, dripping walls, we tried to tie between bollards, but they were 30 metres apart - placed for barges. With the stern line tied on it was still another 18 metres to the next bollard. The lock keeper shouted at us in French from his glass tower and we eventually understood that we had to put

We entered the intimidating cavern with its high, dripping walls.

113

The Pope's Palace at Avignon. We enjoyed a wine tasting on the roof.

bow and stern lines around the same floating bollard. With our hearts in our mouths, the great black gates slowly and inexorably closed. A terrible squeaking and screeching started as water furiously bubbled up around us. CLYPEUS tugged and fought the ropes trying to escape the strong currents which were battering her keel. The grinding and screeching noise came from the floating iron chambers supporting the steel bollards which grated against the concrete as they rose and fell with the water. Once you understand what is happening around you, it all seems relatively safe and easy, but that first lock Beaucaire Ecluse was terrifying.

Only half Le Pont d'Avignon still stands, the other half was destroyed by floods in 1668. Nobody was dancing on it as we tied up alongside the pavement at Avignon which was full of tourists wandering through the medieval cobbled streets. From our mooring we walked into the city through ancient stone arches. The temporary Harbour Office and showers were in the bowels of a barge tied to the roadside. Evidently the original pontoons, office and many of the yachts had been washed away in recent floods. After a rest day we went early to Les Halles, the covered market, but arrived before many of the traders. Sitting enjoying a croissant and café au lait watching the stall holders set up their displays and joking with each other was entertaining. The shops in most French towns, apart from the Boulangeries, don't like to greet the morning before 9. 00 -9.30 am when most shops do open.

We attended a Celtic Concert in the Palais des Popes. A mixture of Scottish, Irish and Medieval ballads played on a small Celtic harp, violin and accordion. The music was esoteric and complex. The aesthetic violinist, dressed in a pale green

Robin Hood tunic and tights with his hair pulled back into a pony tail, took it all very seriously and never managed a smile. The tall dark harpist, a beautiful girl, wore a silky maroon Eastern European tunic with harem type, ankle hugging trousers, suitable for holding the harp between her knees. The smiley accordion player had 'bovver boots' on beneath his gypsy apparel. All were accomplished musicians deftly intertwining their complex melodies making a pleasant noise, but made no actual tune I could follow. During the interval a wine tasting was held up on the ramparts under the moon and glistening stars. It evoked dramatic notions of medieval romance, chivalry and intrigue.

Now a cold north wind was blowing; winter was on its way. We were wearing shoes, sweaters and oilskins and of course lifejackets at locks. Apprehensively we approached Bollene Lock, 23 meters (69 feet) deep, what could go wrong in this mass of churning water? As we neared each lock I would call the lock keeper on the VHF (the channel frequency is listed in the Navicartes) with a "Bonjour Messieur. Nous voulons monter s'il vous plait."

Approaching St Etienne-des-Sorts through farmland and vineyards in a steady drizzle, we tied up at the single pontoon. Two teenage girls who were sitting on the edge, rose and moved back.

"You don't mind the rain?" I asked as I took a line ashore. With lovely smiles they shrugged and happily chattered on, up the pontoon gang plank and down the street.

'Funny way for such attractive girls to spend a Saturday afternoon,' I thought. However, after walking right around and through the charming old village, and only seeing two elderly gentlemen standing talking, sheltered from the drizzle by the roof of a open garage. I told Peter "No wonder those girls were sitting in the rain looking at the Rhone. At least IT was moving!"

At Viviers we moored at the edge of a park, beneath the prominent cathedral where the huge trees seemed to be heaving great sighs as the Mistral gusts lifted and lowered their boughs.

The Rhone is tricky and strong – this is not a relaxing waterway like the canals. You are aware of the enormous power of water. The Mondragon Waterfall was tamed in 1952, and the water diverted into a Hydroelectric Plant which, at the time, supplied 10% of France's electricity. The Bollene Lock was designed to empty or fill in seven minutes. It was the deepest lock in the world when constructed. We were lucky to have learned to tie our lines correctly to the same bollard as we rose up into the sunlight. However the commercial traffic: hotel boats, peniches full of sand, gravel, oil, were always ahead of us in the locks and when their propellers turn to accelerate out of the lock, watch out!

Out on the river the huge ships caused a series of metre-high waves into which we always steered head-on. The Navicartes were essential and we referred to them constantly.

Sometimes a reach of the canal took us high above the picturesque Rhone valley and we could see vineyards of: Cotes de Rhone, Chateauneuf-du-Rhone and Chateauneuf-du-Pape, medieval castles, rocky gorges and wooded hillsides. Red-tiled villages basked in the bright sun. It was a pity there were few places to moor up safely and no way did we feel we could leave CLYPEUS to go exploring or wine tasting.

Large grey and white herons stood on the banks and atop river markers looking like disillusioned old men with their shoulders hunched and straggling wisps of grey feathers flying over their eyes in the wind.

On July 30th we travelled 40 kilometres and traversed four locks – a 'best ever' river day. At Glun (PK58) we were able to pull off the Rhone into a backwater where families were water skiing and zooming around on jet skis. By 7 p.m. they had gone home and we appreciated a quiet night in a lake setting. It was so peaceful after the challenging days behind us. In spite of Peter's derision I put up the Malay mosquito net so that I could sleep in the cockpit. It was cool as I rejoiced in our good fortune and I wondered how many of our contemporaries, in their 70s, are able to stretch out and look at the stars above them until they fall asleep. In the silver pink dawn I could see reflections of trees and bushes mirrored on the surface. A single quack from a duck broke the silence, then two herons flapped by low above the water.

After a lovely hot shower at the 'Port de Plaisance' at La Roches de Condrieu I tried to find an open supermarket. Everywhere was closed – on a Tuesday? There was a Children's Fair advertised and an invitation for all to come to the traditional

Les Roches de-Condrieu village Summer Feast in the market.

Top right:
Lyons and convenient moorings in the centre of town.

Bottom right:
Joining the River Soane we slipped between fields of sunflowers.

Annual Summer Feast. At 7.30 p.m. Local families welcomed us and made room for us to sit beside them at the white cloth covered tables beneath the high wooden roof of the market. We stood in line for food, beer and wine (Cote du Rhone for 5 euros a bottle!) then returned to our table where Peter's neighbour, Antoine, a big handsome chap from Martinique with excellent English, said he had been a chef at the London Ritz under Gordon Ramsey and in other top London Restaurants. His French wife, with their children, had tired of London and their three bed-roomed house in Barking. With the proceeds of the house sale they were able to buy a pleasant five bed-roomed house with a large garden in Condrieu. Antoine now worked in a five star Hotel on the banks of the Rhone and both were happy with their decision.

Next morning the southerly wind was blowing against the current and the Rhone was rough with white horses. There was a long delay of an hour and a half at the next ecluse to wait for a large hotel boat and then for a peniche carrying flammable liquid to go through before us.

Lyon offered easy mooring under plane trees in the middle of the town. Trying to find an email café, I asked some ten year old boys who were dashing around between the trees on their roller blades. Immediately they politely directed me accurately to an Internet Café.

At Lyon the Rhone heads off North East to Switzerland so we continued North towards Paris heading up through the tree-lined River Saone between terraces of vines or sunflowers - a lovely experience in the morning sun as their heavy heads followed the sun – very Van Gogh! This river was obviously shallower and in the late afternoon while steering, I noticed heavily laden sand barges exiting

from a tributary near PK44. They were taking a wide sweep to get into the centre of the river, so I headed CLYPEUS well towards the opposite bank. Then ooops! Judder, judder, thump, thump, the boat stopped. We were aground. Peter rushed up and tried to reverse us off but CLYPEUS was stuck solid on the river bed. As peniches and sand barges swept by, we tried to go astern to coincide with their wash, hoping the odd extra inch of water would lift us. Eventually Peter rowed out to lay an anchor to try and winch us off. Needless to say I wasn't popular!

As it was all my fault I radioed the VNF 'Ecleuse Drace' depot to ask for assistance. "Nous sommes eschaffe." (We are aground)

"Qui Madame…" and a jumble of French."

Not sure what, if anything, was going to happen, I set off in the dinghy, first to the sand quarry to see if they had a work-boat to tow us off. It was deserted now and everyone had gone home for the night. I decided to row downstream to a village where I had noticed a boat yard. It was further than anticipated and I realised I would never be able to row all the way back against the current. Pulling in to the rush-banked shore I hauled out the dinghy. Walking along the path towards the village, two men were in sight, one in front of a VNF white van. As I spoke to him the other man approached, he was from the village Boatyard. Both were on their way to CLYPEUS to give assistance. By the time I had rowed home, CLYPEUS was afloat and a worried Peter was looking out for me. Evidently she had floated free of her own accord when the lock further up-river had emptied. It had happened just as the VNF men were approaching and Peter was able to give them the thumbs up sign that all was well. We continued up river suitably chastened!

At Montmerle that evening after chatting and having drinks on GRALYN, a neighbouring yacht, both crews decided to stay for a rest day so that we could enjoy the 400th Annual Horse Fair to be held in Motmerle on Saturday. The 'Faire du Cheval' had been held every year since 1605. After cleaning the boat and washing the decks I wandered around the delightful village surrounded by vineyards. An unusual illustrated house number which showed a reclining lady caught my eye. It was number 69! Was it a house of ill repute? GRALYN came for drinks and next day hundreds of horse boxes arrived from 5 a.m. onwards.

At Montmerle we were in time for the 400th Annual Horse Fair.

All types of horses, from carthorses, to Shetland Ponies, hunters and thoroughbreds stood patiently in the dappled shade beneath trees beside the river bank. Grooms and farmers sat on straw bales surrounded by dusty green wine bottles, which they opened with alacrity as soon as a friend, or customer, appeared. Market stalls of horse tack, clothes, cheese, sausages and take-away food stalls lined the cobbled streets. Various events took place in the sanded village arena: elegant Spanish Haute Ecole and cowboys lassooing calves.

We pulled ourselves away at lunchtime as we had to be back in Wales in time to receive expected Australian sailing friends to visit in August. In 1996, Lorraine and Brian of MARA, had put their own lives at risk to wait for us when we were arrested and held for a month under suspicion of spying in Eritrea (*as told in Red Sea Peril*). We were looking forward to seeing our stalwart friends very much.

More concentration was needed now to keep within the narrow deep channel – no more going aground on our way to St. Jean de Losne where we hoped to leave CLYPEUS for the winter. We had been told it was a safe marina, off the river, in the ancient Basin which used to be the barge capital of France.

Tournon, town of trees. The moorings were beneath magnificent trees which lined the streets, river and squares. L'Hermitage vineyards surrounded the town. Sitting in a pavement café after dinner enjoying a digestif we decided this was a lovely way to return to England – much easier than fighting our way back across the Bay of Biscay. In the morning after a quick browse around the flea market on the river bank we left for Seurre.

A yacht going downstream suddenly veered towards us, the crew were waving and shouting:

A Google image of the Barge Basin at St. Jean de Losne.

Image © 2005 DigitalGlobe

Pointer 47°06'12.74" N 5°15'39.51" E   Streaming ||||||||| 100%   Eye alt 3462 ft

©2005 Google

"Ahoy CLYPEUS. Ahoy CLYPEUS!"

"Who is it? Who knows us?" Peter muttered.

"Hello", we called back bemused. Peter slowed down. They approached more slowly towards us.

"It us, we used to be on INCENTI. We're on our way to meet Lorraine and Brian of MARA. We are taking them on the river for a few days."

"Oh Hi! Hello. Sorry we didn't recognise who you were. We are just rushing up to St. Jean de Losne so we can leave CLYPEUS there and get back to England to be ready for their visit to us."

"Yes, we know. Great to see you, but can't stop. Have a good trip."

"You too. Give them our love and say we are looking forward to seeing them. Byeee."

"Byeee" their voices faded as they were swept downstream. It seems a small world sometimes.

At an overnight stop in Seurre we relished the brand new showers and facilities. Twenty kilometers on we arrived at H^{2}0 Marina in St Jean de Losne. Captain Bob, the mooring master, said "Yes, there is room for CLYPEUS to winter here." What a relief!

Between June 15th and September 5th we had sailed 1,401 miles from Greece to Port St Louis and then 683 kilometres inland passing through five locks. On our last evening the warm sunlight was a farewell to this year's voyage as the undulating gold of corn heads bent to the breeze. We tied a large red bow on our bowsprit to warn people walking on the pontoon but also somehow to reward CLYPEUS for looking after us so well.

Next morning we caught a train to Paris, then Eurostar and train home.

Peter returned by train during October to winterize the engine and make sure all was well before it became really cold.

We tied a large red bow on our bowsprit.

CHAPTER TWELVE | VALLEYS OF VINES

2006 FRANCE - St Jean de Losne – Seurre – PK 159 – Chalon Sur Soane – Ecluse No 32 de Fontaine – Chagny (terrifying day) - Santernay – St Leger sur Dheune – St Julian – Top of Route – Geoff's Place – downhill to Blazny – Geneland – Paray La Monial – Digoin – Decize – Nevers – Water inlet blocked - Plagny – Histoire de l'Eau – Marseilles Les Aubigny.

St. Jean de Losne 47 06.256N 5. 15.659 E.

Ducks eggs were lying on the plastic cockpit sole.

ON SUNDAY THE 24TH APRIL 2006 we caught the 8 a.m. Dover to Dunkerque car ferry and enjoyed a misty calm crossing while eating a good English breakfast. We had decided to travel by car so that we could load it with some of the unnecessary stuff from CLYPEUS to ensure she floated higher in the water. It was also important to traverse the canals early in the year to make sure there was enough depth for our 1.8 metre keel.

First stop in France was to buy diesel and a picnic of baguette, pate and plonk. As we drove south, we could hear the call of cuckoos above fields of yellow cowslips. In St Jean de Losne, when we arrived at 6 p.m., the boat keys were in the cockpit and all was well with CLYPEUS. She was as sweet and clean as Peter had left her in October. Nothing had frozen or burst and all the bottles of wine, beer and sauces he had carefully fitted into woollen socks and placed in buckets, were returned to their former homes.

Five ducks eggs rested in the cockpit, no nests, just the eggs lying on the sole. I immediately wanted to bake a cake.

"I will make a chocolate sponge in the morning," I said and thought how convenient it was to have eggs home-delivered.

A French neighbour, Siaid, came over to make sure all was well and did we need anything?

"No, not tonight thank you, but I promise you a piece of chocolate cake tomorrow when I use up these duck eggs".

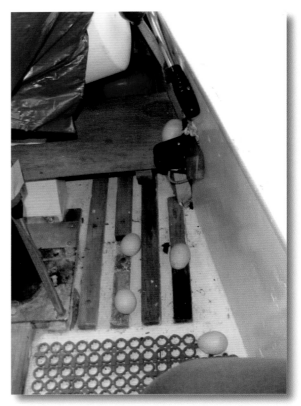

"Mais non." he said, "zay 'ave been there perhaps two, three weeks."

"Ah! Quelle domage!" Shame shame, so - into the dustbin they went.

It was a cold night but we slept well.

The basin at St Jean de Losne used to be the barge capital of Europe. It is out of the main river system and not liable to flood during the snow melt run off from the Alps. Easy access to all the major waterways of Europe makes it an ideal starting point for summer cruises, north, south, east or west. Other boat owners were Swiss, German, and Belgian as well as French.

After washing and folding the winter covers we started trying to lighten the boat, emptying surplus stuff into the car to raise the keel so that she floated higher in the water: spare anchor chain, block and chain (for hauling engines up and down), wind generators, books etc. The maximum canal depth of the Canal Lateral du Loire would be 1.8m and our keel depth was 1.7m at least, and that was in sea water. Now, in fresh water, she would float deeper.

When the car was full, Peter worked out an ingenious way of measuring our depth with a 10' metal pole with string tied on at both ends knotted at 1.8 m. At the bow, on either side, holding our respective bits of string at the knots, we both lowered the pole beneath the keel then walked to the stern. With geometric diagrams he decided we now drew 1.66 metres. – We shouldn't plough too many furrows.

I carried on getting rid of things and cleaning while Peter worked on the exhaust and engine. Loads of books were taken to the Marina Library which was manned two days a week by Volunteers. When Peter tried the engine it started first turn of the key so he was happy. As usual the fresh vegetables, meat and fish available in town were excellent.

I enjoyed a concert in the old, dusty, dark, Eglise St Jean de Losne organised by the local Lions Club. It was held to choose the best young conductor for a scholarship. Five enthusiastic young men, in turn, conducted the young 22 piece orchestra. Beneath the faded wooden painted arch where the gilded leaves appeared to support the organ pipes, the pretty young first violinist, her blonde hair pulled up into an elegant bun, followed each conductors' baton surely and confidently. The winner was a commanding fervent, precise, young conductor who bounced with the music as he conducted Mahlers 5th Symphony Adagio which was the easiest listening.

Every Saturday morning boaters met in the Marina shop for free coffee and croissants organised by Captain Bob, a grey haired and garrulous, slight, American sailor who was formerly a naval aviator in the US Navy. He and his wife Peggy had a beautiful Swan 44, CHAPEAU an unusual boat for inland cruising.

"We didn't mean to stay in Europe," Bob said. "But we have been in France for ten years now. We wintered the boat here one year and the following year I was offered the job of looking after the international cruising folk passing through the Marina during the winters. So, eight years later we still over-winter here. In the summers we cruise Germany, Switzerland, Holland, Belgium or back down to the Med. I enjoy meeting all the different crews and organizing their berths. They don't always appreciate my humour though."

I'm not surprised! He relished his 'Cap'n' position and told jokes and stories endlessly to anyone who would listen.

On Saturday afternoons everyone met for a BBQ. Siaid was a professional chef so he was in charge of the marinades and cooking. As we huddled into our anoraks, chatting over our glasses of wine, we realized Australians Al and Robbie knew many of our Pacific sailing friends..

Robbie was trying to snuggle down into his three coats. "Why did we come over so early? It is still too bloody cold. Next year we'll wait until June."

It was almost too cold to work in the open so we joined a new friend, Sue Boxall, in her car to tour the Beaune Valley to look for suitable wines for her new business. Sue lives on her own on 'GEEDE VARWCHINY', a 50' Dutch sailing barge and as Secretary of the Dutch Barge Association enjoyed organizing and travelling to the rallies all around Europe. Sue was starting up a gourmet and wine tasting enterprise 'Burgundy on a Plate'. At St. Romain the proprietor was friendly and informative. His family had lived there since 1700s. After the degustation we lunched at Relais du Chateau Rochepot, in an imposing room with a high large fireplace and log fire. Later we cycled to her spacious barge for guidance on our route north and to see if Peter could mend her Hotpoint washing machine. He could.

On May 2nd it was still cold but we bought our VNF License for four months for 206 euros and were assured our keel could get through Canal Lateral de Loire to the Seine, the most westerly, rural and deepest way through to Paris. At the bricolage we bought a stout wooden gang plank.

Five busy days later, after parking the car at Robert's farm, we backed out of our secure berth and headed out into the Saone. At last we were off, south at first, back down the Saone towards the heavy grey cumulus clouds ahead. The first lock into the canals worked perfectly. We were through by 12.15 p.m. and called 'Bon appetit' to the lock keeper who had driven in his white VNF van to open the lock for us. Tied to the bank in Seurre we enjoyed our lunch and siesta, relishing the fact that French Canals are much wider than English ones.

The medieval town dozed beneath huge chestnut trees, their pink and white flower candles were in full bloom. Half-timbered houses leaned secretively together with blue jacarandas peeping over ancient walls of thin red bricks. White apple and cherry blossom and mauve wisteria covered timber porches; tubs full of pansies and pink daisies lined the streets and filled them with a sweet fragrance..

A wedding was taking place in the 14th Century Church of St Martin. The bells pealed as the bride and groom came through the great unpainted ancient wooden doors. As the photographer organised the group, it began to rain but nobody noticed. In the family crowd, bossy little girls in their best dresses helped each other and made all the smaller children, look towards

the camera. As the guests departed to the wedding breakfast, a cacophony of car hooters and aerosol horns burst upon the quiet cobbled streets. Faces appeared in windows and even the slumbering cats on inside windowsills pricked up their ears but didn't bother to open their eyes.

The walls of the old red brick houses reflected the day's warmth as we walked back to the Port de Plaisance, the air now filled with the smell of rain on warm dust. A Dutch couple, Canute and Mary, came and talked over a glass of wine and passed on news and boat gossip in perfect English. They happily live on the canal full time slowly travelling from the Mediterranean to the English Channel, or from Switzerland to western France.

It was raining next day, Sunday, so we busied ourselves on board.

Some details of a few days from my Journal:
9th May 2006.
10.45. Let go from Seurre at 10.45. There was nobody else on the river. It seemed as if all of France was ours. CLYPEUS floated along in the heavy smell of white May bushes blossoming along the banks. Frequently white and grey herons took off from the water's edge at our approach dragging their feet behind them. The river wound between bright yellow fields of rape. Loud birds were all a-twitter, and hawks were gliding high. Unusually a lady answered my radio request for the lock to open.

12.00. Through Ecleuse Equelles. We tied up for lunch by a Restaurant at PK 159.

After a rest S. walked along towpath up the Rue du Saone through the village and along the highway to Gergy village. I spoke to a gardener who had fine potato plants already flowering under a plastic arch. He said he liked his 'earlies' as early as possible.

Lovely old pale stone 14C Church. Lilacs,

mauve and white, pansies,wisteria bloomed over old steep-roofed medieval houses. S. walked back down to river through 'sportif' road where boys were playing soccer seriously, and parents were taking toddlers to feed the ducks on the river. The flood plain is used for summer sports and kept in good condition. Quiet night. Peter won Trivia again.

Mon.10/5
We continued up river in cold rain towards Chalon Sur Saone. Many fishermen lined the banks, camping, but few other boats. All day we met only three cruisers and one peniche in 20ks. Arrived Chalon 11.30 tied up in Marina. The office was closed but electricity was available. Walking into town we found it was Liberation Day. Everything was closed except for Monoprix Department Store so we spent an hour mooching around out of the rain and bought bread and a bottle of anti-cholesterol medicine (a bottle of Pinot Noir). The rain increased so we spent half an hour sheltering in shop doorways. When it lessened a little, we walked wetly home to a whisky and a tasty dinner of left-over smoked chicken in a paella.

Tues.11/5.
Cold, raining. Paid dues. Walked to Carrefour Hypermarket where it was deliciously warm inside. We were surprised at so much stuff -a fantastic variety of goods on display including swimming pools with pump motors and chlorinating gear. Solar garden lamps were a good buy, 10 lamps for 15 euros.

We ate an early lunch hoping to leave for Canal du Centre but so cold decided to stay put.
14.40. Weather lightened a little so decided to go.

In preparation for the narrow canals we had made a large board showing our 1.7m depth so that barges would know that we couldn't easily get out

We made a large board showing our 1.7m depth so that barges would know that we couldn't easily get out of their way.

Top right: We tied up safely opposite Le Fontaine lock keepers' cottage.

of their way. Our first lock into the canal system from the Saone had easy floating bollards which were familiar although it took a worrying twenty minutes of waiting around in the river before the lock opened and a smart holiday hotel peniche came towards us.

Next came our first automated lock, all alone. I climbed up the wet ladder clutching the mooring ropes and secured them to bollards. At first I couldn't make the lock open, then realised after pulling the blue rope three times to no avail, they must be pulled slowly and firmly, not tugged sharply.

Thirty minutes later at the next lock there was a steep ladder to climb. The water rose 5.13m (16'). No problem now we were getting used to the procedures.

At ten past seven we tied up safely opposite Le Fontaine lock keepers' cottage (no lock keeper

though). Peter asked advice from the VNF chap who came by in his white van who said we would be safe here over-night. It was a quiet, cold and rainy night.

On Wednesday 10th May it was again cold, raining, and we didn't want to start. It proved a very steep learning curve day. Suddenly, as we were having breakfast, the sides of a big black iron barge were passing us very close, and very fast.

"Crumbs. That's close," I shouted as I dashed out in time to see the stern of a huge peniche side-swipe our bow catching his stern cleat in our anchor as it protruded beneath our pulpit. CLYPEUS was yanked forward fast. Mooring pins and ropes were snatched out of the ground and we were being dragged at high speed through the water. Our bow line was still tied to a mooring bollard and the cleat, Sampson post and pulpit were about to be pulled out of the hull. Fortunately the lad on the barge rushed aft and managed to kick our anchor free. The barge charged on leaving us twisted right across the canal in a swirl of muddied water. It had come out of the lock too fast and couldn't straighten up into the canal before he hit us.

The VNF man happened to be watching and held our lines while, in shock, we sorted ourselves out. We decided to carry on rather than retie up. He said go slowly, 'doucement, doucement' to let the peniche get ahead. Too right! There was only a gouge out of the flare of the bow, something Peter could repair himself eventually.

The locks were a worry. Peter said, "It would be best if you climb up, or down, to work the mechanisms, and I hold the mooring ropes to keep CLYPEUS in place in the moving water."

"Right!" That was fine by me. Holding the boat still against the strong currents in the gushing water

needed all the strength he could muster. Actually, I enjoyed climbing the vertical ladders often with the ropes round my shoulder and held in my teeth as I mounted the dripping lock walls – I needed both hands for the slippery ladders. What countryside was there to see on top of the lock? The 5.20 metre (17feet) ones I found quite dizzying to look down on Peter as the water gushed in, and he clung desperately to hold the lines while the boat bucked and zigzagged in the swirling foaming water. Once the crew has climbed up the ladder they can't get back down onto the boat as it now lies centrally between the bollards and not near a ladder. (All the locks and canals were built for long barges, not pleasure boats.)

It was amazing how few towns or even villages we passed through. We were in real, rural France.

At Ecluse No 28 the blue pull rope didn't work and the gates wouldn't close.

"It won't work," I shouted down to Peter.

"Use the emergency phone then," he shouted back

I pushed the red emergency button and talked to a VNF lady operator but couldn't understand what she replied. Ten minutes later I phoned again. This time I understood something and waited. Twenty minutes later a lock keeper in a white van arrived and with a remote gadget operated the lock, but too fiercely. The sluice gates opened too quickly. Shock, horror, on his face as he saw how CLYPEUS, with her deep keel, gyrated as the surges, lifted and swung her about, and how difficult it was for Peter to hold her in place. I watched anxiously; should a 74 year old, who said his heart kept racing, be taking such a strain?

At the last of the day's locks the same VNF man drove up and asked us to wait for a cruiser to go through with us (after I had climbed the 17'

Our first automated lock, all alone. I climbed up the wet ladder clutching the mooring ropes and secured them to bollards.

ladder). We did, and this time he operated the lock very gently 'doucement, doucement' he said again. We were apprehensively geared up for a crisis, but all went well and after lunch fell asleep exhausted. Our first day in the canals had been terrifying – not the easy cruise we expected.

Chagny had a big basin where the long hotel barges turn around. Alongside the tow-path is a high industrial wall with tiles showing old photos of a previous era when the Tile Company employed most of the town. It is still functioning but there wasn't much activity.

We gave ourselves a rest day; we needed it after yesterday's traumas.

Peter said "You really are a gutsy girl", which pleased me no end.

I walked into town to look for an internet café, but no, there wasn't one. However the Tourist Office had a good exhibition of welded iron implement sculptures which were unusual and creative. I treated myself to an anise while looking at the modernised square where new stepped stone walls lead down towards a line of fluctuating fountains. The walls look most attractive and interesting but had many sharp corners at just the right height for little children to hurt themselves. It looked fresh and clean but an elderly local gentleman explained that "Ze previous trees and grass in summer were better. In summer it becomes very 'ot in the Square and now zere is no shade."

At last the sun shone and we managed the easy automated locks all on our own. Some have floating bollards, but all locks going up need ladder climbing and rope pulling. The countryside is peaceful and beautiful. Serried ranks of grape vines line the valleys. Unfortunately we passed Santenay Winery pontoon at 8.45 a.m., not a convenient time for a degustation. Actually while the weather was

cold, we had decided we prefer 'Oz' wines which are heavier and more substantial. They seem to have more sunshine in them.

"Sacre bleu!" I hear our French friends mutter.

On arriving at St. Leger sur Dheune we paid for our berth and showered and felt as fresh and squeaky clean as a television shampoo advertisement. Together we walked to the Boulangerie for fresh bread and to 'phone our daughter.

An excellent dinner a deux was enjoyed at the riverside Le Petit Kir which included a complimentary glass of kir and a misted bottle of ice-cold tap water on the table – nobody tried to sell us bottled water which we appreciate. We think bottled water, its plastic bottles and the ecological cost of transporting it, in countries with abundant, natural good fresh water, is a ridiculous waste of resources. The attractive English proprietress came and chatted and when we complimented her on the fresh water, she agreed with our views. A pleasant river terrace faced the river and pale sunset, but it was too cold to sit out and still raining.

On Sunday, after buying a baguette, we started at 8.30 a.m. knowing we had a long day ahead as the canal was now too shallow to get close to the banks to moor up. While waiting for a green light to proceed forward into the Lock 13, the VNF travelling eclusier told us "thirteen more locks then you can moor by the Canal Museum". We traversed the thirteen locks by 2 p.m. – up the ladders, down the ladders for me, strenuous rope holding to keep the boat straight for Peter and we were exhausted - mentally more than physically. Every lock is different, sometimes the water enters with great force, spouting with a rushing tidal wave, and at others it bubbles up furiously from the sides and sends CLYPEUS skidding all ways. A stiff drink, a

quiet lunch and for a while the sun shone, boys were quietly fishing on the bank, and we felt SAFE in the quiet, straight canal.

After a sleep we cycled along towpath to see Australian Al and Robbie on ESCAPE with whom we had spent time in St Jean de Losne. After a glass of water, they opened a bottle of champagne and much later we cycled home to eggs and bacon. We found the canals more challenging than anticipated. Between locks is peaceful and delightful but all the locks have different characteristics and there were still 100 odd to go!

Unfortunately The Barge Museum didn't open on Mondays, but before we left we spoke to a rotund little Frenchman in traditional blue overalls who said, "Ah! Une Endurance 35!"

We were so surprised, not many French artisans 200 miles from the sea know yacht types. Of course the Endurance was designed by a Frenchman, Pierre Ibold, and had won an international competition, but even so! Our new friend had a Trapper 24 and took us to see it in the yard nearby. He was a jolly, friendly man. Most summers he takes his boat down to the Med. Cheerily we waved goodbye only to find him at the next lock waiting to help and take our lines.

Eventually we tied up at 'Jeff's' in a Montchanin backwater at the top of the watershed and the end of the Canal du Centre. Carl, from Kent, helped us tie up in thunder and rain. His cruiser was sporting a Welsh dragon flag.

"Why are you flying a Welsh dragon?" I asked.

"Lloyd George (a Welsh Prime Minister of Britain) was my Grandfather's brother." He said "and I'm very proud of him." Carl and Katy loaned us Navicartes and a useful map. They were really helpful with information. The rain settled in and felt as if it was going to stay.

On the 17th May we left for the downhill run passing through Ocean Ecleuses 1,2,3,4,5,6,7 by 12 noon. It was so much easier going down, no swirling, thrashing, water, now it just slowly, calmly, disappeared down a plughole. As pre-arranged, Carl was waiting for us at Blanzy to lunch at The Maryland with them and their visiting friends. It was great! The restaurant was full of French business men gesticulating and talking loudly. Our five course lunch, including coffee and wine cost only 10 euros each, including a splendid cheese

board which was left with us, and as many refills of the wine bottle as we wished.

Australians, Peta and Steve, on the large barge 'HISTOIRE D'EAU' chatted to us and at six o'clock came on CLYPEUS for a glass of wine and to recommend places on our route. We enjoyed each others company. They had so much to tell us, that wine, cheese, pates, baguette and salad just disappeared and before we knew it was 10.30. Time for bed.

Leaving Blazny we tried to stop alongside

the Le Clerc supermarket, but the water was too shallow for our boat to get close to the bank. We could see three large commercial peniches approaching in the rain, one after the other.

"I will have to put her into the mud," Peter said as he slowly pushed our bow further into the reeds. "Hope we can float off again when they have passed." It was raining and cold. We waited for twenty minutes, clutching mugs of tomato soup to try and warm our hands, before we could reverse off the mud

How often a good day is followed by a frustrating one. Next day we met the only awkward lock keeper. The locks close for an hour at lunch time from one until two. We arrived at 12.40 and saw the white VNF van already parked, we thought ready to work the lock.

"Ah! good," said Peter. "Plenty of time to get through before lunch."

But no. The white-haired lock keeper sat in the van with his feet sticking out of the window, studiously ignoring us, until 2 p.m., when he deigned to walk and open the gates of Ocean 14. Peter found it difficult to hold CLYPEUS in position

while we waited for gates to open. Usually he sticks our bow into the mud, but it doesn't always hold and I can't get off to tie up. Still, it gives me time to sit on the cabin top and admire the wild flowers lining the bank: pink ragged robins, white cow parsley and blue forget-me-nots.

At Genelard there was a big deep mooring area. We wandered around the now small town which once supported a huge steel works that used to make equipment for barges. It was our turn to enjoy a delicious roast dinner with Peta and Steve on HISTOIRE D'EAU, their well converted 28m barge was originally constructed in 1907 using iron rivets. It is not only spacious but has everything - including a jacuzzi.

We thought the sun was going to shine at last but it reverted to rain and cold. The interior thermometer in our saloon showed only 14 degrees C.

Chateau de Digoine looked very impressive with black tiled cupolas as we puttered on through the delightful countryside. As I stood waiting to wind the lock gates open, a busy little blue tit with a morsel in her beak flew beside me and entered a small hole in the adjoining disused winding gear. A few minutes later she re-appeared and flew off. I bent down and could hear the nestlings twittering inside the old iron pipe-work. As we continued a pair of hawks hovered overhead and accompanied us for over an hour. An otter swam hurriedly alongside the steel piles, his head disturbing the water into an arrow head of ripples like fletches travelling across the glassy surface. When he came to a break in the bank he scrambled up and disappeared. Stonecrop, cow parsley, yellow iris, forget-me-nots, marguerites, dandelions, ragged robin, purple spears and fields of golden buttercups lined the canal banks. Tall chestnut trees their white and pink candles were bursting forth and the heavy

We tied up alongside 'HISTOIRE D'EAU.

scent of hawthorn blossom hung over the water.

In the late afternoon we tied up at Paray La Monial alongside HISTOIRE D'EAU and woke up amongst four Australian boats and one New Zealander - not a European or American boat in sight. Paray La Monial Basilica is light and beautiful with modern chandeliers and decorations. After shopping at Inter Marche, Peta and Steve came for dinner. It turned out to be one of those meals when you don't try hard but everything turns out perfectly: the melon was just right, the salmon steaks juicy, washed down with a cool bottle of rose, followed by sweet strawberries and cream. The meal had just that certain freshness and tastiness that doesn't always occur no matter how hard I try.

It rained and rained. Peter spent two days changing a fuel filter on the engine, but had difficulty bleeding it. It was Sunday afternoon before he said "All OK. We can breathe again."

The Antipodeans organised a Pot Luck Supper on HISTOIRE and gave us 'South Equator citizenship' to join in the evening: eight Aussies, two Kiwis and two Poms. We discussed mutual friends from way-back S. Pacific days. Cheers to MAIKWAI, VOYAGER and SUTAMON, MARA and TIMSHELL!

Good party, good food, home by 1a.m.

After an early book swap on the quay, we all went our separate ways. We headed for Digoin only three locks and 8 kms away. Wonderful vegetation lined the banks with the strong sweet smell of white acacia blossom, which looked like white laburnum, festooned the canal banks. That night eight of us joined together for Al's birthday supper at La Pierrade where a hot stone block is put on the table with thin slices of meat to cook yourself. In the moonlight we all walked back alongside the Loire to ESCAPE for coffee and birthday cake and admired the well lit Aqueduct's curved arches reflected in the satin-smooth black water of the river.

At last under bright sun, blue sky, and a cold wind CLYPEUS floated over the River Loire in the aqueduct. It does seem strange to be in a boat looking down on the slow flowing river where it tumbles over stones. While waiting at the lock under magnificent plane trees and sweet smelling acacia, we noticed many trees were burdened with mistletoe. I hate to think of the alien stems twisting and writhing up within the boughs ready to sprout out again through the bark. It brings to mind some of the most compelling space creatures. When I consider the shape of prawns, crabs, lobsters and toads and then mistletoe insinuating itself into beautiful trees or ivy strangling them from the outside, I realise there are no monsters worse than those in every day nature on earth.

It was time to stop worrying about nature - the canal was very shallow now. When our depth meter shows 3' we are aground. It showed 2.9' for most of this stretch as we ploughed through soft mud. There was obviously leakage from the canal down into the nearby Loire. It seemed a long day before we moored at Garnat Sur Engievre where a single jetty led to a peaceful, well kept picnic area. We walked into the village to post cards and buy a whole small Alaskan salmon for 2.20 euros (at that time £1.40)

We noticed many trees were burdened with mistletoe.

Right: At Decize, as we locked into the Crown Basin David Ross took our photos.

The following cold grey day was different because the friendly Eclusier, in his white van, rushed from lock to lock to let each boat through. He pointed out a stork nesting at the top of a tree with little beaks peeking over the side "Un nid de sigoine avec les petites" he said. (We looked it up in the dictionary - a nest of a stork with the babies)

At Decize we locked into the Crown Blue Basin while David Ross took our photos. Shookie and Brandolph help us tie up and invited us for drinks on BRANDLE, a 21.4m (62') peniche on which Brandolph has indulged his every whim and fantasy. Attractive, blonde, 30ish Shookie was the paid skipper. We were given substantial drinks and shown around the sumptuous boat.

It was so 'over the top' I noted some details but I have changed the names to protect myself from libel:

It was built in Southampton in 2001 and took two years for the Yard to fit it out with Brandle as site agent. He had planned it all and bought all the bits

> Length: 21.4m depth 1.2m.
> Engines: 1939 Kelvin 4 cylinder
> Generator: Panda 13 KVA
> Auxiliary engine: a Kubota

For those interested in unusual boats it had: hydraulic drive to two wing props. All the electronics were Raymarine. The speaking tubes from the bridge to the engine room were made by copying those on HMS BELFAST, male ones made up and female ones original, with brass trumpet speakers in engine room. The portholes were from a liner being broken up in Bombay. A genuine horn from a destroyer informed people of BRANDLE'S coming. Bollards were made from a design he saw in Amsterdam and had made from cast iron in Ireland. It had a fridge/freezer, gas cooker, oven, grill, microwave, TV etc. The State Room had an en suite, Guest double cabin and shower. The crew had double bunks and bathroom forward.

Videos from an infra red camera system reported in real time to his home in Shrewsbury.

The camera looks inside the boat and across decks.

Returning from the market we took the wrong towpath on the way home and found ourselves on the wrong side of the Loire and had to retrace our steps. I cycled back to picturesque Decize in the afternoon to explore. The 7th Century crypt of a dark, dark, church was really spooky – no one else was there. A climb up to ruins of the Duke of Burgundy's castle gave a magnificent view of the Loire Valley.

Our daughter Andrea's wedding was looming and we wanted to be home in mid-June for two weeks. Where to leave CLYPEUS? Marseilles Les Aubigny was suggested.

On the 28th May, we left Digion and puttered along the calm canal. At 12.30 Peter noticed no cooling water was squirting from the exhaust and the engine temperature was high. We pulled in as near as we could to the shore and heaved the gang plank across to the grass, banged in the pitons and tied up. On investigating under the floor he found the engine water intake blocked with grass and weed. (He is always listening to the engine note and checking that all is working well). Twenty minutes later we were on our way again.

In the next deep lock (9.23 metres about 30') I climbed up the vertical ladder with the mooring ropes as usual. There was a young Londoner in a hire boat behind us who was asked by his Skipper to climb up with the ropes, he said, "You must be joking! I'm not going to climb up that high," which made me feel good!

Next day we pushed on to Marseilles Les Aubigny and found a deep mooring alongside a pontoon. We walked along the bank to organise it with M. Raimondo for 58euros for a month. There was some confusion as, although the pontoon belonged to M. Raimondo, any electricity and water is supplied by the Municipality, and has to be paid for at the Marie.

Peta and Steve had invited us to spend a few days on HISTOIRE DE L'EAU, so in the rain, we caught a bus to Nevers and then a train to Decize. They met us at the station and we walked along the canal to their luxurious barge. On the grass-matting-covered deck, white and purple petunias in tubs surrounded teak garden furniture. From the wheelhouse, steps descended aft to the Owners' bedroom and en suite. It had a well-converted huge lounge/kitchen area, with a guest bedroom and bathroom with a Jacuzzi. Unfortunately it was only warm enough to have breakfast on deck on our last morning. The weather was cold, wet and windy but as the steering wheel was inside the wheelhouse progress was easy. What luxury! The forward part of the bow contained a washing machine and dryer, central heating and air conditioning pumps and motors, water and fuel tanks, generator, deck hose pump etc.

Peta and Steve made us very welcome and we enjoyed three days with them travelling to Fleurie and Nevers. Sunday was spent cleaning the boat ready for their next guests to arrive. Neighbours on HARBINGER came for coffee on deck. They happened to be from Landshipping near our home in Pembrokeshire and their sheep dog Jill was from Haverfordwest. After a few glasses of white wine in the sun, we took them all for lunch at the Marina café nearby.

Later we walked into town to catch the bus back to Marseilles Les Aubigny and CLYPEUS. It was a lovely break with no responsibilities. Peta and Steve are both Australian, born in the early fifties, young enough to be our children! They were excellent boat handlers, efficient and non fussy. They had attended appropriate schools for barge

handling* and maintenance before they took HISTOIRE on the water and for the last five years have spent six months at home in Melbourne and six months exploring the European Canals.

As we had a week before our trip to England we had the opportunity to make more friends and started a boules tournament in the evenings with more Australians, Sue, Richard and Douglas on ADAGIO, another barge. I made a sash to compete for: the CLYPEUS AWARD - LA BOULE BANDE D'HONNEUR 2006. Sue, an artist, lives on her charming red and white barge all year and had rented a garage on the bank for a studio and gallery. Her friends were visiting for a couple of months from Sydney and we were introduced to other local expats.

Marseilles Les Aubigny is a fascinating little village and a centre of the Resistance during the War. On the opposite bank was The Resistance House where a radio shack in the attic had sent messages to London. There were secret tunnels from the cellar under the river and under the canal. The Germans had bombed the tunnels but the entrance was still visible. While we were there the

June full moon made the nights as light as day. What adventures, expeditions had been planned here?

Tuesday the 5th of June was Mary's birthday and we were invited to join in the celebrations. Under ADAGIO'S green and white striped tent twelve of us enjoyed a pre-dinner kir then off to the Auberge Du Poid de Fer, for an untypical, typical French meal. We were warned that the eccentric Proprieteur (and chef) only serves customers he liked. I wrote about the unusual evening:

Auberge du Poid de Fer

Beneath the trees, beside the River Loire sits the old Auberge du Poid de Fer (feet of iron?) The setting sun illumined a white-clothed table laid for twelve, decorated with small vases of lacy white elder flowers just beginning to droop and give off their final sweet perfume like a bridal tribute. A round table beneath the unpainted wooden balcony groaned under a colourful buffet. My first instinct was: "not much food for 300euros."(we had all contributed 25e's each) However, each dish was superb: fresh raw salmon marinated in lemon juice and olive oil, pink roast beef sliced fine so that it melted in your mouth, small hocks of pork slow-roasted until the pale meat fell apart. Rondelles of creamy goats' cheese between slices of red tomato drizzled with oil, vinegar and herbs, crisp green lettuce with walnuts and dressing, slices of sweet melon and strawberries dotted hither and thither on pink and white parma ham. No bread, no cheese board, unlimited cold water and bottles of Burgundy, Rose and Sancerre white wine, satisfied everyone.

The lights were turned out, a birthday cake with flaring candles was brought in to a chorus of 'Happy Birthday' as the singing died so our host fired a two gunshot salute from the balcony. He later descended with a pistol stuck into his trouser belt, blowing a brass hunting horn and carrying a didgeridoo in honour of his Australian guests. Fortunately Richard was able to produce some low reverberations while Sue's 'cooees' and piercing whistles (two fingers strategically placed in her mouth) took us back to the Outback.

Displayed around the garden and riverside were crayfish pots together with anchors and iron buoys which still had bullet holes through them showing how the navigation buoys had been sunk during the war.

Following Jos into a lock.

Somehow we had to get back to our car at H20 Marina 150 kms away to return to England for daughter, Andrea's, wedding. Peter had helped Danish Jos with the engine on his small, fairly old, yacht. He had diagnosed an engine fault and recommended a mechanic who could put the problem right. However they needed a spare part which just happened to be available where we had left our Peugot at St Jean de Losne. Jos offered us a lift as he and his wife, Wenche, were about to drive home to Provence. They had to prepare their home in Antibes for visitors who were to rent their house for six weeks and needed, maids, nannies, a chauffeur and Rolls Royce available.

We stood by their Mercedes at 8 a.m. ready to go. In a few minutes Jos walked up "I need to buy croissants, can't live without my morning croissant" he muttered as he walked off to the Patisserie. He returned fifteen minutes later with four croissants and said "Guess what else I bought?"

"Sausage rolls? Cakes?"

"No bigger than that."

"A bicycle?"

"No, no, no. A house."

"A what?"

"A house. Fifteen rooms, in an acre fronting onto the Loire, for 100,000 euros." (The euro was worth about 60 pence at this time.)

"What? A house? But you haven't had time to look at it."

"I've seen it from the outside. Can't go wrong at that price, whatever the condition. I've given them my attorney's name and details and made a firm offer. Here comes Wenche. Don't say anything."

We all scrambled into the car and set off

"You're going the wrong way," said Wenche quietly.

"I just want to show you something." He turned across the bridge and little way down a promenade: "See that big house on the right?"

"Yes."

"It's ours."

"What do you mean, it's ours?"

"I just bought it when I bought the croissants." Stunned silence.

"Have you looked in it?"

"No, but for the price it must be the bargain of the century. Our boys can come and work on it and make it a B & B and perhaps a restaurant. The price is so low because the 88 year old owner hasn't long to live and he wants to return to his village in Pau in the Pyranees. He just wants to be rid of it."

"Oh!" (Jos had told us the money was available because he wanted to buy a larger, newer, boat and couldn't make up his mind which type, and Wenche didn't want another boat she wanted to stay home and be near her grandchildren.)

By the time we had reached our destination Wenche had decided to have the shutters and front door painted pink.

When we met up again a month later, they told us that the village Notaire and other locals were involved in the house sale and a higher bid had been accepted. But it was a lesson to us on how an entrepreneur's mind works.

Sue promised to watch over CLYPEUS while we returned to England.

NOTE
*Steve and Peta had taken the RYA Inland Helmsman's Course and the ICC International Certificate de Bateau de Plaisance. They had a licence pour La Conduite des Bateaux de Navigation Interieure, and had also taken a course on the CAMBRAI on Canal de St. Quentin (90m south of Calais) office address: CAMBRAI, 12 Lincoln Ave., Twickenham, London TW2 6NP. Tom and Di Murrell of The Dutch Barge Association had been helpful in recommending courses.

CHAPTER THIRTEEN | THE LANGUID LOIRE and A CARDIAC CRISIS

2006 Marseilles Les Abigny – La Charite – St Mammes to Paris

AFTER THE WEDDING we returned to CLYPEUS by Eurostar on 11th July. Fresh sunny days and cool nights were perfect for getting back in the groove.

Peter re-fitted a new Philips GPS and a new bilge pump switch, while I sat guiltily, nursing my aching knees remembering Andrea's wedding. We are so proud of our family and happy for her and Lawrence, her gentle giant of a husband. After they had been cheered off on their honeymoon, Noel and family set off for their villa in Spain and son Paul, with his American family stayed on in Hereford to be with Andrea's boys who were still at school. Peter drove off each day with the Americans to show them some middle England: Shrewsbury, Ludlow, the Welsh Mountains and waterfalls, while Paul and I walked Hereford environs. It was lovely to have time with my eldest son.

However, there should be lessons in growing old! As your body gets older, your mind doesn't, and inside you still think you are that strong healthy person you have always been and can suddenly walk for six miles, eight miles and ten miles on three consecutive days. No warnings are given, you just wake up with a swollen knee and are crippled for three weeks.(and on and off for a year).

Now sitting in 30C in the cockpit, keeping my leg up, and thinking longingly of ice, I remembered an unexpected incident in Thailand when anchored off a remote island in Phang Gna Bay on the inland side of the Phuket peninsula. I rowed the inflatable dinghy ashore on my own and found my way up a small gulley through the overhanging mangrove trees. I was just thinking it was foolish to be alone so far into the jungle, when I came to a clearing and saw a traditional Thai teak fisherman's house with two young women in the garden. One was doing the washing beside the well, the other was sitting on the ground picking cashew nuts from the end of the pear-shaped fruit. I stopped to say hello and was asked if I was thirsty? Then:

"Do you like coconut milk?"

"Yes please".

With that, the young woman called her eleven year old brother, who shinned up the thirty foot palm trunk and threw down three coconuts. While the boy hacked off the top of a green nut the girl disappeared. "Wait ." she said. "Ice"

"Ice?" in this remote spot.

Re-appearing with a plastic bag of ice. "Freezer for fish," she smiled. As soon as I had drunk some of the delicious sweet milky-water she popped ice-cubes into the nut. Delicious! The best drink ever!

No it wasn't! The best drink ever was in Egypt. Anchored off Safaga, with our Australian friends on MARA, we took the local bus into Luxor to explore the Karnak Temple and Museum. It was extremely hot. Next day we decided to be different and take donkeys to visit the Valley of Kings. I fell off mine, well I didn't fall off, the stupid donkey was walking straight at a car coming towards me. I pulled the reins sharply and the saddle slid beneath the donkeys belly and I hung on upside down until gravity took over and I dropped onto the road. (My back was bruised but no big deal, just laughter all round). Back in Luxor on the local bus back to Safaga, the bus windows were down but the oven-hot air blasting through didn't cool it at all. At the traffic lights a street Vendor thrust an icy plastic bottle of Fanta Orange through the window.

"A dollar" he shouted. He got two dollars and

that drink was the best ever. Better than any chilled Ascot champagne. It revived us and our spirits.

Bacl on board Peter continued replacing the bilge pump and still banished from the cabin I sat and thought of Chris Bonnington's remarks in *'Sea, Ice and Rock'* when he is on board SUHALI with Robin Knox-Johnson:

"One of the features, as far as I can see, of life on a boat is that things are always going wrong. I suppose because of the sheer wear and tear of continuous heavy usage in a hostile, corrosive atmosphere. Anyway, Robin just spent an hour upside down in the engine room covered in grease and fixed things. Yet another example of the constant ingenuity that is essential for the long-distance sailor."

For those who are not interested in the daily toil of climbing through France's locks, feel free to skip the next few pages. For those intending to voyage through France they may give you an idea what to expect:

From the ship's log:

15th July

It was time to leave our new friends in Marseilles Les Abigny and head for Paris.

09.30. Through Ecluse 25

10.30 Through Ecluse 26

10.40 Aground mid-channel. Backed off and steadily ploughed through mud.

11.00 Through Ecluse 27(Beffes)

12.00 Ecluse 28 (Argenvieres)

12.30 Pulled into bank for lunch using passerelle to get ashore.

13.00 Ecluse 29 (Rousseaux). The lock opened but we couldn't get off the bank. Peter told the Eclusier. He phoned through for more water to be let down.

13.45 Through 29

14.30 Tied up at grassy bank in 7' of water at La Charite. Hot. Shirley sat on the bank to read under a tree which offered the local insects a substantial meal.

20.30 After dinner on board walked into La Charite across two bridges and had an Abbaye Beer at pavement café.

16th Sunday

Up up and away with the early morning sun shining through the tree trunks. Passed through fields of sunflowers all trying to lift their heavy heads to follow the sun. This stretch of the canal was shallow: 5.9 feet and we draw 6 feet. Sometimes the boat just slowed and we ploughed through the mud. Other times we bumped over mounds with our hearts in our mouths.

Through Locks 30, 31, 32 where we met two boats loaded with musicians playing their way around France giving concerts where they halted for the night.

14.00 Top Spot. Tied up outside St Thibault Port de Plaisance as it was too shallow for us to enter. Pushed my bike down the gang plank to cycle off to find the swimming pool - Great! Cool at last. A splendid arrangement of three pools between well kept lawns and trees, all clean and fresh in the sunshine.

After a dinner we walked into town again in the evening for a riverside beer and Pastis.

17th Monday.

Pushed our bikes up through the historic

vineyards to Sancerre. Pliny had recommended Sancerre wine and goats cheese (Crottin de Chavignol)) in the first century AD. In the 11th Century Augustinian friars developed its cultivation. After an ice cream in the town square we followed the tourist 'pietons path' around town. Splendid views over the Loire Valley. Wheee'd downhill on the main road with the bicycle brakes squealing.

18th July Tuesday.

Lovely morning. Blue dragon flies and butterflies above the murky water and black clouds of tadpoles moving below the surface. The next four locks were a bit stressful as three charter boats shared the lock and there wasn't any room to maneuvre when the water rushed in. That night at Chatillon sur Loire we moored near Jos and Wenche on DAGWEEN III. It was a well kept park-side mooring, looked after by a French yachtsman who was getting ready to ocean

voyage again. The tourist office offered free email so we were able to contact our family. With Wenche and Jos we walked around town and had dinner.

19th July

Next morning emails were waiting from all three children plus others congratulating us on a *Good Housekeeping Magazine* article about our voyage and long marriage.

It was exciting to cross the Briare Aqueduct, designed and built in 1890 by Gustav Eiffel, of tower fame. The waterway is carried for 722 yards over the River Loire in an iron trough supported on stone pillars. It replaced series of locks on each side of the river crossing.
We travelled through eight locks going up that day, and then over the watershed to start coming down. The six locks coming down were so much easier as once the ropes are around the bollards, it is easy to get on board and just slacken off the lines

Left:
The waterway is carried for 722 yards over the River Loire in an iron trough supported on stone pillars.

Right:
The sun shines between the tall trees in the early morning and late evening casting shadows.

as the water goes down.

18.00 Tied up at Rogny les Sept Ecluse, a pretty little town. But we had alternator trouble, the warning light had come on. We decided to have a stop-over day as, not only had we passed through 14 locks, but had also gone aground many times. Peter had strained himself trying to push CLYPEUS off the mud. There were terrific thunderstorms and lightning that night.

20th July

Peter spent all day making repairs to the alternator, 3 diodes had failed. The local electrician couldn't supply replacements so a temporary repair was made. 30 litres of diesel went into the port tank. I did the washing (by hand) and shopping. Voyaging through the French poplar-lined canals the early morning and late evening, the sun shines between the tall trees, casting shadows. Bars of darkness line the calm surface of the water until an intruding boat causes ripples and the serenity dissolves.

I put some thoughts for and against canal cruising to paper:

For:

1) Instant friendships with other friendly supportive boating couples.
2) The interesting variety of nationalities from so many different backgrounds.
3) FUN. All are interested in each others' voyages.
4) Safe. Sheltered,
5) No tides or currents.
6) Weather forecasts are not important – It's either raining or it isn't.
7) A peaceful and unhurried way to see the country

Against:

1) Restricted. Once again in the hands of other men/women at manned locks
2) Can't go overboard for a dip at the end of a hot day or pour a bucket of water over my head. It is much too dirty.
3) In the right sort of boat it would be far easier, the constant worry of going

We passed
through
Montargis,
a veritable
Venice.

aground or hitting our easily shattered concrete
hull, took its toll. A shallow steel,
or fibre glass boat surrounded by rubber
guards would be ideal.
4) The rivers can be dangerous at flood times.

We spent the next morning waiting for the
alternator part, but it didn't come. When putting
water into the port tank, it seemed to be taking a
long time.

"Oops! We seem to be sinking," I remarked,
"I'm sure I didn't have to step up as far as this to get
ashore." Then the emergency bilge pump started.

"Hmm," Peter lifted the cabin sole. "Hell ! The
bilges are filling up. Turn off the water. Quick." He
found a fitting had corroded through and water
was escaping into the bilge.

In the afternoon we traversed four locks one of
which was called Picardie. It certainly did have
roses and it was a very pretty flowered stretch of
canal.

On a quiet reach we emptied the bilges by
bucket and poured it away into a ditch, two metres
from the bank, so that no oil went into the canal.
Then put-putted along through magnificent forest.
Now the lazy River Loing was on our right.

Another eight lock day. Although going downhill, it was still stressful and tiring wondering what
was going to go wrong at each lock. We scraped the
sides of the last two locks and had a quiet, early
night.

For our 52nd wedding anniversary we
breakfasted at a picnic table on the bank. Passed
through Montargis, a veritable Venice, and moored
at Dordives to find a restaurant for an anniversary
lunch. Back alongside the boat, I sat on bank and
splashed my feet in the water to try and cool off. I
was sitting in the shade reading my book when a

fiftyish, slim, smart Dutch lady with a bouffant hair
style cycled by, stopped, and introduced herself as
Marghe. It proved an interesting chat. Because the
Seine winds extravagantly within its valley, I didn't
realize we were close to Paris but Marge mentioned
that every month she had her blonde hair styled by
Pierre at Gallerie Lafayette. Then she usually spent
two hours in the Musee D'Orsay, the Louvre or the
Orangerie. She had raced in the San Diego ladies
Dragon Boat team in Singapore when she was
45 in1975 (which made her 75), and climbed
Kilimanjaro at 50. Her 92 year old mother had died
in Neimegen last October. Marghe had been home
to look after her for the last year visiting her every
day in the nursing home. Now she was clearing her
mother's house to sell and wanted to invest the
money in a house in France but it was taking too
long. She couldn't understand the lack of drive of
the French Estate Agents who didn't give her
properties to look at or make appointments for her.
She was staying with a friend on a barge while she
looked around but was about to give up.

Lily pads were on our left as we cruised beside
the slow-flowing River Loing which seemed to be
covered in lilies. We passed through thirteen more

locks before we came out into the River Seine at Nemour where the depth rose to a nice safe 12 feet and carried on to St Mammes to fill our water and diesel tanks again as now the hull could float lower in the deeper water. The hot humid night reverberated with more thunderstorms.

We allowed ourselves a rest day on the Seine to

Champagne 2 Lock and continued on down the pretty Seine valley through Fontainbleu, through La Cave Trois Ecluse in Chartrettes which we had all to ourselves. The huge lock was filled just for us. It seemed wrong to let so much water down river for one small yacht. In the evening we rejoined GWEN L alongside the new quay at Melun.

Yippee! We'd almost made it to Paris. The penultimate goal of our 25 year Round the World voyage.

Gwen of GWEN L kindly woke us up with very welcome fresh baguette and we left Melun by 8.30

clean the boat, fill the water tanks and get used to being on a flowing river again. The cruiser alongside wanted information about the canals to the south, and we were delighted to go on board for a glass of wine and tell them. However, Peter suddenly shot up and said

"My God, I've left the water running." The tanks were overflowing and CLYPEUS was filling up fast. The water was over the starter motor. We pumped like mad to clear it then he took the starter motor off and dried it out immediately. On a boat you can't relax for long. Water, inside or outside, is a constant problem.

Fortunately, as I will tell later, we met and chatted to the couple on GWEN L and their guests before taking on 150 litres of diesel and pressed on towards Paris. At 14.45 we went through the huge

following them. The voyage was easy. They arrived at the locks first, we followed about 20 minutes later and a huge sand barge followed us, usually another twenty minutes later. The wooded hills sloped down to the Seine where splendid properties supported turrets and tiles. Their lawns dipped to the riverbank and weeping willows trailed their supple pale green leaves in the water. GWEN L forged ahead but had to wait in each lock for us and we, in turn, had to wait for the sand barge which chugged sedately downstream to slowly, slowly manoeuvre itself into the lock behind us.

At 3 p.m. we were going so well we decided to carry on to the Arsenal marina in the middle of Paris. By the time we arrived, 58 kms and four locks later, about 5 p.m., we had to wait forty minutes for the Marina lock to open. The cold wind from the North was roughing up the north flowing Seine. For an agonizing time we had to hold station in the strong current between the unforgiving stone walls. CLYPEUS rolled extravagantly in the wakes of deep laden barges and fast tourist boats. When the green light shone we moved forward in line into the dark narrow entrance to the Arsenal Marina Basin Lock and only just squeezed in beneath the Metro station. Trains were screeching to a halt above us and main road rush hour traffic was roaring and hooting across the bridge. The dripping black walls showed no bollards or rings to tie up to. I hung on with the boat hook hooked into a cranny. Then major PANIC. Peter could see the ends of our masts were going to be trapped between the lock gates as they closed. They would be squashed between the thick iron gates.

"We've got to get further forward," he shouted. "Quick, quick."

I pushed us along the wall with the boat hook, right up close to the boat in front, but didn't quite

make it far enough and our radio aerial was squashed flat as the heavy gates banged shut. It was frightening being so close to other boats as the water surged up and tried to push CLYPEUS around with the aerial still caught between the gates, until it broke off.

Eventually we were in the blissful calm, and directed to a place opposite the Capitainerie where the only land access was up steep stairs to the road. Peter looked exhausted but our neighbour, a Guernsey R.N.L.I. Bosun and therefore due the utmost respect, was determined to immediately demonstrate his new Romy Rig sailing rig design on his model boats. Peter was interested and had a go at radio controlling them and appreciated the

versatility and extreme maneuverability. As I hummed '*The Blue Danube*', he could make them waltz and dance around each other with amazing ease.

After showering in facilities built into cellars under the tree lined road. Peter looked very tired but happy. We opened a bottle of champagne to celebrate a major milestone in our homeward voyage. After dinner we had an unusual glass of

A Guernsey RNLI Bosun demonstrated his Romy Rig.

brandy after the long, long, day as we thought it would do us good! An early night and I slept well, but in the morning Peter looked tired and grey.

"Don't feel too well," he said weakly. "Had bad chest pains and felt sick in the night, but I sprayed my pink stuff (glycery trinitrate) under my tongue and the pain gradually went away and I went back to sleep. It was probably indigestion after our celebration dinner."

"You stay in bed while I shower, then I'll go and do the shopping and leave you in peace."

In the showers I told Matt of GWEN L that Peter had had chest pains and how poorly he looked and felt. "I think yesterday was too long and too stressful," I said.

An hours or so later when I returned from the market, GWEN L'S guests rushed to meet me saying,

"Don't worry. He'll be all right!" which of course immediately made me panic.

"What's the matter? What's happened? Where's Peter? What's going on?" I questioned as I rushed along the pontoon.

They followed saying, "the emergency medical team is there. Gwen is waiting with them."

CLYPEUS, was full of black clad and booted Pompiers et Sapeurs with the emergency medical team and their equipment in the cabin. There wasn't room for me. I glimpsed a pale Peter, with an oxygen mask over his face, lying on the little settee behind the immovable folded saloon table. Gwen indicated I sit beside her on the cabin roof and told me she had been a Sister in the Accident & Emergency Department of Rotherham General Hospital and had visited Peter after Matt had told her what I had said. She immediately knew that he could have had a heart attack and came to see him in the cabin. When she saw his colour and talked to him she told him to stay still and not to move,

then immediately called the emergency services. They had arrived within ten minutes and were now assessing him. More medics arrived with more equipment. This was the A & E Doctor from the local hospital. I was told Peter had had a heart attack and needed hospital treatment as it was still happening. He had put himself behind the immovable folded saloon table which made it really difficult for the medics to get to him.

While I was walking home with the shopping the Pompiers & Sapeurs van had screamed past with sirens howling and their white and blue lamp flashing and I had wondered who was in trouble?

I sat in the cockpit watching them administer an array of tests and injections. I was told in French that they would let me know which hospital he would be taken to as soon as it was arranged. The Doctors left with instructions that he mustn't move a muscle as he was still having minor heart attacks.

Strapped onto a stretcher Peter was lowered into the RIB and ferried across to the waiting Ambulance.

In staccato French, the senior Sapeur gave his instructions. With amazing teamwork in such a small space, talking quietly to each other and kindly to Peter, they gently sat him up and lifted his rigid body onto a stretcher and carefully straightened

Left:
CLYPEUS was full
of black clad and
booted Pompiers
& Sapeurs.

Right:
He was rushed
to the Cardiac
Wing of the
Salpetriere
Hospital
(where Princess
Diana had been
taken after her
car accident).

him out. Then they inflated the neoprene sides and strapped him into the cocoon. The team manoevered him sideways out through the narrow cabin door into the cockpit, then lowered him into the red Emergency River Rescue craft which had been radioed in from patrolling on the Seine. I didn't manage to get near him to touch his hand or let him know I was there. He was zoomed across the harbour to a waiting ambulance and I was told to wait to hear to which hospital he had been taken. Gwen stayed with me and was very supportive and helpful and knew what was happening - I didn't, I was just guessing (not very positively). It all went very quiet!

Gwen waited with me on CLYPEUS, while I tried to get my head round what would need to be done here and at home. How sick was he? How would I get the boat back to England if he couldn't sail anymore? What was the best way to let the children know what had happened?

At last a Pompier stepped on to the little along-side pontoon (heavily, and almost toppled into the water, he wasn't used to narrow floating pavements) and told us where Peter had been taken. Fortunately

he was at the Salpetriere Hospital – the world renowned University teaching hospital, where incidentally, Princess Diana had been taken after the Paris car crash. Apprehensively I packed his pyjamas and washing things and we climbed up to the roadway where Gwen hailed a taxi. I thought I was managing calmly and efficiently until I stepped out of the taxi and slipped and fell. My glasses banged into my cheek as my head hit the kerb and I gave myself a black eye. Then when I looked for my Visa card with the thought I would need to get more euros for fares and possible payments, I found that my Barclay credit card had been lost? stolen? It must have happened when shopping.

At the hospital nobody in Reception knew where Peter was. No, he hadn't been taken to E & R, I didn't dare ask about the Mortuary. Eventually after a harrowing thirty minutes he was located in Cardiac Intensive Care, which in this hospital was a whole separate new building. Hurrying through the long polished corridors, with Gwen's help we arrived at the right section. Peter was wired up and laying pale and disinterested. I just had to stand and wait while he was being investigated and treated. For what exactly? Eventually a young doctor who spoke some English came and took me outside and explained what was happening, that he had had at least one heart attack and may be having more.

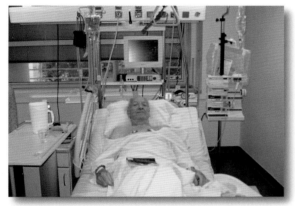

Peter was kept in Intensive Care for four nights and once again, if something bad has to happen, we were lucky enough to be in the best place and have caring friends to help us. Gwen and Matt loaned me their spare mobile phone so that the hospital could reach me if necessary. They also let me use their onboard email facility so that I could alert our children and cancel my missing Visa card.

On the second day GWEN L carried on with their voyage to England. They had flights booked to Singapore to see their son and couldn't delay any longer. We can never thank them enough and felt very lonely when they left. I was allowed to visit Peter at any time, and spent some hours in the Hospital Administration Department with our 'E1-11s'. They said they wouldn't need any money now, but a bill would be forwarded. (When it came three months later we paid it, then Peter sent the account on to The UK Department of Health and we eventually received almost full compensation). Peter continued to improve and the doctors kindly

kept me informed of his progress and various procedures. It was decided not to operate as too many arteries were narrow and he would do best on medication for a while.

The other yachts' people were a great help. Jos escorted me to the Capitainerie to ask if they could give me a special price for our enforced stay. The French officials allowed us to be one size smaller for the daily mooring fee for the whole of August. All through our two summers in France we met nothing but kindness and friendliness.

I had time on my own to worry and plan and think about Peter, my husband and best friend. We met when I was 15 and he 18. How could I live without him? I tried to be positive and describe him in a poem:

> *A quiet man, a patient man*
> *Gentle, tall and fair.*
> *A cautious man, a careful man*
> *An inveterate investigator.*
> *How does it work? How was it made?*
> *Is it efficient? Can it be improved?*
> *Or better still, does it need mending?*
> *A natural engineer, blessed with an enquiring*
> *mind,*
> *But singularly self sufficient.*

Our children were marvellous. Paul offered to come and help from America, if he could be of use. Noel insisted they would pay for us to recuperate for a week in a good hotel (as long as it wasn't' the George V!) We enjoyed a quiet and restful seven days in the Novotel. The following weekend Andrea and Peter's sister, Liz, came to escort us back on Eurostar to spend a month at home and Rosemary met us at Waterloo and drove us home to Pembrokeshire. They did everything possible to

Back in Paris CLYPEUS was fine in the Arsenal Port de plaisance.

and crew for us to help bring CLYPEUS home? A rush of kind friends offered to help, but when it came to the point they all, justifiably, had commitments for the last week in August and first week in September. He decided he didn't want anybody else on board, it would just compound the problem by having to rush so that our crew could fit in with their 'home by' dates By the time we arrived at the mouth of the Seine it would be spring tides and the start of the equinoctial gales. Should we try and bring CLYPEUS back to England or should we just get her out of the Arsenal and find somewhere quiet and safe on the Seine?

We enjoyed walking along the flat areas of Pembrokeshire's coastal clifftops to gently recuperate and build up his strength.

So, on 30th August, severely chastened and no longer so sure of our capabilities we returned to Paris and enjoyed five days resting and settling down. We were aware of the fundamental change in ourselves and our loss of confidence. It was lovely to be back on board CLYPEUS and we appreciated each day, each meal, concentrating on a more rigid diet and less alcohol. One evening though we did have a lovely meal al fresco at the restaurant in the Arsenal Gardens in the balmy twilight - Paris at its best!

Peter did maintenance and repaired the alternator, while I cleaned the boat and restocked. We took time to visit the Louvre and Tuillerie Gardens and the excellent Sunday morning market by the Place De La Bastille.

help us. How fortunate we have been to have such caring and considerate children. We were quite loth to leave CLYPEUS as we love living in our little boat and life is very easy if we are not going anywhere. However there comes a stage in many parents' lives when you realise you are no longer 'boss' and we complied. It hurt a bit that CLYPEUS was having six weeks sitting in the centre of Paris and we were not enjoying it with her.

The doctors told Peter that as long as he didn't get over-tired or lift anything heavy he should be OK.

During a month of frustrating indecision at home Peter gained strength. Who had time to come

CHAPTER FOURTEEN | THE VALLEY OF THE SEINE

2006 Paris to Limay – home for the winter – 2007 Limay – Rouen

FOR 482 MILES THE RIVER SEINE snakes along between spectacular castles and abbeys, set against a backdrop of plunging white escarpments and thick woods. It wells up thirty miles North West of Dijon to start its journey. A third of the French population live within reach of the Seine and they make the most of it. On warm days Parisians strip down to nothing and sunbathe on its warm stone banks Twenty five locks gradually lower the river 1,600 feet before it reaches Rouen. It can look a calm, deep, translucent blue/green or it can look like café au lait on the boil.

The Arsenal Marina, near the Bastille, was the site of a medieval cannon and powder factory that accidentally blew itself up in 1871. It is a calm and peaceful sanctuary with only a few peniches chugging through. Even the tourist boat commentators keep their voices down low – they have just come through the Marne Tunnel in their Bateaux Mouche, so called after the flies (mouche) which whine around their heads.

Now, in September, the Parisian boats were returning to claim their winter berths. We must move on. Feeling very apprehensive we untied our lines and prepared to re-enter the Seine to find somewhere to moor CLYPEUS for the winter.

On Monday 4th September at 7.45 a.m. I quietly let go the lines whileand Peter backed out of our berth and waited for the lock to open at the advertised time of 08.15. We gilled around trying not to hit anything. Nothing happened. Evidently, we should have made a radio request to the Marina Office for the lock to open. Eventually we were let out into the calm and peaceful Seine in time to catch the river traffic lights around Notre Dame. They allow downstream traffic for 25 minutes at 35 minutes past each hour. It was drizzling gently and

Peter back in charge as Paris's Statue of Liberty fades in the mist.

the top of the Eifel Tower was lost in cloud.

The Bridges of Paris all look very similar from the top of a bus, but at river level, each has a story. Pont Alexandre III with its four golden winged horses, was the centrepiece for the 1900 Paris World's Fair. It was meant to outshine the 1989 Eiffel Tower. The bridge still symbolises France's grandeur at that time.

Underneath Pont de L'Alma is a sculpted soldier in flowing cape and fez. A sentry of the Paris floods – if it wets his spats, the river is fast and furious. If the water leaves a ring around his neck, the banks are awash. They say it will be a terrible day for Paris if it ever reaches his moustache. We had noticed, on the wall of the Arsenal Marina, a high plaque to mark the level of the 1910 flood which must have been at least to the sentry's lip

147

Left:
Renoirs
'Le Dejeuner
des Canotier'.

Right:
And here we
were on the very
verandah where
it was painted
with our beloved
boat in the
background.

level. Pont Neuf is the oldest bridge started by Henry III in 1578 and Petit Pont is the bridge that Abelard nightly slipped across to see Heloise every night.

Leaving Paris, the abandoned hulk of a Renault Factory on the Ile Seguin looked sad and derelict. They now have a modern factory further (where our car was made) down river. Smart laden Peniches slurped by, with the capitaine at the wheel, his wife polishing the windows or sweeping the decks. Most have a small car sitting on the after deck where geraniums and petunias flutter in the breeze.

At Neuilly, we passed the stone gazebo on Ile de le Grande Jette, the Temple of Love, where King Louis-Philippe enjoyed his fanciful, romantic, Venetian parties.

I started practising my French VHF message for lock keepers "Bonjour M'sieur, nous voulons avalant, s'il vyous plais." - (we wish to go down-stream please). Through the Suresnes Lock hoping to find a stopping place at 17k at Clichy, but the Marina was full, so we carried on and moored at Reuil Malmaison, It's a new town with fountains and attractive gardens leading down to the river. On

the opposite bank was the Isle des Impressionistes and Chatou which was the terminus of the Paris suburban railway when it was built in the mid 1800s. It encouraged the young Impressionist artists to take the train out of summer-hot Paris to spend the day, or night, on the cool rural riverside. They would meet and paint at La Maison Fournaise:.

Renoir, Degas, Monet, and Maupassant used it as a scene for many of his stories.

As soon as I realised, the restaurant on the opposite bank was where Renoir had painted his 'Le Dejeuner des Canotier', which had always been one of my favourites depicting relaxed, happy, young people enjoying a drink on a riverside balcony. Iit was definitely a 'seize the day' moment. I walked across the bridge and booked us into La Maison Fournaise for lunch next day. It was delicious - the best French meal I've had. The dessert was 'to die for': roasted figs topped with raspberries, blackberries and deep red coulis oozing down the topping of vanilla ice cream. Particularly the dessert of roasted figs with raspberries, blackberries and coulis poured over vanilla ice cream - to die for! It seemed wonderful to clink our glasses to toastwith

CLYPEUS our dear boat tied up on the opposite bank. It was a perfect. day in a perfect setting.

Next day We left Rueil Malmaison in bright, hot sunshine. Cormorants were nesting high in the trees which were now turning yellow, red and brown. At Ecluse de Bougivel the Lock Keeper called out "Au revoir. Retournez vous un jour." which was nice to hear. The French people, all through our journey were kind and friendly. Perhaps our appalling French, which we try to use all the time, makes them want to help these poor, simple, boaters.

At noon we stopped for lunch at barge-lined Conflans where, in the past, 40,000 barges travelled each year. While Peter rested, I climbed to the fascinating Musee des Battaliers which explained the history of the river and barges. Conflans was very important because it is at the confluence of the Oise and Seine. All the coal which Paris needed in the 19th century, came through here.

Looking for somewhere to moor overnight at Andresey we explored around the back on an island and notice that Andresey, gradually CLYPEUS was slowing down.

"I think there is something around the propeller," Peter said. We pulled into the bank just outside the Hotel de Ville and pushed and prodded with the boathook from the cockpit in the murky water, but couldn't shift whatever was there. "Well have to launch the dinghy." He pumped it up and we lowered the Avon into the scummy water.

"Coming round the back of the island wasn't a good idea."

"I've caught something that feels like plastic around the prop." I said. We pulled and prodded with a metal hook, but still no good.

"Would you mind awfully going over the side? I think it's the only way." Peter questioned me.

Over the side again to clear a large sheet of plastic from the propeller.

I'd been putting off even thinking about getting into this filthy looking water which was bound to have a horrible mucky, muddy, bottom. Looking at the dirty wateI did think I was getting a bit old at 73 to be diving to clear the propeller, but heigh ho! There was nobody else to do it.

"I guess there's no real problem as long as I keep my mouth shut and don't swallow any of that poisonous looking water," I said as I went to change.."

I quote Peter's entry in the log:

'15.50 Launched dinghy and prodded with boathooks. We could feel something but couldn't move it. Brave Shirley donned bathers, goggles and armed with the bread knife, dived under the stern. It took her 7 or 8 dives to get the tangle off. It was a large sheet of clear plastic plus some thick rope/netting. It is a wonder we moved at moved at all.'

A mile further on we tied to the bank for the night.

Early next morning we were off, and ten minutes through later we were followed into Andresey Lock then by a, huge barge. It took twenty minutes before we motored out into the pleasant river, past Poissy and the modern Peugot

Factory. Splendid houses lined the banks.

Passing the entrance to another Port St Louis we could see it had mooring spaces but it seemed too soon to stop. On past Melun to Limay at PK109, apprehensively, we cautiously slowed to go through the arch of a ruined bridge afraid the river it might be too shallow, but no problem. We tied up to Limay Halte de Plaisance, a free pontoon, for a late lunch and surveyed the pleasant town on the opposite bank – Mantes La Jolie.

Later in the afternoon we explored the pretty town and its huge recently restored church with a 90' high nave which had been bombed during the war. but was now beautifully restored.

In front of CLYPEUS we could see a few pontoons with, what looked liked, 'live-aboard' boats moored up, so next morning we wandered.

Next morning, after enjoying our warm croissant and coffee we wandered along the river bank to see if we could stay there. It was a small Marina with a sign "Les Marins de Limay". Finding. We found our way through a garden, our feet crunched onwith walnuts covering the ground beneath the trees. A huge Alsatian put himself between us and the stairs up to an office door.

"Good dog, good dog, bon chien," we whispered as we cautiously edged around him.

M. Ardoin the proprietor, full of Gallic charm, greeted us and made us welcome. Yes, They did have room for us to winter there. However Peter, but we decided we should go and see Port L'Ilon first. It is only five miles downstream first, and has it is a new Marina set in a disused, now flooded, sand and gravel pits out of the mainstream of the river which would be away from out of any of winter's raging torrents, should it prove a wet and snowy winter.

It was it was pleasant cruising down river with

the sun and the wind behind us past a stately home the palace Chateau de Sully home of the Duc de Rosny, and the high white escarpment at Rolleboise crowned by a famous hotel.

A sign on right hand bank indicated Port L'Illon through a narrow gap in the opposite bank.

"Do you think we have really really got to cross the back of the weir and go through that narrow gap?"

"Looks like it."

"Hope we don't get swept down onto the weir. What if the engine stops? I'm nervous with no sails. now we have no sails up."

"The engine won't stop. Go on the bow and see if you can see any shallows in the channel."

It did look a bit dodgy, but the Perkins engine steadily ploughed us across the river and in among trees which met overhead. We threaded our way through, nosing around corners beneath the trees into a big expanse of rough and windy water with a modern Marina on the far bank. Eric, the manager, was pleasant and helpful and told us it would cost 1,400 euros for 6 months, with an extra 5 euros each time to use the washing machine.

We thought about it overnight, (and put and load through the washing machine). However the Marina seemed very isolated. There was no village nearby. We found a British couple and chatted to them.

"It would be very difficult to stay here without a car." John advised.

"The bus only comes to the crossroads twice a day and it's quite a long walk from there, especially if you are carrying shopping," his wife added.

We decided to have another look at Les Marins de Limay.

On the 10th September, after breakfasting in the cockpit on a lovely sunny quiet and still morning, we showered, then fed greedy swans and cygnets with stale bread.

Fortunately nobody was watching our farcical departure. which was a farce because I didn't notice that I hadn't untied one of the bow ropes! Peter put the engine into gear to back out from the pontoon and nothing happened. Investigations into the gear box performance, the propeller etc. before I noticed the offending rope. Shamefaced, I had to endure Peter's unflattering comments. But it was such a lovely morning and place, my spirits lifted and I sang all the way back up river. Peter even joined in.

We tied up at Limay Halte de Plaisance again, and after lunch explored the reconstructed town where Corot had painted, and confirmed that we would be well protected behind the island out of the main stream. There was also a large Power

Station a couple of miles upupstreamriver which used the river water for its cooling system which and Peter thought it would keep the water from freezing around us. Hopefully CLYPEUS would be sheltered, warm and safe. Walking beneath the walnut trees and around the quiet Alsatian, we climbed up wooden steps into M. Ardoin's office

M. Ardoin agreed CLYPEUS could winter at his yard and came on board for a Pastis.

The Yacht Club opposite tried to have an end of season race but no wind.

again and settled for a winter mooring: 990 euros for six months. At 6 p.m. we motored CLYPEUS was moored to the to a berth on the outside of the pontoon where we were concerned that she would be vulnerable to passing traffic and their wash. M. Ardouin and his son Pierre helped us to tie up, then came on board for a pastis and promised to move us to an inside berth when a big white motor yacht moved out in October. (He didn't). Later we phoned our family to let them know we had found a winter home for CLYPEUS.

On Sunday at 11 a.m. a fleet of 33 yachts, from sailing club opposite, set off to race with their colourful spinnakers up. They eventually returned at 6 p.m. There was less than a little wind. We chatted to pleasant a French lady owner from a red yacht who confirmed it would be 'tranquil' here.

We enjoyed a peaceful time during the season of mists and mellow fruitfulness – a damp haze huangs over the Seine, the morning bird calls were lazy and dimmed. The muted dull roar of traffic hummeds gently in the far distance. The market wasis full of ripened fruit and large vegetables at the end of the season. Some apples and peaches had already lost their freshness and juice. We spent a whole week doing nothing much, making friends and arranging Eurostar tickets. The yacht club

opposite tried to have an end of season race. They left mid morning to drift down river and some were still paddling back at 6 p.m.

Each morning and evening I walked along the river bank with neighbouring Ann of JAO and her three boxer dogs.

Ann invited us to supper on the pontoon with Sarah (who taught English at a Parisian school) and her daughter Anna. Ann served, from her small boat a delicious summer supper starting with a kir apertif, then melon, cucumber and basil salad, followed by roast chicken with potatoes in garlic butter and mushrooms; followed by prickly pears or a slice of petite gateaux made by Anna and coffee Great! We talked poetry "Apolinaire." Fortunately I had just been reading some French poetry and was able to join in the discussion briefly.

Ann gave us a helpful hint when buying red wine. A good cheap Burgundy will have "Recolte" written on top of the cork.

Neighbour Anne invited me to walk along the river bank each morning and evening with her boxer dogs and she gave us a delightful BBQ on the pontoon in the warm evening air. Other new friends, Therese and, Dennis, with daughters, Alizee, Laurence and Aurelielyce, lived on the big white catamaran behind us.

I asked Dennis what was his dream? Expecting him to say – to sail to the South Pacific or something, but he said: "That is my dream" pointing to his boat which he and Therese had built themselves. himself. "I had the dream to build it and now we have done it and we have been living on it for six years and I'm happy." he continued "Perhaps when our daughters have left home I will sail my wife back to her island of birth, Mauritius."

On the 20th September, confident we had left CLYPEUS in good hands we took a fast train ride

Top left:
Leaving CLYPEUS
for yet another
winter.

Bottom left:
The hewn chalk
staircase up to
the cliff top.

Top right:
The large
Pigeon Loft.

into Paris and then Eurostar to London andand then homea National Express Coach brought us safely home to Pembrokeshire.

In November we returned to Limay by car and ferry, to check that all was well. with our dear boat. A grand display of chrysanthemums lined the bridge across the Seine into Mantes La Jolie as we walked to the market. With the car filled it was great to have the car to fill up with wine and

cheeses and we explored the surrounding countryside. La Roche Guyon was spectacular and exciting with its secret stairway cut through the chalk cliff to the top of the escarpment. There were many

Bottom right:
La Roche Guyon
had a secret
tunnel to the
Tower on top of
the cliff.

tapestries and elegant furnished rooms. The pigeon loft was spacious. Pigeons were probably a major part of the diet. The views down to the pas terre and across the fertile Seine valley of the Seine were as spectacular. Down in the cellars, the story of the Nazi regime and the French Resistance was graphically told. Further down in the dungeons was

Our presentations about our voyage on The BOUDICCA wereappreciated by staff and passengers.

an iron Chronoscaphe – a time machine used in the *'Adventures of Blake and Mortimer,'* a Sci Fi film.

The only bad thing was that our best bicycle was stolen and, of course, leaving our boat afloat to groan and shiver at her mooring in another country is a constant worry.

During the winter Peter returned to distributing Meals on Wheels and I returned to teaching Keep Fit to ladies. It was now a class 'For the Gracious Years' and contemplated what were we going to look forward to after our circumnavigation was completed? I was afraid that we would grow old very quickly once we stopped sailing so, with a friend in my Writers' Group having given me the name of an Agentthe help of a friend from my Pembroke Dock Writers' Group, in January I applied, with a comprehensive CV, to an Agent, to find out if we could become guest lecturers on Cruise Ships.

It all happened very quickly. Two days after posting off an application letter, the Agent telephoned to ask if we would like to be Guest Lecturers on the Fred Olsen Cruise Ship BOUDICCA. Could we be ready to fly to Costa Rica in three weeks' time to join a 25 day Caribbean cruise? We would need to have six forty-five minute Power Point Presentations on computer as there was no other equipment for showing slides on board. (Evidently Kodak replacement carousel projector spare parts are not made any more longer made so slide projectors are no longer viable).

Of course we said 'Yes', looked at the slides we had been using to give talks for the last five years and realised they were not good enough for a professional presentation. Peter researched, then bought a new laptop capable of handling the thousands of bytes for photographs, while I sorted through the last 25 years of slides, negatives and

photographs for the most suitable images. Many negatives were in poor condition after being on a small boat in the tropics for over twenty or so many years, but the prints had survived better. So Peter re-scanned the photographs over 1,600 images while I wrote the scripts. It was a lot to do in three weeks as well as organise medical insurance, clothes and transport to Heathrow and Southampton.

Full of excitement we left for Heathrow with a laptop and three memory sticks of our presentations distributed about our clothing and bags, so that we would still have our programme if bags were lost, or one of us became ill.

No problems. We were met at Costa Rica's Airport by a man holding up our names on a large card and driven to a luxurious hotel on the Pacific coast. The next day we were chauffeured over the mountain range, through the rain forests, and right across to the Caribbean side of Costa Rica to join the BOUDICCA.

The wonderful 25 days passed with no problems and an opportunity to see islands and places we had missed during our own voyage – the contrasts in cruising styles was amazing. The luxury was very acceptable, the only thing we missed was being able to stay long enough to get to know local people and be invited to their homes. That and the necessarily regimented deadline to be back on board seemed very restricting.

CHAPTER FIFTEEN | TOWARDS THE TIDES

2007 Limay – Vernon – Givernay - Rouen

ON MARCH 17TH 2007 we drove back to Limay via Rouen so that we could take advice from the Harbour Master at the Port de Plaisance about the worrying 83 kilometre long stretch from Rouen to Honfleur. In this tidal stretch of the Seine there are no safe places to moor and few emergency stops. He was very helpful (01 35 083 394) and gave us tide tables and tips. At Limay we spent a week on CLYPEUS making sure all was well and paid our dues.

We returned for another week on April 16th.

I wrote in my journal:

The silent Seine slides by our hull. Not a sound except the 'curreek' of ropes as they hold CLYPEUS to the pontoon while the River pulls her towards the sea. It's only the second week in April. The willow is bursting pale green fronds which drag on the river surface. The chestnuts are spreading and bronze-tipped leaves emerge from the brown sticky buds. Dandelion fluff floats across the river catching in the cobweb traces hanging around the boat rigging.

A brown, bright-eyed duck sits on her eggs on a feather nest in a flower pot on the adjoining boat.

The dawn chorus twitters first, then is joined by a mixture of quacks, squawks, splashes and more melodious songs from branches above the river.

Hot sun by day, cool nights. Our kind neighbour Anne invites us to another BBQ on the pontoon between us and introduces us to her friends. M. Ardoin (Jean Pierre) joins us with a bottle of Cabernet Savignon and enjoys the BBQ with us.

Back home for a month then on 23d May 2007 we took the Portsmouth-Le-Havre Ferry for, hopefully, the very last lap of our voyage. The French trains to Rouen were efficient, clean and on time.

We were becoming more apprehensive by the day – so were our family. After last year's health

A brown, bright-eyed duck sits on her eggs on a feather nest in a flower pot on the adjoining boat.

scare they obviously thought we were too old to be safe. Andrea and Lawrence kindly decided to spend a week of their holiday to come and assist us on the long down-river leg. In Rouen Peter bought our River Licence and I booked a hotel where our crew could stay for a couple of days before rushing them into on-board living.

In Limay our French friends welcomed us back and invited us to join in a party in the boat shed around the keel of Sebastian's boat. M. Ardoin welcomed me in true Gallic manner. It made me laugh that none of the ladies took the slightest

M. Ardoin, the proprietor, welcomed me back in true Gallic manner.

notice of his gallantry – on looking at the photo, neither did I! We enjoyed meals on other boats and they came on CLYPEUS for dinner. The weather was still cold. Each morning Peter cycled off for our croissants and I walked with Anne and her three vigorous Boxer dogs along the river bank. Therese drove us to Carrefour and Auchan supermarkets and thirteen year old Alizee made us a delicious tarte au peche. Producing fresh and tasty dinners for them all on board was quite a challenge.

Peter and I busied ourselves with maintenance, reading and walking. The municipal trees lining the streets were mainly walnuts and festooned in fresh green nuts. Peter has a passion for pickled walnuts. As nobody seemed interested and many were dropping to the ground we picked a few kilos and he pickled them – very successfully. Walnuts remind him of his boyhood in Surrey where a big walnut tree grew in the garden. During WW2 squirrels filled up his father's Riley 9 (which was up on blocks for the duration of the War) with walnuts. His mother pickled walnuts very successfully and Peter has enjoyed them as a rare treat since.

While oiling and preparing the shrouds and masts for re-rigging he replaced the missing radar reflector which had fallen off somewhere along the way, and the VHF antenna which had been flattened in the Paris lock gates.

Therese and Dennis invited us on their catamaran for a BBQ with their three charming daughters: the oldest was a commercial airline pilot, the second a lift service engineer with her own red Ducati motor bike and Alyzee was still at school but thought she would have a flower shop – a fascinating, confident, trio.

On our last day we gave a BBQ party for all the Limay Mariners – which went well. They seemed to enjoy it. I know I did. I wanted to make sure we had

property – a small pillared house on Villeneuve, an island near Paris. His father, a retired doctor, wearing a battered panama hat, was kneeling trying to dig out old bamboo roots. Sebastian's charming mother made a large potato omelette and then we tucked into the whole round of brie which we had brought, a left-over from our party. How I wish my French was better and I could have had a real friendship with this lovely contemporary – it would have been great to share life-time experiences and draw some conclusions together.

Next day, the 11th June, we left Limay with a crowd of friends on the pontoon to wave us goodbye – au revoir, I hope.

I sat on deck and wrote:

The silent Seine slips by.
No mighty warrior but
A gentle lady steeped in silk.
A tapestry of trees surround her.
Pristine lawns and weeping willows
Trail their pale leaves across the surface
Waiting for the breeze

Impressionist France
Translucent light sparkles and glistens
on the water
Ducks make their unromantic harsh quack
Swans, their giant wings thrash the air as
Webbed feet brake in a splash
To fight off encroaching geese.

What will winter bring when the Seine's
Flowing clothes have left her bare?

Down river, past the elegant Rosny-sur-Seine Chateau, and a right turn, through the leaf arches

a party sometime, just in case we sank somewhere between here and home or Peter wasn't well enough to cross the Channel. It did however highlight that not all sailors are instant friends – they were to us, but not to each other. Some sat in a group excluding others. Only Jean Pierre Ardoin, the proprietor, seemed able to mix freely. Therese said none of the other Marina ladies say 'Bonjour' or talk to her. Anita said "it is the French way", but it seems odd to me that three ladies, all at home all day, don't share their joys, problems, or cars.

Sebastian, took us to meet his parents at his

157

**Top left:
Peter sat beside
the Seine and
contemplated
our last lap.**

**Bottom left:
Barges can just
squeeze into the
Locks side by
side.**

**Top right:
Moored in
Vernon I visited
Monet's house
at Giverney.**

**Bottom right:
The famous Lily
Ponds.**

We arrived at the lock at 10 a.m. but it was mid-day before we were through as we had to wait for three peniches to lock downstream: commercial vessels have right of way, leisure vessels must wait.

Mid-afternoon we tied up at Vernon. Water skiers were churning up the water and making the boat roll, but they all went home at 6 p.m. when it started raining.

into Port L'Ilon to take on 70 litres diesel and spend a tranquil night and a rest day to try and be sensible and gain some confidence. Peter sat beside the Seine and contemplated our last lap. We walked through ripening cornfields, and were invited to drinks on CAPELLA (an adapted Fisher in beautiful condition) Liz and Douglas from Cheltenham, welcomed us on board. We found we had a mutual friend in the talented marine artist and author Claudia Myatt.

Fog covered the lake in the early morning but lifted by 9 a.m. and cautiously we left safe, calm L'Illon and headed towards Ecleuse de Mericourt.

Monet's house and the lily ponds he so famously painted in his lifetime from 1833 to 1926, are at Giverney which is not exactly on the Seine. You stop at Vernon, once a Norman village where

pretty houses line cobbled streets, but now a large town. Just look away from the purification plant and power lines across the river and all is honeysuckle, clover and conifers. At Le Frete Restaurant you can lunch beside the river and watch slow traffic idle its way to the sea. I took the local bus to Monet's house and garden which was crowded with hundreds of tourists, particularly Japanese, many of whom were sitting painting the famous lily pond and bridge. The house was furnished as it had been in Monet's day, including the yellow and blue painted kitchen, set out ready for a meal.

Peter spent the day around town and checking the boat. He found two of the four propellor shaft coupling bolts were loose, so tightened them - another potential crisis averted.

Another lazy day when we just walked over the bridge to the quaint Mill and Castle. On the way back we noticed tiny CLYPEUS in front of the huge hotel boat, 'the CEZANNE'. It shocked us and we both said at once 'Did we really sail around the world, on our own, in that small boat?' We promised each other to try and not make any more mistakes, but go slowly and carefully everywhere,

Left:
The quaint Mill over the river.

Top right:
The Castle which had no signs or identification.

Bottom right:
Vernon Market was great and fish stalls excellent.

159

cruising, or crossing the road.

On Saturday there was an excellent market. In the rain we bought oysters, and asparagus, walnuts, and a lush pizza.

At 11 a.m. still in the rain, we pulled away from Vernon jetty. Nimbus clouds were rushing east overhead. At Ecluse de Notre Dame de La Garenne we locked in after a sand barge whose bow was being taken by the wind right across the lock. We kept well behind him – there was plenty of room, then waited until it was clear. Under showers and sunshine we continued to Les Andeley's and tied up under the ruins of Chateau Gaillard.

In a break in the clouds I explored the village and watched guests, and the bride, arrive for a wedding. After our meal of oysters and fresh market food, washed down with a cool bottle of Rose, we sat on deck with the last of our wine watching swallows, herons, cormorants and ducks settling down for the night. After a game of Trivial Pursuits we happily retired, admitting to ourselves that "life doesn't get much better than today".

Sunday dawned a lovely summer morning. I strolled up to Chateau Gaillard, sniffing the glorious smell of the patisserie's hot bread, before

toiling up the tree-arched lane towards the Castle. A magnificent panorama stretched out across the Seine valley with tiny CLYPEUS moored alongside a pontoon. There were illustrated panels in French and English to give the history of the valley below and the castle.

"When this valley was formed La Manche (The English Channel) was dry and the river that eventually became the Seine, then followed the course of the Loire to the sea.

In 1190 Richard the Lionheart, King of England, Duke of Normandy and King of France, and Phillippe Augustus, went together on 3rd Crusade. Richard was taken prisoner in Austria and Phillippe Augustus took the opportunity to seize part of Normandy. On release Richard decided to build this fortress to protect Rouen. Stakes were embedded across the River to stop unwanted boats coming down from Paris. A castle was also built on the island but this was destroyed by fire. After Richard's death his brother Jean Sans Terre – bad Prince John, of Robin Hood fame, held the castle and then in 1203 the wicked Earl of Chester who, when under siege, expelled 1200 unnecessary occupants (the locals) who were seeking refuge, out into the cold, cold, snow where most of them starved to death because the French didn't want to feed them either but wouldn't let themcross their lines. In 1204 the Castle was re-captured by Philippe Auguste's soldiers and miners who undermined a strategic wall. In June 1204. Rouen was thus recaptured by the King of France and ceased to be needed as a fortress and the whole of Normandy, except for the Channel Islands, returned to being French.

The castle was used as a Royal residence and then a prison for famous people e.g. Marguerite de Bourgogne who was held for being unfaithful to her husband Louis X (she was later strangled in 13l6

CLYPEUS looked so tiny moored alongside the pontoon.

because he wanted to marry Clemence of Hungary.

During the 100 Years War the castle changed hands again between England and France. Later robbers, murderers and counterfeiters found refuge in the castle. Henri IV was requested to demolish the fortress in 1598. Stones are taken for local abbeys and castles until 1611 when it was declared a National Historic Ruin.'

Just as we were preparing a martini before going out to a much anticipated dinner in the Three Michelin Star restaurant in the village, we heard a shout. A crewman was standing on the foredeck of a big sand-barge pusher tug pointing to the pontoon where we were tied up.

"Messeiur, Messieur" Nous voulons aller la. C'est chez nous." - We wish to go there. It is our home. You must leave. NOW." The French crew shrugged, raised their palms to heaven. "Pardon, Pardon," they said.

"Oh dear! There goes our dinner."

"We'll have to move. Now." Peter said as he turned the ignition on and I untied the ropes. Off we go again in the rain.

"Can we tie up outside you?" Peter asked.

"Mais non. There is another tug coming now."

"OK, we go" – and go we did, in the rain and rising wind. Friends had told us of a safe anchorage, with enough depth for our keel, behind Ile Morelle further downstream. We found it, went around the far end of the island then sneaked up behind it.

"Thirteen feet. OK?" I shouted from the cockpit as I carefully watched the depth sounder.

Peter lowered the anchor and I put the engine into reverse to tug it safe. "All OK,"

Lightning flashed and thunder roared so loudly it sounded like grand pianos falling downstairs, then settled to a softer continuous rumble which was almost drowned by the sound of the gusting rain sweeping up the river. CLYPEUS danced from side to side while the anchor and chain groaned and grumbled all night in the storm.

Monday looked a poor day – a hundred per cent cloud with wind and rain. White horses raced up river as the wind beat against the current. We watched peniches chugging downstream with waves breaking over their bows in a smash of white foam and decided to stay were we were, although CLYPEUS was still dancing from side to side of the narrow Channel as the wind tried to push her upstream.

At 14.00. the wind died and the sun almost shone.

"Shall we go?" Peter asked. However the engine starter failed to get the engine going. Peter took it off and rotated the contact engagement adjustment and solenoid slightly. Then cleaned all terminals and the solenoid and made sure everything was tight. It started first time, but we decided tomorrow would be a good day to leave.

It was a pleasant restful evening until we tried to move the anchor ready for tomorrow's departure. It was stuck firmly. The chain had

Les Andeley village lies beneath Chateau Gaillard.

Top:
Peter rowed ashore to see if he could get help.

obviously wrapped itself around something BIG. Peter pulled, then cranked, hauled in the trip rope.

"Absolutely solid! – we're not going anywhere. Let's try motoring."

With the engine slow ahead we moved a few feet, but the drag was tremendous.

"OK. We're staying the night to think."

We thought and planned. "Easiest way, is to cut the chain and lose the lot – about five hundred quid's worth. We'll try and find a famer with a tractor."

"There's cows in the field alongside, perhaps there's a farmhouse nearby."

We slept little, worrying all night. Peter woke me at 8 a.m. with our usual morning drink of a mug of hot water with honey and vinegar.

"Let's see how close we can get to the shore, launch the dinghy and I'll go and look for a tractor."

Bottom:
We dragged our problem to the bottom of the garden where, Christian with his low loader-lifted the anchor above the water while Peter pulled the chain.

We waited until the rain eased a little, then slowly, slowly we towed whatever it was towards shore and tied up to an overhanging willow tree branch. In the inflated dinghy we prodded the underwater load with the boat hook, peering down into the murky water. It was impossible to see the problem. The water was too muddy from last night's heavy rain for me to see anything even if I did dive down.

Peter rowed ashore to see if he could get help. He walked to a farm but they couldn't assist so he tried to find the owners of a tractor we had seen in a garden up river. He found the tractor garden and knocked on the front door and managed to explain our problem. A retired couple, Christian and Francoise Geugat, were welcoming and couldn't have been more helpful.

They said "Come".

Christian was a retired master tractor driver

and had been foreman of the maintenance department at the local ALCAN factory. We dragged our problem to the bottom of his garden where, with his low loader he lifted the anchor above the water while Peter pulled the chain, detached the anchor, and re-attached the chain to the back of the tractor. The tractor slowly rumbled forward dragging the taut chain across the grass. A huge tree root gradually emerged. M. Geugat steadily held the chain taut with the tractor, while in the dinghy, Peter managed to untangle the chain which was wrapped round and round the root.

"We've got some champagne," I whispered.

As soon as it was free, Peter called out, "We will bring the champagne if you bring the glasses." Five minutes later we were sitting on M. and Madame's patio sipping champagne and chatting in fractured French. Oh! So relieved! We must be the luckiest couple on earth. Imagine finding someone competent, who had been foreman of a local aluminium works, now with his own tractor with a hydraulic lift, within a hundred yards of our problem. It took another couple of hours to replace ropes, anchor and chain to CLYPEUS, then we were on our way again.

As we tied up at the Posse Water Ski Club, Peter said "Today has been a busy week."

Unfortunately 'today' wasn't over yet. The Ski Club was in a lagoon off the river just above the last lock on the Seine. It was very shallow, just enough depth to accommodate our keel. However the water level kept changing as the nearby lock filled and emptied and the keel bounced on the bottom. The last thing we wanted was to go aground, so moved off and anchored in the middle of the lake to study the tide table and decide the best time to enter the tidal Seine to catch the last of the flood, then ride it downstream. It was a calm night water-wise, but frogs started croaking as the sun went down and then… It must have been a frog orgy. The crescendo of croaking was deafening in the warm night before heavy rain and lightning.

On a beautiful sunny morning we passed through the last lock: Amfreville Ecluse, and re- entered tidal waters. I couldn't help calling out

"Au revoir la belle Seine."

The lock keeper wished us "Bon Voyage."

CLYPEUS picked up speed with the tide and whizzed past Elbeuf Quay at 11.8 knots and arrived in a wet and windy Rouen by 12.30. It was Midsummer's Day and a Festival of Music was being held over midnight. A musical group of some sort played in every square and many street corners: jazz, a madrigal group, a classical quintet, Pop, Rock & Roll, Reggae, Trad Jazz and a group playing an instrument we had never seen before – they looked like hand-cranked violins. We were told they were the original hurdy-gurdys.

On June the 24th Andrea and Lawrence arrived and after a couple of nights in a hotel and sightseeing together, they joined us on CLYPEUS.

A huge tree root gradually emerged.

163

CHAPTER SIXTEEN | THE SEINE ESTUARY and ENGLISH CHANNEL

2007 FRANCE Rouen to Honfleur via Tancarville – Honfleur – Trouville – Ouistreham – Channel Crossing – E. Cowes – CLYPEUS for sale.

Left:
In Rouen a mummified cat was displayed in the wall of the Arts Centre which had previously been a Charnel House during the Plague.

Right:
Our crew took turns steering and both handled the boat well.

ON JUNE THE 24TH Andrea and Lawrence arrived in Rouen and stayed in a hotel for a couple of nights. Together we explored the ancient town with its cathedrals and markets. In a charnel house where the bodies were buried during the plague, and which is now an Arts Centre, there was a mummified cat displayed in the wall – ghoulish, but interesting! Peter found a fascinating, for him, Key and Lock Museum.

Andrea and Lawrence moved on board and apprehensively, with all the up-to-date tidal information we could muster, we prepared for the long 83 miles journey down river to be completed all in one day. At dawn, next morning, in the rain, CLYPEUS cleared Rouen and the unusual lifting bridge. The river was busy with many large cargo vessels laden with cars, or oil, or stacked high with containers.

Our crew took turns steering and both handled the boat well, keeping a good look out and a straight course. We anticipated taking about eight hours with the outgoing tide to reach Honfleur. A beam of sunlight leaked through a hole in the clouds and was quickly hauled back again.

At ten, in the rain, clutching hot toddies, we celebrated being on the same longtitude as Chichester Harbour and reminisced about various adventures in our Folkboat and the children's Emsworth Slipper dinghy. We passed pretty riverside towns and villages until as we came closer to the sea the horizon widened and the flat country began to look bleak. The tide was rushing out with the river and we were being swept along faster and faster, ten knots, twelve knots

The weather deteriorated with cold rain and wind and the tide had turned. As we neared the open estuary the sky looked like a Constable painting with many cumulus clouds. A north wind began to blow against the tide and the brown swirling river became rough. We were apprehensively beginning to have doubts about getting to Honfleur.

By 15.15 we passed under Tanquerville Bridge and the entrance to the Tanquerville Canal but it was dead low water. The lock was closed and mud-bound. With the rising wind biting our faces we splashed on. Then the boat began to dip and roll so the masts started shifting in the trestles as CLYPEUS plunged through the oncoming waves.

The strong incoming tide was now fighting against the outgoing Seine. The wind and up-going current were becoming dominant. Hills of brown water with vindictive white lips began to rear up against us. CLYPEUS dipped and lifted, the masts moved restlessly against the ropes which tied them to the bow rail and stern cross-supports. Wind against tide we could deal with, and had done so many times before, but never with a creaking, straining and wobbling deck cargo. The supports Peter had made in the sun at Port St. Louis had never been designed for this duty.

Andrea and Lawrence were looking rather green and worried. CLYPEUS was rolling from side to side as well as pitching.

"We're going to lose the masts if we carry on." Peter shouted above the wind. "We can't get to Honfleur, we must turn round and go back."

I could see that turning broadside on to the wind was going to be a problem.

"OK folks," he called out "We're going back."

"Good," said Andrea and Lawrence in unison.

"But where to? I asked. "There's nowhere to go until the tide comes in and Tanquerville Lock opens."

"We'll find somewhere. We certainly can't go on into the estuary. We'll lose the masts and that would be a tragedy, and an expensive one, and possibly extremely dangerous. OK everyone. Ready about."

As CLYPEUS turned so the wind and waves caught her broadside and she rolled dramatically to starboard and took some time to right herself. I heard Andrea and Lawrence gasp and looked at their terrified faces. They didn't have the complete faith in CLYPEUS and Peter's skills that I did. The boat did roll so far that the lee combing was swishing through the foaming water and then, as she came round, she gradually righted herself and with the wind and new tide behind us, we returned up river.

But, where to go? It was another three hours before the lock opened. We motored close in to the brown creeping tide line, looking for somewhere sheltered to anchor. Past the mud banks of the new lock entrance and there, at last, was the entrance channel to the old lock where the tide was already filling the muddy puddle and reaching the old timber gates. It offered a space just large enough for us to get in and the small pond was calm and smooth.

Peter went forward to prepare the anchor. At the wheel I cautiously edged us forward until CLYPEUS slid into the mud.

Peter called "OK", and let the anchor rattle out for just a few seconds.

"Reverse," he called.

I reversed a little way, not wanting to get out of the shelter of those lovely stone walls.

"OK. Let's wait and see what happens. Keep the engine running Shirley."

We sat on the cabin top ready to fend off with our feet, and breathed again in this small calm oasis. Wind buffeted down the sides but the water was flat and gently lapping its way up the grey seaweed covered walls.

Spasmodically the sun peeped out and with a cup of tea and fruit cake life picked up.

A scared, white-faced and tearful daughter looked at Peter and I, appalled.

"Why do you do it? she demanded, beginning to sob. "Why do you it?"

"Do what?" we asked.

The main mast was lowered carefully into its tabernacle.

"Put yourselves in such danger."

I felt like saying "Poof, that was nothing. We've been in far worse conditions than that for much longer, eight or nine hours, or even days, of crisis," but decided I had better keep quiet.

Sheepishly we tried to tell her, it wasn't that dangerous – worrying, yes, but in the general scheme of our voyage – not that bad. We didn't know what to say. We hadn't considered NOT doing it. We were nearly home.

"Well, I think you are mad and so does Lawrence."

"Mmm," he agreed, "if that's sailing fun, then it is probably the first and last time I'll try it." He looked at Andrea. "Let's buy a camper van." They grinned at each other in agreement, gradually calming down.

"Will you please sit on the side decks and push off if we get near the walls," Peter asked.

"And I'll go and make us a hot toddy."

CLYPEUS gradually rose calmly with the tide. We fended off with our feet as she swung from side to side in the down draughts.

At last, at 6 p.m. two barges passed, obviously going into the new Lock.

"The lock must be open. Start the engine Shirley."

Peter pulled up the anchor and came aft and took the wheel – he steers CLYPEUS backwards better than me. I used my nautical French on the VHF, I thought for the last time "Nous voulons entrer le Canal du Tanquerville s'il vous plait. Nous sommes un bateau de voile qui a onze metres." (We wish to enter the Tanquerville Canal please. We are a sailing boat measuring 11 metres.)

As the lock filled, an official came with forms to fill in. We couldn't understand why officialdom had suddenly taken over, until we realised we could have come in from over the Channel and Customs and Excise needed to be satisfied.

Eventually at 18.45 we were safely tied up alongside a white steel yacht in Les Tourpelliers de Tanquerville. There was nobody around to ask if it was OK, so we all sat in the cabin and relaxed and listened to the weathers forecast which was "gales up to Force 10."

"We're safe and we're not going anywhere for a couple of days, so let's open a bottle of wine while I get dinner," I suggested.

Two days later, when the wind died down sufficiently, we entered the dock for the masts to be lifted. It was still blowing a gale and all that Daniel, the master rigger, could do was use his crane to lift the masts on to prepared trestles on the dockside and with Peter's help, sort out the rigging ready for when it was calmer.

On the 28th at 9.15 Daniel returned. He hoisted the masts very professionally, prodding the buttons on a yellow plastic box belted around his ample waist. The main mast was lowered carefully into its tabernacle. Andrea and Lawrence were stars, not letting Peter lift or stress himself and being in

thank him for his expertise and help we gave him a rose and bottle of wine as well as his fee.

It is difficult to tell all of the traumas we went through on that day from Rouen to Honfleur. If the masts had fallen into the sea and dragged all the ropes with them we would probably have sunk, or at least lost the masts and the ability to get home and possibly all drowned in the brown swirling, cold, water.

Two days later the weather calmed and we locked back out into the Seine. I noticed the first seaweed floating past for many years (there isn't much seaweed in the Med.) As we approached Honfleur, the Channel Ferry left for England with

We gave Daniel a rose and bottle of wine as well as his fee.

Honfleur Harbour.

the right place at the right time. The mizzen caused no hoisting problems.

However their time with us was over. They had allowed themselves two days proper holiday for their First Wedding Anniversary, and had sensibly booked a Hotel in Honfleur before they had to catch the ferry back to Dover. So after lunch they caught the local bus to Le Havre and then a taxi to Honfleur.

We stayed on board and watched Daniel lift himself in his cage to retrieve a line which was misplaced. (It cost 130 euros for both masts to be replaced and to stay for four nights – a bargain!) To

**Left:
Grandson Freddie
climbed the mast
to re-reeve the
staysail.**

**Top right:
Grandpa
demonstrates a
bowline.**

**Bottom right:
To leave or
not to leave safe
Ouistreham
Marina on
the Eve of
Bastille Day?**

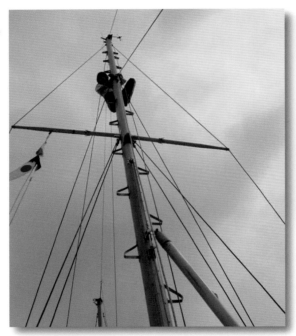

Andrea and Lawrence on board.

The weather was terrible but there are worse places to shelter from gales than Honfleur. For ten days we enjoyed ourselves in the shops, museums and library. The Municipal indoor swimming pool was particularly inviting: when it was windy but not actually raining the roof slid back; as soon as the sun shone and the wind died the south facing glass walls also slid back - an excellent compromise for Northern Europe!

At one stage we were the only yacht left with anybody on it – all the other owners had left their boats and returned to their European homes. Grandson Freddie arrived for a week to add some muscle across the Channel. He also climbed the mast to re-reeve the staysail halyard through its block, a job which Peter had been thinking about for some time.

It was great to spend time with Freddie and he took me to Jazz Bars and places that Peter doesn't enjoy. One evening, in front of the Town Hall on the harbour side, a group of student dancers from a gymnasium in Bruges gave a brilliant dancing display, mostly twirling and swirling colourful flags to match their medieval costumes and then an exuberant Tarantella.

Unfortunately the weather didn't improve and

after more wet and windy days in a grey dawn we set sail for Ouistreham. There was a grim simplicity about the grey scene, apart from an iron-dark line at the horizon, the sea and the sky were much the same porridge colour, a muted faintly radiant grey, expectant, as if waiting for something to happen.

On this short voyage we crossed the Greenwich Meridian so had OFFICIALLY CROSSED OUR OUTWARD TRACK. The lock eventually opened into Ouistreham and we tied up thankfully in the pleasant rural marina.

However the storms started again. A rainy day trip to Caen to explore William the Conqueror's Castle wasn't a brilliant way for a sixteen year old to spend his time. The WW2 Museum reminded us that 28,375 men are buried along this Normandy coast where the Mulberry Harbours supported the invasion from the South Coast of England in June 1944. (When I was ten and living in Milford Haven I remember the convoys assembling in the wide deep estuary). Another blowy day in Trouville where Freddie enjoyed his first gaufre (with Chantilly Cream) We did try to leave on 9th July but talking to the fishermen when we were already descending in the lock they said it was going to be

Force 4-5 from the North. We headed out into a squally and lumpy sea with the wind dead ahead. Peter on the foredeck tried to raise the staysail in the rising wind, not a job for a man who has had a heart attack, so we turned back and Freddie returned on the ferry to Southampton, then Hereford for his school 'end of GCE year' parties.

Ouistreham Marina was pleasant and clean and the excellent fish market beside the harbour was almost deserted – which meant good fish and shell fish at reasonable prices for us if not for the fishermen. One trawler came in with an abysmal catch.

One trawler came in with an abysmal catch

We set course of Poole in a calm sea. Wind SW2-3.

After a good sleep on the 13th of July we awoke to sunshine and a slight wind from the south so we started preparing CLYPEUS for sea, and checking tide times and heights. Being the eve of Bastille Day the Marina Staff were preparing a barbecue party. To leave or not to leave?

I did last minute shopping of more wine, oysters and clams just in case we did go. We couldn't help worrying about where we would land when we arrived in England as we had told Salterns Marina in Poole, that our estimated arrival date was the first week in July. We were fretting that they may not have room for us if we delayed our arrival into

Top left:
By 0200 the engine was off and we were making five, six then seven knots with the main, staysail and yankee up.

Bottom left:
Freddie looking west for Ouistreham.

Right:
By 4a.m. we were scooting along at 7.2 knots on rough seas.

school holiday time. At the London Boat Show they had been kind enough to offer us free mooring for the attendant publicity.

Crossing the Channel is not a matter of departing on the crest of a wave. Peter planned to cross the major shipping lanes in daylight, which entailed started at night, so at 20.00 we locked out of Ouistreham and set our course for Poole Harbour in a calm sea with the wind from SW 2-3. With all sail up and keeping the engine on, we were making 4.4 knots

By 10 p.m. France was ablaze with lights, and at midnight, an explosion of bursting fireworks

heralded in a new Bastille Day for them and a cold night with a rising wind and sea for us. By 0200 the engine was off and we were making five, six then seven knots with the main, staysail and yankee up.

By 4 a.m. we were scooting along at 7.2 knots and the sea was ROUGH. Peter decided we were going too fast and downed the staysail in a squall. Standing at the wheel while he struggled on the foredeck I couldn't help thinking how foolish we were. He shouldn't be doing this at 76 with a bad heart. Both of us were on tenterhooks, not with our boat or our seamanship, just could we cope physically? It was time to stop this game. Then he decided to put a second reef in the main, hanging on tightly as waves hit the starboard bow and foamed back down the cabin top where he was holding the sail to the boom with his elbows while trying to tie reef knots. My knuckles were white as I clutched the wheel ensuring we didn't jibe on the surfing crests and praying. CLYPEUS settled down to plugging along at over five knots. When we were younger this would have been a great crossing – speed, excitement, no problems with the boat, but age changes everything – like love!

As daylight dawned we were in the shipping

lane at three knots and rolling on the big grey seas blown in from the west. We restarted the motor and changed course to ride with them. Back to 6.9 knots in the squalls but, ever the optimist I noted that it wasn't raining! As the day progressed high mares' tails and cirrus clouds in the sky forewarned of more rising winds. Oh dear! We endured a morning of rough seas and kept careful watch to look out for shipping. Neither of us felt like breakfast or lunch but we nibbled cream crackers and a bit of cheese, then hot chocolate with ginger snaps. It seemed a long, long day and we took turns to sleep. Nothing must go wrong now. Did we really used to do this for fun? How fortunate we have been to experience the balmy Pacific and warm seas and winds.

At 1400 I woke Peter so that he could steer us into the lee of the Isle of Wight – we were nearly home and should both be on deck for these momentous minutes of our lives. Forty-five minutes later we were in relative calm at last and motoring towards Cowes in the familiar Solent chop.

Peter took the sails down as a cold sun shimmered through high cloud. The sky looked cold, even the sun looked cold. Although we had started out on a compass course for Poole, we had been driven east and finished up rounding the eastern end of the Isle of Wight. This was no time to try and be strong, this was a time to go with the flow.

The Solent was full of boats racing in a major event. We hadn't seen so many yachts and motor cruisers all slicing through the water together since Australia.

At 15.30 I radioed East Cowes Marina who told us to come in and report when closer. As we listened to the VHF we heard them turning other yachts away. I'm afraid I was pathetic and pleaded,

"We really do want to come in now. We have had a rotten Channel crossing and are very tired."

The pleasant staff offered a pen on the starboard side of a pontoon. What a relief! However it was immediately obvious why they were turning boats away as the last of the ebb was swirling out and it was very difficult to steer slowly between the pontoons without being pushed down by the tide. We managed it and eventually tied up our dear boat CLYPEUS up in England again after her 24 year, 65,000 mile voyage.

East Cowes Marina was excellent with free email facilities so that we could let our children know that:

"At last. We've done it. We are back in the UK safe and well." (we didn't add 'just'). Good hot

Eventually we tied up our dear boat in England after her 24 year 65,000 miles voyage.

Top:
Now that's what we call a proper Sunday Roast Beef lunch.

Bottom:
Sunday papers and lunch in a Cowes Waterside Pub

waterside pub for a delicious British roast beef lunch with all the trimmings.

On Monday Peter walked into AAA Yacht Brokers and put CLYPEUS up for sale. We both agreed we had had enough, we would just hang on for our official reception in Poole then return to Cowes and sell our beloved and trusty boat. It was hard and I cried when the salesmen left after taking details and photographs. I gave the Broker a copy of both my books '*Seize The Day*' and '*Red Sea Peril*' and he said that having such good provenance would help sell her. We agreed that for a quick sale £22,000 was a reasonable price, and they would moor CLYPEUS for free until it sold. If we managed to sell it ourselves then they would reduce their commission. It was a great bonus to know she wouldn't cost us an arm and a leg while waiting to be sold on England's ridiculously expensive South Coast.

showers restored us for dinner in the Marina Restaurant and a blissful night's sleep. We had covered 514.6 miles since Limay.

Next day was Sunday. We relished walking into Cowes, crossing the Medina on the chain ferry, buying the Sunday papers and relaxing in a

Our five nights in the Marina had cost £122, but again, worth every penny for all we had achieved whilst there, which included restoring our bodies and our egos.

CHAPTER SEVENTEEN | HOME IS THE SAILOR, HOME FROM THE SEA.

JULY and AUGUST 2007. Cowes – Poole – Newtown Creek – Cowes - Pembrokeshire

O N THURSDAY THE 5TH JULY, twenty-five years to the day that we bought CLYPEUS, we apprehensively set sail for Poole in bright sunshine and little wind. Nervous that something stupid might happen in these last few miles? As we sailed past Newtown Creek, Yarmouth and Hurst Castle we recalled our happy family sailing days in SARKA. We then belonged to Chichester Cruiser Racing Club and had spent many weekends under their auspices racing from port to port around the Solent. How useful the chart on our laptop would have been then!

Beneath the Cruising Association burgee I proudly raised my fathers' Yacht Holidays Company House Flag from the crosstrees above the Darwin to Ambon Race flag. How pleased he would have beenwith our achievment. He had been intensely interested in our voyage and had posted off copies of my letters to many friends.

Left:
Our lap top showing the Solent – What a difference in technology since we left – before computers and mobile phones!

Right:
I flew Henry Offord's (my Father's) Company - Yacht Holidays House Flag from the cross trees under the Cruising Association Burgee.

The Log reads.

1200	*Motored out of Cowes into Solent. No wind*
13.30	*Newtown Creek abreast,*
1400	*Yarmouth on port bow. Cold, cloudy. Strong tide with us.*
1500	*Passed through North Channel (Hurst Castle) 6.3 Knots at 1500 rpm.*
17.15	*Entered Swash Channel behind Brittany Ferry. Called Salterns Ch 80. The SUN is coming out. Phoned Mary and Derek (friends who lived in Sandbanks and had seen us off in 1983)*

Left:
Our last sail
back to Cowes –
Peter Relieved.

Top right:
Shirley – Happy!

*18.15   Arrived Salterns Marina. Mary and Derek
here to meet us Yippee! Boatmen and
Simon Chalk welcomed us in.
Shared a bottle of champagne on board
with Mary and Derek*

In Poole Harbour as we cautiously made our way through the lines of anchored expensive boats, all quietly depreciating; it reminded us of how many people have boating dreams, but find it hard to give up land and familiarity. How lucky we were to make our decision when we did.

Mary and Derek had been our first married friends when we moved to Rugby in 1954. They had seen us off from St Katherine's Dock in 1983 and now, here they were, to see us back in 24 years later. Peter gave a great sigh of relief, as though twelve tons of concrete had been lifted from his shoulders.

over all the years (and for allowing us to mess up their address books). Unfortunately it was the week of dire floods in the Midlands and many roads were closed. Even Andrea couldn't get to our party. So no family were there to welcome us back.

Steve Butcher
greets us with
a bottle of
champagne.

He lightened up and was a happy man at last! The last few years had been a trial for him.

We arranged a private party for friends who had kept in touch with us, with all the different addresses all over the world during the past years. We can never thank them enough for keeping faith

Salterns PR Agency had organised our Home-coming Event. On the 30th July we sailed out of the Marina to pick up a mooring and raise our flags: the traditional dressed-overall flags, plus courtesy ensigns of many of the countries we had visited plus a large Welsh Dragon. We had so wanted to sail

In 1947 the Company restarted and prospered with cruises up the Seine to Paris and the Rhine to Basle.

When Salterns called us on the VHF, we motored back into the Marina for the BBC cameras and a television interview. A host of friends were there to party with us together with the Mayor of Poole. After another day of celebrations we were taken to the ITV studios and to Radio Solent.

Top left:
Friends came for a party.

Bottom left:
Sailors all help us celebrate.

Top right:
The Captain talks on Radio Solent.

Bottom right:
The crew adds her bit!

back to Milford Haven but decided 'discretion was the better part of valour.' Sailing west, into wind, to Lands End was bound to be a problem. The weather was so unpredictable, who knew what traumas we would have to go through. We knew our Welsh friends would understand. I proudly raised my father's Yacht Holiday house flag. I know he would have been pleased. (In 1937 he had started Yacht Holidays, offering luxury cruises through the bulbfields of Holland. During the War the boats had been used as German Officers' clubs.

**Top right:
Now we must
start emptying
our bedroom and
home.**

The celebrations were not quite over. The Mayor of Poole invited us to his Parlour for tea next day. Wearing his chain of Office, Jeff, the Mayor, and the Lady Mayoress informally welcomed us. We sat on comfortable chintz covered armchairs and relaxed as they told us of their day. They had been up at 4.30 a.m. to attend the dawn ceremony on Brownsea Island to celebrate the 100th Anniversary of Scouting. Baden-Powell took twenty boys to Brownsea Island to camp in August 1907. 400 scouts were now on the island celebrating and another larger number were attending a Jamboree in Chelmsford. Jeff said it was inspirational. The scouts on the island were of all nationalities and enjoying being friendly equals

**Left:
25 years of
'stuff' to be
unloaded.**

life, our way, in charge of our own destiny with no interference.

Giving the Seagull outboard motor away was a wrench – we had been using it since 1971. Its story started when impecunious Peter saw the advertisement for Seagull Outboards on sale from a Yacht Chandlers in Marlow, on the Thames. He was working in High Wycombe and at that time Seagull outboards were £39. The special offer was 'no down payment, no interest - just pay instalments of £4.50 for nine months.' We wanted it for that evening as it was spring tides and a long

**Bottom right:
Giving our 36
year old Seagull
outboard motor
away was a
wrench.**

Then came the sad task of emptying our home. Steve Butcher, Salterns' Marina Manager, kindly drove Peter to Pembrokeshire to collect our car and then Peter loaded our estate car and took it home returning next day after a very frustrating slow drive on choked roads. We were back in the real world! In the 90's my Mother had written to say we were losing touch with the reality – she was right. We had had nearly a quarter of a century living our

row with three children and the weekend's stores down Thorney Channel to SARKA. Reluctantly the salesman eventually let him leave with a sales contract signed and the outboard over his shoulder but no actual money changing hands. Those were the days!

Another load filled our car – how had we crammed all this stuff into a 35' boat? We couldn't fit everything in so Trish and Ray, friends in Bishops Waltham, stored a load in their garage until we could pick it up in September. I had met Trish in the Cruising Association Library in St Katherine's Dock when we were both studying charts for an Atlantic crossing. On arrival in Antigua on Boxing Day 1983 she was the first person to greet me as the anchor went down with "Hello Shirley. Do you remember? I met you in the Cruising Association Library. We arrived last week." Twenty four years later here she was kindly giving me a birthday party with cake and candles.

On August 5th the last load was squeezed into the Peugot. We celebrated with a lunch at The Harbourside Hotel with a delicious English summer meal of fresh crab, and summer pudding.

Around 7 a.m. next morning we left the Peugot fully loaded in the Marina car park and untied our mooring ropes and sailed for Cowes.

It was a glorious day for our last sail on our beloved boat. We were almost overwhelmed at the thought of our achievement. I wallowed in emotion in the hope of getting this farewell out of my system, saying to myself 'this is the last lunch I will make on CLYPEUS,' 'this is the last noon position written in the log.' Tears of excitement and sadness flowed. Anchoring in Newtown Creek for lunch we were able to reminisce. We had spent so many weekends here with the children, walking, swimming, rowing; what wonderful memories our

boats have given us. We sat and watched another yacht from our era where the skipper manually winched up his anchor, rocking the handle back and fore to see-saw the chain up, hoisted the jib and mainsail and set off without turning the engine on, gently steering his craft by tiller as his wife cleared the cockpit of their lunchtime picnic.

The Solent was full. It was Cowes week with mega yachts and little dinghies seriously racing. It required diligence and care to keep out of their way and for the first time I didn't want to join them. Peter was right (as always) it was time to look at a new future with different interests.

However we did approach Cowes with the smug feeling of something achieved, another hurdle crossed in the long battle for experience, the long battle to prove whatever it is that each of us has to prove to live life to the full.

It was 4 p.m. by the time we entered Cowes amidst hundreds of other yachts returning from their glorious day of racing. Hooray Henry's shouting to each other and raising glasses; prim classic yacht owners disdainfully quiet; and family boats just trying to get home without hitting anything.

Cowes week. We returned amidst hundreds of other yachts.

177

We called Triple A Marine on the VHF and were led up to their pontoon ready for us to leave her there the following day. Anita of TALISMAN rowed over and introduced herself. She had come to ask us to come for a cup of tea, but by the time we had talked and talked she stayed for tea on CLYPEUS and we were invited to supper on TALISMAN where we met her husband Simon. They were hoping to sail to St Helena and work there. It was a wonderful last 'instant friendship' the memory of which we will treasure. We also chatted to an eel catcher whose patch was from Bembridge to Yarmouth. He had done his apprenticeship on the Norfolk coast and said he now made a reasonable living on the Isle of Wight.

In the peace of early morning I sat and watched

waders, oyster catchers and whimbrels lift their feet high off the mud as they stepped forward looking for breakfast, and was mesmerized by the suck and gloop of the falling tide.

Before we left, Francis Chichester's GYPSY MOTH V came in and moored in front of CLYPEUS. It was good to know we were leaving her amongst such exalted company. We couldn't help feeling a

little superior when the crew told us that GYPSY MOTH'S circumnavigation had had to be abandoned when she was holed on a mid ocean reef – we knew the feeling, but our concrete boat construction had allowed Peter to mend the hole sufficiently for an 800 mile voyage back to Australia, and to continue without outside help.

We were immeasurably sad leaving our beautiful boat, her golden masts sparkled in the sunshine. Wading curlews called and sandpipers twittered on the nearby mud bank. It was like losing a family member. We bought CLYPEUS on the 5th July 1982 and moved on board in September 1982. We completed our quest on the 30th July 2007 and left her on the 8th August 2007. A quarter of a century of adventure and freedom. We do hope the next owner has as good a time in her as we have. I sat in the cockpit and threw flowers from my welcome bouquets into the outgoing tide, one by one, with tears streaming down my cheeks. The red petals slowly floated out to sea. (I saw no reason for a British 'stiff upper lip' on this occasion – nobody could see me.)

The Harbour Master's Launch picked us up and ferried us down into Cowes to give up the keys.

The Speed Ferry zoomed across to Southampton and then a bus and a walk in pouring rain to pick up the car from Saltern's Marina. It was a quiet drive to our now permanent home beside Milford Haven Estuary.

I wrote in my journal:

'Hello house, hello hydrangeas'. A feeling of peace and safety lifted our spirits as we entered and look around our clean, light castle. It's only a modest 1970's bungalow but with big windows in the kitchen, dining room and lounge all facing south across the River Cleddau and west down the sparkling Haven. Dried, pink petals of the bougainvillea are scattered across the conservatory floor, but the plant is still flowering happily, thanks to kind neighbours, who have also put a bowl under a leak in the roof.

It is so good to be home. A walk around the garden shows the lawn was obviously mown yesterday and brown, dried, cut grass rests on top.

Roses, cosmos, hydrangeas and hibiscus are trying to push their way up through the enveloping ferns, nettles and 'sticky-willy'. All is well. The grape vine is bursting out of the greenhouse and the raspberries will be ready for picking next week. Tomorrow I must put a net over them. In my study I notice a quote from Thor Heyerdahl's 'In the Footsteps of Adam' which I had written out: "I have tried to find out the secret of the groups of people who smile most. The smile is a gift of the God that comes from within." I was walking around with a huge smile, pleased that we had survived to be home together and looking forward to the next phase in our lives.

On the 20th September Peter returned to Cowes to hand CLYPEUS over to her new owner and show him how the boat worked. He had also written an instruction book to cover the modifications that had been made.

As sailors 'home from the sea' we had a Party at our local Neyland Yacht Club in November which helped mitigate our disappointment at not sailing all the way home to show to our friends our sturdy boat.

Top left:
We were
immeasurable
sad leaving our
beautiful boat.

Right:
Homcoming party
at Neyland Yacht
Club, table
decorations.

CHAPTER EIGHTEEN |
SOME HIGHS AND LOWS OF OUR VOYAGE WORLD WIDE

THERE IS SO MUCH MORE to sailing around the world than sailing, if you take time. As for the sailing itself, I would rate it as:

20% Glorious
60% A good, satisfying, exhilarating, economic and rewarding way to travel
15% Ho hum! Rough, queasy and sick making
5% Absolutely bloody terrifying!

A few highlight and anecdotes some of which are in *Seize The Day,* or *Red Sea Peril.*

I sat in the cockpit crossing the Atlantic on dawn watch on a calm Christmas morning after 30 days at sea, the sun rose pink, gold and duck egg blue as carols sung by the Choir of Kings College soared up to heaven from the radio thanks to BBC World Service. Tears streamed down my face for joy at the beauty of the morning and home-sickness for my children.

Smelling the sweet scent of earth and vegetations as we approached Antigua after over a month at sea.

In Mexico, catching a ferry and local bus to the ancient Mayan city of Chichin Itza. Touching the stone altar of the Mayan's God Chacmul who demanded a still beating human heart be placed on his flat stone belly in appeasement for a good harvest. Examining the carvings around the Ball Court where the Captain of the winning team in the tournament was beheaded on the spot as an honour at the supreme moment of his life.

When touring around America stopping at Lee's Ferry across the Colorado River and noticing five little children's graves and reading that when a Wagon Train crossed the river, the Ferryman was given a bundle of children's clothes with no warning that their previous owners had died of small pox. Consequently all the children of the Ferryman and his wife died the same way. It was a lesson for me and I made sure all the second hand clothes I passed on to island children were well washed and disinfected.

On Isla Providencia in the Caribbean we made an unscheduled stop and, after being inspected by Customs and Officials, rowed ashore and stood before a baker's window. The delicious smell drew us to a display of fresh iced buns with a cherry on top. A young girl came up and introduced herself as Audrey. We said how good the buns smelled and looked.

Audrey said "Well, why don't you buy some."

We explained we had no local money yet. With that she went into the bakers and bought us a bun each. They probably only cost a few pence, but to be bought buns by a stranger who wore no shoes gave us food for thought.

Through the Panama Canal, we deviated on the way to The Galapagos Islands to uninhabited Cocos Island. Few vessels ever visit, but there were seven other yachts anchored in the bay when we arrived. The American couple on "GUITAR" from Florida invited us all for an Easter Saturday 'bring a dish' party on their spacious foredeck. We sat contented, on a balmy starry evening, sipping iced drinks, listening to our host playing his guitar and softly singing cowboy songs and '40's melodies. The moon came up over the mountain to shimmer across the water to us. Cocos was so perfect we stayed seven days and enjoyed the other happy, satisfied sailors. It seemed a great achievement to be in, and enjoying such a remote place. Everybody was self-sufficient, in their own space-capsule, and while anchored we could allow ourselves to relax and enjoy the moment. We gathered dinner-plate size oysters at low tide. I caught a lobster by hand.

Sudden terror as we noticed hammer-head sharks skulking along the bottom beneath us. I've never managed to get into the rubber dinghy as fast, before or since!

Anchored off Hiva Oa in the Marquesa Islands CLYPEUS dragged her anchor while we were at church enjoying the harmonious Polynesian hymn singing. Rowing back to where we had left our boat, she wasn't there. Then Peter noticed a feint light out at sea. "That must be CLYPEUS. I left the galley light on." With that he rowed furiously towards the light. It was CLYPEUS. We climbed aboard and motored back and re-anchored but had nightmares for weeks, because if it hadn't been our boat we could never have rowed back against wind and tide, just drifted downwind in the rubber dinghy for 3,000 miles towards Australia.

In the Tuamotos, the Dangerous Archipeligo, I was sitting on a log chatting to Honore while she picked tiny seed oysters from a twiggy branch which had been lying in a sheltered corner of the lagoon. She carefully laid the half inch diameter oysters in a plastic bowl of sea water. In halting French, we exchanged names, ages, the weather, the last island we had visited. She told me that a new life is about to start for her island. A black Pearl Farm was being set up. A Japanese expert will come and insert a little plastic ball. It will annoy the oyster so much it will cover ze ball in black pearl. "C'est bon," she said. "Soon we will not need French money or French atomic explosions. Now we will have more than coconuts to sell."

A beautiful, and very pregnant, young women with long black tresses and a flower behind her ear walked by. She waved and shouted "Bonjour Honore," My companion waved back, and proudly said to me, "That's my baby."

"What do you mean, your baby?"

"That girl wishes to go to college in Tahiti. We like our young people to have many lovers before they marry. We like to make sure they are fertile and can have children. So, I will have her baby and bring it up as my own. She will be its first mother and I will be second mother. I'm lucky to have been promised the baby. Zer is great competition for it. We all love children. There is always room in every house for one more child."

"What about the father? Who is he? Doesn't he want the baby?"

"Who knows which of her lovers is the father? Does it matter? We are one big family on this island."

"But what about inheritance? What if he has money or property?"

"No problem. We all own everything and share. He, or she, who needs something uses it, then passes it on. Young people are sometimes accused of stealing when they go to Tahiti. But they aren't stealing, they don't know what stealing is. If they need something they use it, then give it back.

"What a pity the rest of the world doesn't live by your rules. You make us seem so selfish. " We sat companionably in the sunshine. Honore serenely continued her task while I contemplated her people's generous and uncomplicated lifestyle. She confirmed our experiences that the poorer the people, the more eagerly they shared their few belongings.

Snorkelling in the lagoons of various islands, where the water is so clear and the fish and coral so colourful, was delightful, beyond my wildest dreams. However getting rolled on the reef in Tonga was not, and I nearly met my end. Be warned! I sat with my back to the ocean to take my swim fins off when a three foot wall of water, a king wave, swept me over and over on the sharp coral. I was being sucked down beneath the coral shelf by the receding wave when Alofi, who had been teaching me to fish with a spear, managed to run back, put his hands under my armpits and hold me until the next surge lifted me up again. Susan, an American nurse on a nearby yacht answered Peter's radio call for help, and came each day for two weeks to scrub out the cuts with hydrogen peroxide then break open anti-biotic capsules and pour the powder into the cuts. Thanks to her I have few scars.

New Zealand and Australian hospitality is legendary and rightly so. Our first day in Australia in Coffs Harbour after a rotten, rough, fourteen day voyage from New Caledonia we took the wet and salty clothes to a laundrette. Walking back with pillow cases full of lovely fresh linen, we were offered a lift by a stranger, 'CJ', in his brand new four wheel drive Mitzubishi Pajero. He came on board for a cup of coffee and a chat and invited us to supper. At 7 p.m. he came and collected us and drove us about three miles to his home. He happened to be a wine connoisseur and we dined on lobster and prawn salad by candlelight while deciding which wine complemented the seafood best. At 11 p.m. 'CJ' declared he had had too much to drink to drive us home, why didn't we drive ourselves back to the Marina in his new Pajero. Peter protested we couldn't possibly take his new car, with only 70 miles on the clock, but eventually gave in. We drove home, collected blankets and a flask of coffee and drove up into the hills to look down on the black velvet ocean with the silver path of a full moon lighting the bay. In the morning bright sunshine bursting through dappled leaves woke us while Kookaburras and Lyre birds cackled and sang. The wet grass was delicious between my toes – something I hadn't felt for a long time. The

Pajero was returned bright and polished by 10 a.m. and we had a new life long friend.

Sailing around the islands in Vanuatu I noticed 'Waterfall Bay' marked on the British Admiralty Chart. "Can we go?" I asked Peter. "No reason why not," he said. The freedom sailing your own boat where and when you want is wonderful. (However you must be aware of the impending cyclone season and be careful not to eat too much of the food your hosts generously share – they may not have much more.)

Anchored in the bay I took a towel ashore as a gift (I usually go ashore on my own as Peter would rather stay on the boat. I had read that cannibals don't eat women, - we are unclean!) and met a charming couple on the beach, about our age, who were happy to accept the towel as a token of friendship. They let me do our washing downstream of the natural swimming pool. Victor who still hunted with a bow and arrow was the patriarch of this isolated family with whom we stayed for a week. Issor, his son-in-law, appeared on the third day after spending five days walking to the next village for a can of paraffin for their hurricane lamp.

One evening when Peter tested my little tape recorder to record them singing their songs he said "One, two, three, four…"

Victor snatched it from his hands and said "Five, four, three, two, one, testing, testing." He had been an aircraft spotter for the Americans and had kept them informed of any Japanese aircraft movements during WWII. One thing he said surprised me. He asked "and was England in the War?" He had never even heard about the European conflict.

On another Vanuatuan Island, when we arrived I was welcomed, then asked if I wanted to join the other ladies to say goodbye to a young wife who had died. Unfortunately I declined as I didn't wish to intrude, but afterwards wished I had witnessed what happened, the sound of them crying and ululating was heart breaking. The life expectancy of women in Vanuatu is only 48. Having babies in a grass hut with no sterile equipment or medical help or after-care is hard.

The Vanuatans speak Bishlama pigeon English which makes it easy to converse. Guess what a 'bra' is in Bishlama? – A titty basket!

In Papua New Guinea the headmaster of the local school took us into the bush to show us useful plants. He picked up a skull from a tree bole. "My parents would have eaten this chap," he said as he tossed it back into the bush. "Only brave warriors were given a proper burial, as we hoped to ingest their courage as well as their protein, and of course we don't eat women."

At a night club in Pago Pago in American Samoa, a party of ladies were celebrating a 50th birthday. It was a very friendly occasion and slices of birthday cake were passed to us. Some of the celebrating guests performed dances and sang on stage with the band and they did have rather chunky calves and large feet, but Samoans are big people and we though no more about it. However, as we were leaving, after an exceptionally happy evening, an expatriate whispered in our ears, "They're all men you know."

No, we didn't know, but had admiration for the 'ladies' the way they had coped with the gender forced upon them. We would like to know more details of the hows and whys, but have never managed to find out. The 'ladies' are known as 'fatufeenes.'

Sailing friends stayed to work in Pago during the cyclone season. Susan taught at the High School. The staff were asked to choose a Graduation Queen. Their choice was turned down.

"But why?" they asked. "We think she is the most beautiful girl with poise and charm."

"Because you can't vote him as the Beauty Queen," was the reply. The American teachers had no idea that many of the young girls were actually boys, designated from birth to be girls by their families if there were not enough females to do the chores.

In Fiji, Tonga and Samoa, white people are still called 'long pig' while in China we are called 'long noses' and sometimes rebuffed, as to them, we smell of sour milk. In 1989 in Taiwan the Chinese still didn't use milk, cheese of dairy products or wheat flour, just rice. rice and more rice with meat or fish protein and excellent vegetables.

We happened to be in the right place at the right time to work in Asia for Peter's previous American employers. We spent two years in Taiwan where they wished to start a joint venture, and then for three years needed technical help in Singapore. Later we took another two year contract with them in Shanghai. Part of the usual expatriate deal is an annual home-leave flight. At the firm's Travel Agency, standard economy rate tickets could be exchanged for the cheapest Round the World flights, so I've flown around the world more times than I can remember, probably eight or nine, to see family in the USA, UK and Australia on my way round. Something I never dreamed would happen to me. Peter has flown for the Company so far and so often to different continents he has no idea of his flight record.

In Taipei I worked in the American School; an excellent expensive private school, originally started by the Occupying Americans after the war. Now it caters for international students, children of the executives of Japanese, Korean, Italian, German,

French and Belgium companies flourishing there, together with some Taiwanese children who had conveniently been born in Australia, America or Singapore, as local-born children were not allowed. The law concerning multiple wives had just been changed. Now only one wife was allowed but previous polygamous marriages were still acknowledged. Fathers would come to school Parents' Evenings with different wives for different children.

The Middle School Headmaster and his wife organised a school trip to the States. Mrs Jones was explaining to the students that in America a man is only allowed one wife, so please be discreet about your home arrangements. A fourteen year old boy looked her up and down and then said, "Do you mean Mr Jones, only has you!"

While in Singapore we took holidays in Borneo and Sumatra, went elephant trekking in Thailand and sailed up to Tioman Island off the east coast of Malaysia. It is reputed to be the most beautiful island in the world, where Bali Hai was filmed and where the old sailing ships took on their last water before Canton.

In Borneo we travelled up the Strang River to visit Head Hunters in their Long Houses. Nets of skulls still hung above each family's section of the Long House, but now young men can marry without having to produce a severed head as proof of their manhood.

In Sumatra near Lake Toba (which is bigger than the whole of Singapore Island) we visited a Batak village where previously, if a criminal was found guilty by the jury, he was tied to a tree and the family of his victim could, slice by slice, cut and eat him. Evidently the tender thumb and its joint were usually reserved for the Chief and his wife to sprinkle with lemon juice and sambal sauce before eating. The imagination takes off when one thinks of what could happen if a man is guilty or rape of adultery!

The talkative Guide in the last King's Palace, was the son of a junior wife and he had actually lived in the Harem until he was six years old when all children must leave their mothers for the outside world. The list of Kings since the 10th Century was displayed. A long history about which knew nothing.

A news story in Singapore was different, about a 2.5m. (8 foot) python slithering around up into the toilet bowl of an old people's home!

So many natural catastrophes have happened in Asia about which I was ashamed to be totally ignorant. These days, if the television cameras are not there, it hasn't happened. Did you know 1,900 Balinese died when Mount Agung blew in 1963/64. Do you know that 60,000 people died of starvation on Lombok in 1966? The survivors ate mice.

On many of the Indonesian islands the ladies had a white mask pasted onto their faces. I think it was to make their skins whiter – I showed them my suntan lotion which I put on to make my skin darker!

Tsunamis, volcanic eruptions, cyclones and earthquakes are all part of life in Asia and the Pacific Rim. How fortunate we are in Britain, where few extreme natural problems occur.

In Bangkok, the Teak Palace is the home of the previous King and Queen of Thailand and is open for visitors. On the walls pictures hung of the King's 100 odd children. At one stage over twenty of his sons were at Eton at the same time. They are grouped in a photograph in their top hats and short jackets. The Teak Palace is only a few yards away from the Grand Palace and also the house where the King's fifty or so concubines lived.

I went elephant trekking in Thailand, up in the hills between Burma and Thailand. One day my steed, who was usually the leader, was kept back as I was a single amongst five couples (Peter decided to rest and enjoy the Guest House and pool.) We started last and finished first. My elephant, with the help of his mahout, charged up hills past all the others, often taking to the verges and, with his trunk, pulling up any small trees or shrubs that got in his way. On my own, sitting on a flat tray of a seat, I hung on for dear life at first, but by the end was enjoying the chase and the thrill of the elephant's shoulders moving beneath my feet.

The Indian Ocean was an untidy sea with waves going all ways. In Oman a chatty taxi driver took us from the harbour into opulent Salalah. On the way we passed many fine large hacienda type houses. I commented on this to the taxi driver. "Well," he said, "if you have four wives and twenty children you need a big house. They still have a woman's room you know." I imagined a sewing room or somewhere the four wives sat together.

"Yes," he continued, "if a wife displeases her husband he can have her put in the woman's room which has no windows and she must stay there for a day, a week, a year or the rest of her life, whatever he decides. It is up to the other wives to feed and look after her." He added "It pays to be a good wife."

In Al Mukalla in the Yemen with Lorraine, an Australian friend, we explored the back streets. Ladies behind small barred windows called 'Hello' and stretched out their henna painted hands for us to hold. "Would you like a drink?"

"Yes please." They passed out coloured sweet water and we tried to converse. "No, they couldn't come outside. The strong, solid, garden gates were all locked. They had no freedom to roam.

Women generally are so lucky to have such a strong empathy and understanding of each other even without a common language. In my book *"Red Sea Peril"* which is about our travels and arrest as spies in this Middle East area, I have tried to set out some of the problems of female circumcision and how poorly these women are treated.

In Aden, now a grey ashy ruin of its former self, a be-whiskered elderly Arab came and asked where we were from? On saying "England", he gave me a big stubbly kiss and a hug and said, "English please come back. We need you."

Before we left on our travels I was rather ashamed of being British for the way we exploited the Colonial people in the 'Empire', but now I realise, yes, we did treat them badly, but not nearly as cruelly as some of the other colonial powers. At least we left them with established Governments and Civil Servants, roads, rubbish collection and sanitation.

Being taken from our boat in the middle of the night at gun point and being forced ashore into a small beach army camp in Eritrea, was terrifying. Basically because we hadn't a clue what it was all about. They had taken our passports the day before and we thought everything was OK. However it was a month before we were released, by which time we had made friends not only with the young National Servicemen but also with Azib, the kindly wife of the owner of the Khartoum Hotel where we locked up. Our prospects had not looked good when we were bundled onto a plane with one way tickets, and under false names, to undergo further interrogation in Asmara, the capital. We thought that when the authorities realised we were only ordinary sailors they might shoot us and dump us in a ditch somewhere.

Once released we carried on up the Red Sea to see Egypt's magnificent Karnak Temple, Cairo

Top right:
Letters from
home.

Museum and the Pyramids. Through the Suez Canal we turned right to Israel and, apart from over-enthusiastic gun-toting soldiers and bomb squads, we felt safe and almost back in Europe. A trip to swim in the Dead Sea, climb Masada to Herod's Palace, visit Qmran where the Dead Sea Scrolls were found, and on to Ein Gedi National Park, was an unforgettable experience. As was driving to Aqaba and then Petra to see that 'Rose red city half as old as time.'

A two day sail from Ashkelon to Cyprus brought us to Larnaka and this last, more conventional, lap of our voyage. We felt that travel had made us flower, we had expanded to the world and even learned the hardest lesson of all: to accept ourselves as we are.

**Top right:
Letters from
home.**

**Bottom:
Tiny CLYPEUS in
front of the Hotel
boat CEZANNE.
Did we really sail
around the world
on our own, in
that small boat?**

186

CHAPTER NINETEEN | CONCLUSIONS

TWENTY FIVE YEARS OF ADVENTURE! It has been a wonderful life and for us 'seizing the day' was the best decision we ever made. We have lived the simple life, close to nature and learned to rely on and trust each other. We have had undreamed of joys and adventures. Once you have bought your boat and sailed away, living is economic - no council tax, gas or electricity bills, no cars or their insurance and when we started, few expensive marinas. The other ocean yachts people you meet are friendly, supportive, resourceful, full of fun and eager to share their adventures.

However, without the good will and encouragement of our children and family, it would not have been such a happy experience. We came across many couples who had to return home because 'Mother needed them', or children were in debt, or not managing their lives well. Quarrels and anger split many crews. Part of our joy was sailing to see our eldest son who was living in New Orleans and my parents and sister in Rockingham, West Australia. But, if it hadn't been for our sisters Liz, Hilary and Sheila, who took on the responsibility of caring for our parents and told us to 'push off and not to worry' it would have ended much sooner. We can never thank them enough for their generous spirits.

We have been 'free as air', 'free as the sea'. I appreciate that I've probably had more freedom than most. We have travelled the world without a ticket – we needed visas to land in different countries at their Port of Entry, but in your own boat the sea is still yours. Leaving New Zealand was the first realisation that we could go anywhere – where ever we wanted, only common sense, navigational hazards and later, political problems, influenced our decisions.

And what did that freedom give us? Responsibility. There are no lifeboats mid-ocean. We had to be totally self sufficient or perish.

What else did that freedom give us? Time. All twenty four hours were ours. Weather deadlines had to be considered in weeks or months, not days or hours.

And what was the product of that freedom? Self-sufficiency and a non-judgemental attitude to all who are not fanatical; a deeper love and trust in each other, and a tremendous gratitude for the kindness of strangers.

In the time we were away, the changes on land have been enormous: credit cards, personal computers, internet, mobile phones, IPODs, and cheap air travel. Changes in the cruising world seem even more significant: bigger better-equipped boats, stronger and more efficiently cut sails, Kevlar, roller furling, rod rigging, GPSs, affordable RADAR, more electronic navigational aid and books giving information on ocean routes and weather windows. Organised Rallies enable sailors to cross the oceans in company and relative safety and, of course: Marinas.

For all that, I think we were the lucky ones; almost the first generation to have wind-vane self-steering and SatNav (although we often had to wait 90 minutes for a fix which occurred when the requisite satellites rose above the horizon). Some islands in the South Pacific had never before seen a yacht or white people who were not Traders, Missionaries or Government Officials. We were the first visitors to come as friends and felt privileged to do so. I enjoyed managing our simple life on a very modest income (less than £6,000 a year including inland travels).

I'm sure ocean voyaging is more fun now with radio telephones, mobile phones and email on board. Owners and crews can keep in touch with family, friends and investments. Once we had let go of land we were on our own: for thirty one days crossing both the Atlantic, from Teneriffe to Antigua, and thirty across the Pacific, from the Galapagos Islands to the Marquesas.

But, however sophisticated the yacht may be, the life and death decisions still have to be made and with global warming, the sea and weather seem to have become even more unpredictable. Soldiers, sailors, mountaineers and small boat sailors are some of the last groups left who know that companionship in danger is one of the things that makes life worth living. So often we were by ourselves in the whole world – and now, a picture comes to mind as I wait for sleep of our two faces and gloved hands dimly reflected by the swaying surface of the compass bowl.

We have learned to value green and pleasant Britain for its stability and moderation and realise how lucky we are to have been born into such a privileged society where clean drinking water is taken for granted. We appreciate the opportunities for everyone to continue their education, read erudite newspapers, listen to Radio 4, and most of all, to realise that a loving family is the greatest of life's gifts.

We do have some regrets: not being around to help when grandchildren were born and not being close to them as they grew up. But, we have watched from afar and seen our children develop on their own to become useful, independent and sensible members of their communities. We can never thank them enough for letting us go and then welcoming us back when we did come home.

Another regret was when house prices rose dramatically between 1982 and 1986. The five bedroomed house we sold in Wokingham for £84,000 was on the market four years later, for a quarter of a million pounds. How were we ever going to afford a house again? We should have decided to change down to a 'house to let' before we left, but tenants and estate agents are unpredictable. Buying the boat and investing the rest made us feel we had more control. Thank goodness Peter's contracts and wise investments allowed us to buy outright a house to let and then later our home bungalow on the banks of Milford Haven Estuary.

Our friends still welcomed us back in spite of our modest life style. They deserved their bigger and better houses and cars – they had worked all those extra years at the top of their professions while we had been adventuring.

Travelling or living abroad you have to find your own way. In the new country you have no past, no social crutches to lean on. You are what you are and it's up to you to earn friendship and trust. Nobody cares where you are from or what you did before – fit in, or fail, and be lonely. It's the same too when you eventually settle down. Nobody, well very few, actually want to know where you have been or what you did.

In 1999 we had no idea how much it cost to live in a house in Britain any more. How much would rates, electricity, heating, health insurance, dentist, a car and its tax and insurance cost? Each winter for the last seven years we have tried to splice together the frayed ends of our land life trying to live as economically as possible. Peter has kept accurate accounts, putting all bills and receipts into a data base on his computer. We found we could manage living simply. Living on the boat each summer actually reduced our expenditure by always anchoring off; shopping in local markets and having no car or telephone with us.

Now, while we have been sailing through the

Mediterranean during the summers I've spent the winters studying and at the age of seventy, gained a Master's Degree in Creative Writing. I can hardly believe it, but I felt I had something to say, something to pass on to who ever was interested about the joy and beauty of our planet and the endless kindness of ordinary people. My books give an opportunity to go to Boat Shows and encourage other sailors. Our 16' fibre glass dinghy, kept in the Boat Club in front of the house, allows us to gently

Now its all just talk at the boat show.

Our present 15' dinghy at the bottom of the garden.

As the Greek philosopher Horace said in the 3rd Century BC:

"Happy the man, and happy he alone,
He, who can call today his own;
He who, secure within, can say,
Tomorrow do thy worst, for I have lived today.

John Dryden translation from Horace Bk III.

cruise up river for a picnic on sunny days.

The Cruising Association provided a backbone to our cruising life. It has given us a respected image when entering foreign yacht clubs all around the world and we have always been welcomed. Being able to stay in the CA cabins at Limehouse has simplified travel arrangements and we found it comforting to be among like minds and glean up to date information. Giving talks of our experiences to Members is always a satisfying experience and good practise for our latest career as guest lecturers on Cruise Ships – what a wonderful opportunity it is to tell of our voyages and experiences, and in such luxury!

After CLYPEUS was sold we gave ourselves a year to decide what we wanted to do with the proceeds, and for a similar price have bought a Bessacar Camper Van to give us, hopefully, five more years of adventure to satisfy our wander lust, by which time Peter will be 83 and we may want to settle down!

Don't end your days regretting the things you haven't done, it won't always work out, but 'Go for it', at least you will have tried. Our life isn't a rehearsal. This is it. Every day leaves a day less of your life to enjoy.

CLYPEUS PLANS
CLYPEUS a 35' Ketch. A ferro-cement Endurance 35.

Parameters for our Ocean Voyaging Boat:

PARAMETERS FOR THE BOAT were that it be strong, have a deep keel, two masts, small cockpit, and at least two rooms so that we could close a door between us - to sulk if necessary. We also both wanted our own work space. And, no way, did I want to have to make up beds each evening in the main cabin. We are untidy sailors at sea and the bliss of sinking into a tidy, dry bed would be heaven.

A 36' yacht was as large as we felt we could manage both physically and financially. A bigger boat would bean a larger anchor to heave up and down, bigger sails, additional marina charges, higher insurance premiums. Also we wanted to be sure either of us could sail it single-handed in case of accidents or illness. We wanted to do it all on our own, no crew.

Peter also felt simple equipment was safest, to ensure easy ocean maintenance and minimal reliance on electricity and batteries: no roller reefing headsails and a manual anchor winch.

A steel hull would have been our first choice, but those within our budget already had rust problems and osmosis threatened the older fibre glass yachts. Wooden hulls need too much maintenance in the tropics and the fate of the Robinsons in their 43' LUCETTE which had sunk in three minutes after being holed by killer whales was fresh in our minds. After thirty years CLYPEUS'S ferro cement hull has proved stable, inert and easy to repair, but she is relatively slow - a matron amongst sophisticated modern Ms's.

A 35' deep keel yacht is not really suitable for cruising the canals. With her six foot depth she was difficult to control in the turmoil of filling locks and her keel did plough a few furrows!

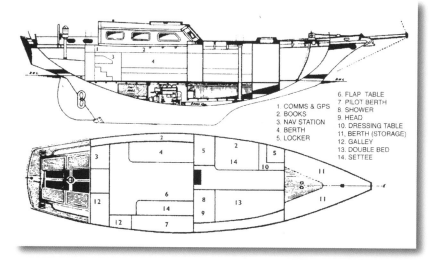

1. COMMS & GPS
2. BOOKS
3. NAV STATION
4. BERTH
5. LOCKER
6. FLAP TABLE
7. PILOT BERTH
8. SHOWER
9. HEAD
10. DRESSING TABLE
11. BERTH (STORAGE)
12. GALLEY
13. DOUBLE BED
14. SETTEE

APPENDIX TWO | PETER'S TECHNICAL NOTES
2.1 CONCRETE HULL MAINTENANCE

WE SPENT MANY HAPPY HOURS wandering around yards looking at yachts which South Coast yacht brokers thought would be suitable for our epic RTW adventure. We had firm views on what would be suitable and nothing we inspected over two years looking was anywhere near our ideal.

Eventually we saw an Endurance 35 at Brighton Used Boat Show which appeared to fit the bill perfectly. Needed a bit of TLC but nothing a new Perkins engine and a new set of sails wouldn't cure (Gulp!!) But it had a ferrocement hull.

We decided to go ahead and thus a new phase of learning started. We chose to have the chlorinated rubber paint on the hull grit blasted off, as it was a bit untidy, and have an epoxy paint job done. A well known Hamble boatyard did the job using a famous Portsmouth made paint and we set off on our journey.

First stop was Guernsey for a refit. We had formed a company in Guernsey to buy the new engine and other gear as there were tax advantages. After a month or so in St Sampsons, working hard, Shirley noticed one low tide that the new paint job was coming up in blisters. After much debate we wrote to the boatyard who had done the work and they sent a surveyor to see the problem.

The long and short of it was an offer to do the grit blasting and painting again if we took the boat back to the UK. Off we go then with the boat full of non-VAT paid equipment on board back to the Hamble. A month to grit blast and dry out then repaint. Everything must be OK now.

About 18 months later we were antifouling in Gulfport, Mississippi and the new epoxy looked definitely poor. No time to worry tho', the Pacific beckons. A year goes by and we are in New Zealand for Christmas, hiding from the South Pacific hurricane season. The boat looked very tired, with ferro rust streaks everywhere. A yard in Opua, North Island gave us a good quote so we went up on their slip.

Now the New Zealanders know all about small boats and how to look after them. They told us that ferro hulls and normal epoxy paint do not mix well, and the evidence was there in front of us. They recommended an Altex Devoe modified aliphatic epoxy, specially designed to paint the inside of big ship cargo tanks. This was called Bar-rust 235 and they put a number of lovely thick coats on. Then a good local antifouling and a white two-pot polyurethane above the waterline. This set with a beautiful gloss and was as hard as steel, ideal on a hard concrete hull. The yard workers were marvellous and very skilled and it was a pleasure to have the work done there.

The original Bar-rust coating was still there 22 years later when we sold the yacht and the white topsides had only needed odd touching up on the corners.

A different type of maintenance was needed when we bounced off an isolated coral reef one dark night and knocked a hole in the hull about a foot below the waterline, near the bows. Obviously there was a lot of drama involved as water was coming in faster than the electric bilge bump could get rid of it and if one of the crew of two is pumping furiously on Mr Henderson's best pump and the other crew is trying to guide the boat then there is nobody left to mend the hole.

All these fabulous hole repair devices one sees at Boat Shows are pretty useless when one has what amounts to a circular depressed fracture about 9 inches diameter with a star shaped pattern of cracks round a central hole. and water squirting in thru' all the cracks. We had prepared a solution to this

situation before we left home, and that was to keep a number of hermetically sealed plastic bags of Portland cement on board together with a Concrete Accelerator liquid made by SIKA. When mixed with cement to make a stiff paste it will set in a couple of minutes. We had never actually tried this out before and being squeezed into the bows of a small boat in a bouncy sea was no place to do the first trials. The water blew it all out as fast as we pushed it into the cracks. A cushion and a piece of plywood and a strut to the other side of the cabin proved a much better solution.

Eventually daylight came with the electric bilge pump still running and one crew hand pumping. We were heading for a known anchorage on this atoll but it was midday before we found it and joy of joys some of our Australian friends were anchored there. We all dragged CLYPEUS into shallow water, luckily it was high tide, and encouraged her to lay on her side with the hole uppermost. At low water I set to with a lump hammer and a cold chisel to trim away all the fractured cement and expose the wire cage. Then mix up a thick paste of clean washed beach sand and West epoxy resin (everybody has a couple of litres of epoxy and hardener on board, don't they!!) and plaster over the hole. The water came up and went down and none came in, so just to make sure, at next low water we put a layer of woven glass cloth and epoxy over the damaged area.
Next stop Australia, about 1000 miles away.
We were in delayed shock for many weeks tho' as we had come very close to losing our lives in a very remote place.

Top, Filling sandbags for Clypeus to lean on.

Bottom: Kind friends pull us ashore.

APPENDIX 2.2 | KEEPING THE BATTERIES CHARGED

WHEN WE LEFT THE UK IN 1983 we inherited the electrical system that the two previous owners had conceived which was based on a dedicated battery for engine starting, plus two domestic batteries selected by a normal red battery switch. The only way to charge them all was by running the Perkins diesel with its 70 amp alternator. We also added a Honda petrol generator to charge batteries if we ran out of power completely and could not start the main engine.

This was quite inadequate for a long distance cruising yacht because the whole object was to sail, not motor. So we added an Ampair 50 wind generator with an alternative water propeller as well. This proved to be useless as a wind generator, but with the water propeller we got a steady 4 amps all the time we were sailing above 4 or 5 knots. That is nearly 100 ampere hours of charge per day, well above our consumption.

Our power demands were very low at sea. The VHF and echo sounder were normally off but we did have a Walker 801 Sat Nav which drew about 1 amp. We did not use navigation lights at night whilst sailing as we were resigned to the fact that large ships never kept a lookout and it was up to us to keep a 24 hour lookout, 3 hours on, 3 hours off. When we were in the Indian Ocean and Red Sea we kept the lights off so that any pirates would not see us. Odd cabin lights were on and off during the evening but we were normally too weary to sit up reading.

We were given an American Wind Bugger generator which had a four foot tip to tip, carved wooden propeller which was absolutely lethal. We tried it a few times but noise, vibration, and danger were against it.

We put up with this situation for 3 or 4 years then, when in Australia, purchased two 45 watt

Solarex solar panels from Bias Marine in Brisbane. These were fantastic and gave a total of about 4-5 amps in clear sunlight.

Later on we got a solid state cooler unit (Peltier effect) and fitted it into an Australian Esky - an insulated cool box - and for the first time had some cool drinks. This drew about 4 amps continuously. It was a low cost solution to cooling food but very inefficient electrically. To keep it supplied we added an 85 watt solar panel which, with the first two, gave us about 10 amps charge in the midday sun.

This setup solved all of our electrical power problems, so long as we stayed in sunny places. In fact we had to fit a so-called Charge Regulator to avoid boiling the batteries. It is just a voltage sensing circuit which operates a relay when the battery voltage rises to 14.3 volts, or so, and disconnects the panels from the batteries. When the batteries discharge a bit and the voltage drops then it reconnects the panels again.

During our 25 years living on CLYPEUS we went through a variety of battery types. For the starter battery there was little choice. It was just whatever was available where we were at the time. Always a 70 to 80 amp hour battery rated for starting the diesel, which would go in the space available. The choice of domestic battery is more of a problem and is dictated by funds available at the time and what is for sale locally. In Australasia the 6 volt 200 amp hour deep cycle golf cart batteries were available. They are probably good where there is a fixed discharge and recharge regime in force but cruising yachts are not like that. Every day is different. We tried them once but they showed no economic or electrical advantage over mass produced, and much cheaper 125 or 150 amp hr 12 volt truck batteries. These are about the maximum weight one person can lift which is another consideration. However well we treated them they only had a life of 4 years or so normally but this was quite acceptable to us.

Whenever CLYPEUS was laid up, during the hurricane season for instance, when we would travel on land, I would reconnect the solar panels so that two were used to keep the batteries charged and one used to supply two 6 inch computer type fans which we fitted in the forward hatch. These were the brushless type with ball bearings and ran continuously, all the hours of daylight, blowing air thru' the boat to keep it ventilated. If you try this yourself remember that the panels put out anything up to 20/25 volts if not connected to a 12 volt battery and this will destroy a 12 volt fan. It is necessary to add a series resistor so that only 12 volts appears at the fan.

On CLYPEUS this is where we fitted our solar panels.

APPENDIX 2.3 | BILGE PUMP EXPERIENCES

WE STARTED OUR JOURNEY with a standard Henderson hand bilge pump fitted in the front wall of the port side cockpit locker and a second pump in the toilet which cleared the toilet and, if a 3 port valve was turned, could suck from the bilges. There was also an electric bilge pump of unknown make which sucked from the bilge under the engine. This pump went to a 1½ inch Y fitting so that it could use the same skin fitting as the cockpit pump.

A number of problems arose from this arrangement. With a deep keel boat such as the Endurance the lowest point in the keel is nearly 6 feet below the outside water level and then to lift bilge water the extra 1 ½ to 2 feet to the skin fitting makes a total lift of nearly 8 feet. When the electric pump stopped running there was sufficient volume of water in the delivery pipe to run back through the pump into the bilge and re-operate the level switch and start the pump again. So we put a Whale one-way valve at the pump outlet to trap the water in the pipe to stop this happening.

The second problem is that the average submersible electric bilge pump is normally described as "xx gallons per minute" but this does not take account in this case of a vertical lift of 7-8 feet This can reduce the pump outlet to a fraction of the advertised flow.

If the pump is only trying to get rid of some accumulated rain water it doesn't really matter if it takes a bit longer. However if you are hundreds of miles from safety and have a continuous inflow of water from some damage then you become very interested in extracting the last bit of flow

This effect is made worse by the effect of voltage drop in the wiring between the batteries and the pump. The centrifugal pumps that are used for bilge pumping are very affected by speed of

rotation of the impellor. A small voltage drop of say 10% could easily reduce the flow by 20% or more. Pumps normally draw up to 10 amperes and a combination of inadequate wiring and odd voltage drops in fuses etc could result in 10 volts or less appearing at the pump itself, seriously reducing its output.

Whilst having an under floor inspection one day I saw to my horror that the green plastic Taiwanese bilge pump had assumed the shape of a Rugby ball and the impeller was jammed. One night some days previously we had noticed a curious smell and could not find any reason. Putting two and two together and adding some logic we decided that the level switch had operated but the pump was jammed due to corrosion of the shaft. A high current flowed limited by the resistance of the pump armature and the cables from the battery, but this was not sufficient to blow the fuse. The current overheated the pump to the extent that the pump casing softened, the heated air inside the pump expanded raising the pressure and the pump swelled up.

We replaced the pump with a high quality RULE 1500 pump and at a subsequent refit added a second pump, a RULE 3500. I was determined not to be caught out again. This second pump was mounted at a higher level than the smaller pump so if this one was working correctly then the second pump would never even get wet and corrosion would be minimal. If the lower pump failed then the bilge water level would rise 6 inches or so and operate the level switch for the second pump Both pumps had completely separate outlet hoses and non-return valves so that no failure or blockage in one could affect the other.

Level switches are another interesting topic. I reject immediately any switch which has mechanical bits rolling around inside it. Those with tilting floats and mercury switch capsules are better but the flexible wire pigtails to the float only last a few years before corrosion gets them. We settled on a solid state switch from West marine. It was a plastic box about 2x3x1 inches with metal buttons on two opposite faces. When the bilge water rose to these buttons for more than a few seconds the internal circuitry would sense this and complete the +ve feed to the pump. Unfortunately the water in our bilges had a layer of oil on top of it and this coated the switch body and made a connecting path between the metal buttons so even though the water level had dropped the switch did not turn the pump off . The solution to this was to fasten a 6 inch long piece of stainless steel strip to each metal button hanging downwards. The bilge water only ever touched the tips of these and never rose to the level to make the switch body oily and wet.

The larger pump was operated by a RULE heavy duty mercury capsule type float switch which, on the basis that it would seldom get wet, would last for many years. Success at last, but not the end of the tale.

I was still worried about voltage drops affecting the pumps so I ran a dedicated pair of heavy wires carrying 12 volts direct from the ships battery to a position near the bilge pumps. To avoid the heavy pump currents passing through the level switches we used the level switches to control a pair of car headlamp type relays which then sent current to the two pumps via two domestic 10 amp circuit breakers. These have magnetic trips to look after high fault currents and thermal trips to look after long term marginal overloads. We felt we could sleep easily after all this.

The only time the upper pump actually ran was when we overfilled the freshwater tanks by accident and put over 50 gallons of drinking water into the bilges

We sailed halfway around the world over a period of 15 years or so with this system installed and it was completely trouble free.

APPENDIX 2.4 | GAS AND GAS BOTTLES

APART FROM WIND, CLYPEUS has three fuels on board, Diesel, LPG (Liquefied petroleum gas) and a small amount of petrol for the outboard. LPG causes most of the problems for cruising yachts. Every nation appears to have its own standards for container size, what gas is in the bottle, and what the connector/regulator looks like.

Let's assume you sail happily away from the UK with 2 blue (Butane) Calor Gas tanks. When the second one runs out (You did not worry when the first one ran out because it happened in the middle of cooking dinner and the skipper gets all sort of flack for not being able to find the right spanner quickly, and anyway we've got a second full tank) you are in a French marina and all you are offered is Camping Gas-or GAZ. These tanks hold less gas than the Calor Gas, but are greater diameter and less height. So, assuming that it will go in the gas locker, you are probably committed to buying a full Gaz tank and a regulator to go with it. If you will not be coming back to the UK for some years then resign yourself to dumping the empty Calor tanks and the Calor regulator into the nearest bin. Do not invest too much in GAZ equipment either, as, when you leave France you may as well throw them away as nobody else uses them until you get to Tahiti or New Caledonia.

At this stage we were approaching Spain still using GAZ. When it ran out we bought a Spanish domestic size bottle and regulator and lashed it on the afterdeck with an extended gas hose. This saw us all the way to the Caribbean and USA but even though we had painted it with epoxy paint it rusted through eventually.

In USA one can buy stainless steel gas cylinders which are obviously ideal except that the USA tank is much larger and almost certainly will not go in your gas locker. It will also have a POL connector, the USA equivalent of the Calor Propane connector. A bullet nosed brass connector with a free nut. Although this connector looks like the UK propane connector there are small dimensional differences and they are not safely interchangeable. However this tank is the most sensible choice for world travel as most countries can fill them. They are available from West Marine but cannot be economically shipped to other countries.

We were lucky enough to find some aluminium gas tanks in a scrap yard in Singapore. They were ex BP and had not been commercially viable, I was told. They had Singapore connectors of course and I had them refilled whilst we were there and got a local regulator. Realising that I would not be able to get them refilled again after we had left Singapore I purchased two USA POL tank fittings which I found in a gas shop hoping to be able to change them later. (The shop was not allowed by law to change them in Singapore). First World countries have very strict laws about the public playing about with gas but away from these areas things are much more lax.

I refilled these tanks in Thailand myself from Thai domestic tanks I rented. This procedure is probably highly illegal so cannot be recommended. First remember that the pressure in the gas tank is solely related to the composition of the gas, and its temperature, and not related to the quantity of gas in the tank. At 20 deg C butane has a pressure of about 16 psi and propane 109 psi. At 40 deg C the figures are about 40 psi and 190 psi respectively. This latter is a very high pressure and any fittings for propane must be well made. Propane is not much used in the tropics as its low-temperature capability is not needed.

I managed to buy high pressure connectors for

both my Singapore tanks and for the rented Thai tanks which allow hose connections to the tanks without going through a regulator, then linked these with high pressure gas hose. Then hoisted the full cylinder upside down, using the main halliard, so that the liquid gas could run into the lower tank on the deck. Wrap the empty cylinder with a wet sack to lower its temperature and let the sun shine on the full cylinder. Open the valves and hey presto, the gas all transfers to the lower cylinder in a few minutes. Care must be taken not to fill the lower cylinder more than about 80% to leave room for subsequent expansion of the gas. Do all this at anchor away from other yachts and with a breeze blowing

Whilst in Oman I found a gas depot which would take the old Singapore tank connectors out and fit my USA POL connectors. A group of happy Arabs spent a whole Saturday morning on the task, as the connectors were originally put in using a Loctite sealant, and were very, very tight. It took three men with a spanner and six feet of steel pipe to undo them. Then they refilled them via the new POL connectors, they had adaptors for every connector ever invented, and charged me about $10 for the mornings work and the gas. It was the best entertainment we had had for a long time!

These aluminium cylinders stayed with us for many years and were refilled for the last time in Cyprus which is where the simple world finishes and the rule laden EU takes over.

gas bottles

APPENDIX 2.5 | VENTILATING THE BOAT DURING LAY-UP

WE LEFT CLYPEUS TO HER OWN DEVICES many times in SE Asia. Most times she was hauled out and fitted with three heavy duty welded plastic covers (One over the staysail boom, one over the main boom and one over the mizzen boom). These were waterproof but were mainly to keep the tropical sun off the woodwork.

We were worried about mildew forming in the unventilated boat so decided to fit two 6inch diameter computer fans in the forehatch to blow air through the cabin. Our forehatch was of the type which could be securely clipped but open ½ inch or so.

I bought two computer fans from a pleasant vendor in Sim Lim Tower, Singapore. They were only about $5 each and had 12 volt DC brushless motors and ball bearings, both aids to a long life. The Sales lady said that if either failed within a year she would replace them. These were fitted side by side in a piece of ¼" plywood which was sized to rest on top of the hatch frame and a piece of plastic mosquito gauze put on top of the wood to keep the "mossies" out.

To power the fans I reconnected our three solar panels so that two were used to keep the batteries charged and one connected to the two new fans. It is not desirable to connect the fans directly to a solar panel as with the fans consuming only about 250 milli amps the solar panel voltage can go up to 20 volts or more and this could damage the 12 Volt fans. So we need a bit of resistance in the circuit. We have to drop the 20 volts to 12 volts with ¼ amp flowing. Knowing that R=E/I then we need 8/0.25 = 32 ohms resistor. If you are in civilisation you could possibly buy a 33 ohm 5 watt resistor which is a standard value or make one yourself from a piece of coiled resistance wire

normally sold to repair simple electric heating rings. To decide how long a piece of resistance wire you need, wait for full sunlight on the solar panel, connect the whole length of wire in series with the fans and measure the voltage across the fans. It will be much less than 12 volts so gradually move one of the connections along the resistance wire so that less of it is in the circuit. Keep an eye on the voltmeter and when it gets to 12 volts cut the wire off. You can make the connections to the resistance wire using standard small plastic terminal blocks. The resistance wire will get warm (6 volts across it with 0.25 amps flowing will generate 1.5 watts), so ensure the wire cannot touch anything flammable. (PS If you have not got a voltmeter you shouldn't be sailing around the World).

We left CLYPEUS in Singapore (Near Changi) for over four years with this arrangement and no trace of mildew developed. Singapore is only 60 miles north of the Equator and very humid, so it was a good test.

After being used for every lay-up for the last 20 years the fans are still running happily!

If you have not got a voltmeter you shouldn't be sailing around the World.

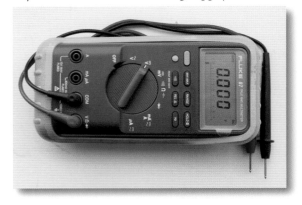

APPENDIX 2.6 | THE DRIVE PLATE SAGA

THERE SHE WAS, MOORED NEATLY alongside the pontoon with her gold anodised masts glistening in the bright sun. We approached her with mixed reverence and awe. She was to become our home for the next 3 years and take us around the World.

We clutched the all-important Blue Book, and the Bill of Sale, tightly in our hands as we climbed carefully on board, unlocked the stable door into the cabin and went inside, each sitting on one of the two side berths, facing each other. We could not really believe what we had done.

What we had done was to resign from our jobs, sell our 5 bedroom house in Wokingham, sell everything else that was saleable, keeping a small amount of furniture in case we came back unexpectedly, and spent one third of the proceeds on a 35 foot ferrocement ketch. She was not ideal but she was the best we had seen in spite of the combined efforts of virtually every yacht broker on the South coast trying to sell us something quite unsuitable.

This story is going to be quite different. Shirley has already written in detail about the places we went to and the people we met in her three books, *Red Sea Peril, Seize the Day and Passport to Adventure.*

This is the story of how we kept this ageing 12 ton ferro yacht in working order, safe enough for us to risk our lives by setting out across the largest oceans in the World, and not only succeeding but living, and sailing, in her for 24 years. I am going to tell this story in a completely unexpurgated way and tell the reader everything that went wrong, or broke, and how we put it right. The hope is that some reader will learn from our mistakes and realise before he starts what he has to learn before he sets out and be prepared to learn continuously

every day that he is at sea. We left the UK on the basis that we would do every thing ourselves and that we would never call "The man" to help us out. The first occasion we had to break this rule was to occur fairly soon, but more later.

We had decided to spend 6 months living on board before we left the UK, mainly to prove that we could live together in such a small space and stay friends. We decided to stay in the Cruising Association marina at St Katherine Dock from Autumn 1982 to Spring 1983. I had organised a 6 month consultancy contract in Watford which was less than an hour by car and Shirley was initially going to work in the CA chartroom to plan our 3 year voyage. We considered that being in the right place at the right time to take advantage of local weather patterns was a primary goal.

We plucked up courage and one sunny morning in September 1982 left Wickor Marine, at the north end of Portsmouth Harbour to sail round to the River Thames and up to Tower Bridge. We went into Dover Harbour for a nights rest and spent a pleasant evening at the Cinque Ports Yacht Club. Next morning we motored toward the Harbour entrance but just before we got there the boat seemed to slow down. A quick check on prop shaft couplings and saw that the gearbox output shaft was not rotating even tho' it was in gear and the engine running, A quick call on the VHF radio and the Harbour authorities towed us back to the marina. This was obviously going to be our technical honeymoon as far as CLYPEUS was concerned. I had never owned a diesel engine before and certainly not one with a Paragon(USA) hydraulically operated transmission and we had no choice but to call for the local mechanic.

This is when the first serious learning session took place. CLYPEUS is not easy to work on as the engine is beneath the saloon floor with access via an 6 foot by 4 foot sheet of ¾ plywood with acoustic insulation glued to its underside and 4 inch square Wood parquet tiles on top. The tiles proved not to be very secure and all the time the floor slab was propped up against the saloon table odd tiles were dropping into the depths of the bilges. Well, the mechanic, we'll call him Joe, looked at the symptoms and decided that as the engine was rotating and the gearbox output shaft wasn't there was something amiss with the gearbox, so out with it. Here the swearing started. The rear mountings for the engine/gearbox unit are on the sides of the gearbox so the rear of the engine had to be supported whilst the gearbox was removed otherwise the engine would drop into the bilges. So sheer legs were erected in the cabin with a 1 ton chain block (which just happened to be on board) to lift the engine. At this stage it became evident that to get at the bolts holding the gearbox on to the back of the bell housing the engine had to be lifted anyway as the sides of the hull were too close to get spanners on to the bolts when it was in position. Well, lifting your Hurth gearbox may be a one-handed job but Mr Paragons' gearbox is definitely a 2 person job; however we eventually had it out on the floor. Here we had our first bit of luck as Joe, looking at the drive plate, which is fastened to the rear face of the flywheel and which transmits engine power through to the gearbox input shaft, saw it appeared to be damaged. So, just undo a ring of Allen screws (very, very tight & fitted with Loctite. You need proper carbon steel Allen keys for this, your Lidl ones wouldn't have a chance) and the drive plate was in our hands. It had actually fallen apart and some of the drive springs were laying in the bottom of the flywheel housing. Providentially a new drive plate was available

nearby and a couple of hours later everything was back in place and we were ready to go. Recompensing Joe was a pleasure as I had seen everything that he had done and I wouldn't have the slightest hesitation in doing it myself next time should the need arise.

One gets plenty of spare time to think when sailing across the oceans and when we had the transmission/gearbox separated from the engine in Dover I had noticed that the narrow splines on the projecting gearbox input shaft were very worn and this worried me as we would lose the drive permanently if they wore away completely. We used the engine primarily to just push us along when there was no wind and usually ran the engine as 1200-1400 rpm giving about 5 knots. There is quite high cyclic vibration at this rpm and the torque being transmitted by the drive plate is not enough to start compressing the cushioning springs so in effect the so-called resilient drive plate was locked up solid. This means that all the crankshaft vibrations were being transmitted directly to the heavy gearbox internals via the spline coupling and wearing it to bits.

The next episode in this particular story was some years later. I had seen at a boat show a different type of drive plate with a very soft resilient polyurethane drive member instead of metallic springs. This isolated all the crankshaft vibration from the gearbox splines at low speed and torque but as you increased the rpm and the propeller torque requirement increased the drive would stiffen up and become nearly solid. Anyway, suffice to say, I purchased one of these new drive plates and Shirley and I lifted the engine, removed the gearbox and took off the drive plate. It was still in fairly good condition and the spline wear was still not disastrous. We fitted the new drive plate together with a good smear of anti-scuffing compound on the splines to minimise the wear, popped the gearbox back on and put the engine back in its hole.

It would be nice to think that this was the end of the story about gearboxes but it does go on a bit longer.

Whilst we were in Singapore I tried to interest some Marine Transmission specialists in overhauling the gearbox for us as I had the feeling that it was slipping sometimes and we still had to travel nearly halfway around the world. "Ridiculous" was the reply. "It is obsolete. Throw it away and get a new Hurth box". This was not an option for a number of reasons. One was that the engine would have to be lifted 2 1/2 inches and the valve rocker box cover would be sticking up in the middle of the saloon floor.

So we ploughed on, Sri Lanka, Aden, Red Sea, Egypt, Israel, and at last many years later Cyprus, and into Larnaca Marina. Our son Paul is a marine surveyor in Milwaukee USA and we faxed asking him to look up any Paragon Transmission spares stockists. He came back with a priced up list of parts for a normal overhaul so we sent off an order. The stockists came back saying they would recommend a few extra parts so we said go ahead and in a week or so we had all these lovely new parts in our hands, the main one being a new input shaft with brand new unworn splines. This shaft is the first component you put in the gearbox when assembling it so it all had to come to pieces first. Now you have to be a bit brave to take the end cover off a hydraulic transmission and shake all the parts out on to a large tray but we, very carefully, did just that. We found rubber O rings which had hardened and cracked and were leaking, worn oil seals and worn bearings and hundreds of needle roller bearings. In the fullness of time it was all assembled again with no parts left over, It was put back on the engine and IT WORKED! What is more it was still working 10 years, and 5,000 miles, later.

APPENDIX 3 | Insurance

NO COMPANY WOULD INSURE just the two of us across the Atlantic or the Caribbean. We eventually managed to get a Lloyds Insurance Policy through Lloyds Brokers. But in Tahiti the cost increased to over a third of our income so we continued voyaging uninsured. In the Mediterannean it is compulsory to have Third Party Insurance for all EU countries. Panateus offered good third party cover and sent us copies of the policy in different European languages. We didn't need to use it and were never asked for any proof of insurance, but we did hear of boats who did have to produce insurance papers.

If your National Health contributions are up to date and in order, emergency treatment is free in countries belonging to the EU. For Peter's hospital stay in France we did have to the pay the costs but were able to reclaim them through the Ministry of Health in Newcastle.

APPENDIX 4 | OUR ROUTE THROUGH FRANCE

MOST BOOKS GIVE THE ROUTE SOUTH from the North. I have decided to follow our course from the South at Port St. Louis to Honfleur in the North.

We chose the most westerly route because it looked the least commercial, had no tunnels and a minimum depth of 1.8m.

We planned our route using 'Through the French Canals' originally by Philip Bristow but the tenth edition is a revision by David Jefferson; Published by Adlard Coles Nautical. *'The RYA European Waterways Regulations'* and the Cruising Association's *'Notes on the French Inland Waterways'.*

The French 'navicarte' *Voies Navigables* were invaluable. They give an informative kilometer by kilometer map of the river or canal with the directions for approaching bridges and locks. They also show the surrounding towns and villages and give descriptions and history of places of interest. They are in French but with English and German translations. For our route we used:

Navicarte 16 *Le Rhone de Lyon a la Mediterranee*

Navicarte 10 *La Saone de Corre a Lyon La Seille*

Navicarte 19 *Bourgogne Est de Joigny a Chalon-sur-Saone*

Navicarte 20 *Bourgogne Ouest d'Avon a Digoin*

Navicarte 3 *La Marne de Paris a Vitry-le-Francois.*

Navicarte 2 *La Seine Amont de Paris a Marcilly.*

Mavicarte 1 *La Seine Aval Du Havre a Paris*

Start	Destination	Locks	Kms	Miles
Port St Louis to Arles		0	40	25
Arles - Lyon		6	270	168
Lyon-Chalon Sur Saone		3	143	89
Chalon sur Saone-St Mammes		148	411	230
St Mammes-Paris		7	90	56
Paris - Honfleur		0	364	222
		164	1,318	690

This most westerly route proved an easy, rural and pleasant way home along the Rhone, Saone, Canal Lateral a La Loire, Canal de Briare, Canal du Loing to the Seine. Turning south, from near Chalon Sur Saone, the canal climbs up across the Massif Central to the watershed near Mont Chanin before descending. At Paray le Monial it starts going North again which was interesting. It would have been good to go through all those delightful vineyards later in the season and wine-taste our way through France but we were worried about the depth of our keel and how low the water might get in a hot, dry, summer.

The locks do close for lunch from midday to 1 p.m. and are not open at night. A gangplank of some sort is necessary as it wasn't always possible to moor close to the bank. We went to a Briccolage and bought a 5m x 0.5m wooden plank.

A Licence must be purchased from a VNF (Voies Navigables de France) Office for a year, 30 days, 16 days or a single day. There are 35 VNF Offices and licences can be applied for by post to: VNF 175 rue Ludovic Boutleux, 62400 Bethune, France, and must be accompanied by a photocopy of the Registration Certificate, the International Certificate of Competence and a cheque in euros payable to the VNF. Current rates are available on their internet site: *hhtp://www.vnf.fr*

We were surprised how rural the scenery was, but as France is twice as big as Britain with about the same population, it is not surprising that they are more spread out. It is a safe and usually easy way to travel to and from the Mediterranean.

APPENDIX 5 | BIBLIOGRAPHY

THERE ARE BOOKS to read before you set off; those necessary for the voyage; the travel guides and fun recreational books to enjoy on the way.

Reference Books:
Atlas
(French Almanac & Cruising Guide) Bloc Marine
Cruising Almanac Cruising Association
Celestial Navigation – Mary Blewitt
Cruising for Seniors – Paul Keller
Cruising Under Sail – Eric Hiscock
Dangerous Marine Animals – B. Halstead
Dictionaries: English, Turkish, Greek, Italian, French. Thesaurus
Field Guide to Seabirds – Capt G.S. Tuck
First Aid Book – Boots
Fitting out Ferro-Cement Hulls – Tucker
Flags – Granada Guides
Guide to Shells of the World Hamlyn
Guide to Minerals, Rocks and Fossils Hamlyn
Marine Life – The Young Specialist – W. De Haas
McMillan The Weather Handbook – Alan Watts
Metal Corrosion in Boats – Nigel Warren
Ocean Passages of the World
Ocean Routes – Jimmy Cornell

Pilots and Charts (British Admiralty)
Turkish Waters and Cyprus Pilot – Rod Heikell
Greek Waters Pilot – Rod Heikell
Italian Waters Pilor – Rod Heikell
Mediterranean, France and Corsica Pilot – Rod Heikell
Thomas Cook Travellers Cyprus AA
Turkish Coast Baedeker
Turkey Lonely Planet
Mediterranean Europe Lonely Planet
Sardinia Lonely Planet
12 Volt Doctor's Alternator Book – Beyn
12 Volt Doctor's Practical Handbook – Beyn
Sell up and Sail – Bill and Laurel Cooper
The Glassfibre Handbook – R.H. Warring
Trees and Shrubs of Greece – George Sfikas
Through The French Canals – Philip Bristow revised by David Jefferson
West Marine Catalogue (much info)
Where there is No Doctor
Yachtsman's Handbook
Bible and Shakespeare
Roget's Thesaurus

Cruising Tales
Across Europe in a Motor Boat – Henry C. Rowland
Companion Guide to The Greek Islands – Ernle Bradford
Isabel and the Sea – George Millar
In the Wake of Ulysses – Goran Schildt
Floating Through France – Brenda Davison
The Greek Islands Companion Guide – Ernle Bradford
The Iliad – Homer translated by E.V. Rieu
The Journeying Moon – Ernle Bradford
Lugworm Homeward Bound – Ken Duxbury
The Odyssey – Homer translated by T.E. Lawrence
The Secret Life of the Seine – Mort Rosenblum
Ulysses Found – Ernle Bradford
The Wind off the Island – Ernle Bradford
White Boat from England – George Millar

APPENDIX 6 | Shirley Billing WHY I LIKE CRUISING – MY FEELINGS.
Mostly written sailing from Rethymon to Chania 3rd July 2003

PEOPLE OFTEN ASK "Blue water sailing. Why do you do it?" Talking to Christine made me put into words why I love the cruising life.

I love the sea, being on it, in it, and under it. On shore watching breakers crash onto cliffs and the receding tide sweeping the beaches clean, or at sea as the sun sparkles on each deep blue faceted ripple.

In spite of major problems, like missing our children and grandchildren, and the rise in house prices, we are pleased we seized the day while were still young enough to make the most of it. Today many forty and fifty-year –olds look with dismay at their future prospects – perhaps it would be better to seize the day and enjoy twenty active years of happy freedom in charge of your own destiny. Most of us are lucky enough to have an extra ten years to enjoy life. As Tchekhov wrote 'Life does not come again'.

We chose to explore this wonderful world by boat, but a mobile home would give similar adventures without the worry of drowning!

The sea is in my blood. Grandfather was a sailing ship captain. My father always had a boat of some sort.

My mother often told the story of her screaming baby sitting in the water's edge when an angry matron strode up and admonished her: 'How dare you frighten that poor child by putting her in the sea.' My mother abjectly replied,

"I'm not putting her in, I'm trying to get her out."

As a child who wasn't clever or beautiful, I learned that it was up to me to make the first efforts towards friendship in each of the eleven schools I attended during WW2. Those experiences have stood me in good stead when rowing ashore alone to a remote island, armed with the knowledge that cannibals don't eat women (we are unclean) and hoping the islanders think the same way. Sometimes they ask 'but where is your husband?' To which I usually reply that he has maintenance work to do on CLYPEUS, but really he is a shy, self-sufficient man who doesn't enjoy making new friends. I do.

I enjoy cruising yachtsmen and women. They have a passion which they are pursuing having defied convention and let go home, salary and friends. I appreciate their supportive and competent wives and their confident, sensible children. Their resourcefulness and courage shown facing dangers and their endurance during bad conditions are all considered worth-while for being in charge of their own destinies and decisions; also their pride in their boat and their humility. All have been, or know they will be, humbled in the face of turbulent wind and water and by the extremes of natural beauty, peace and wrath.

I like the simple life, close to nature, eating the food available to the local community or foraging and fishing for it ourselves. The forces of nature give a kind of security having to wait in frustrating calms, or, skimming the sea's surface as the wind billows and fills the sails and fills our hearts with joy and the thrill of speed. Or, during gales, closing down the hatches, furling the sails, and cowering in the cabin.

Having lived fairly separate lives in our first 28 years of marriage; Peter, never a chatterer, had worked hard in many countries, much of his working life away from home. I hadn't realised what an uncommunicative man he had become – it showed on the boat, without the children to fill the gaps. He seldom spoke to me on more than a 'need to know' basis – if I didn't need to know he wouldn't bother to tell me. Now we had to adjust, no more Keep Fit classes to teach, or friends to chat to. No more like-minded engineers with whom he could discuss his latest project. So now, this was the rest of our lives. Would we overcome our disparity? Fortunately we seem to have done so, with much effort on both sides.

Entering a country by the side door in a fishing harbour or Marina is more pleasing than the crush of bodies at the airport, waiting behind the white line for the Immigration Officer's silent nod, searching my face, then inspecting my passport, stamping it, then handing it back with a curt nod. We have to anchor, row ashore or moor up to a quay. Scan the shoreline for Harbour Police, Immigration and Customs Office before presenting ourselves and our papers; perhaps stopping for an ice cream or beer between offices; then walking to buy fresh bread, fruit and vegetables from the real people, rather than the tourist-tricking taxi drivers and slick receptionists. Of course it isn't always a good experience but we are usually welcomed with courtesy and friendliness.

We feel privileged to have had the opportunity to sail to remote corners of our planet and meet people still unaffected by material wealth, television or tourists; to enjoy the simple life close to nature, eating the food available to the locals.

I enjoy lying beneath the shade of the sails as the deck dips and ploughs through the oncoming tropical swell or motoring over a glassy surface of the Med. Perhaps dolphins will come and swoop and play and stand on their tails – what show-offs they are! At night, they make a tunnel of phosphorescent bubbles beneath the water to burst into a showering star-filled silver fountain. There is an expectant thrill when scrambling over deserted ruins of Crusader Castles in Turkey; swimming into a mysterious and forbidding cave, or into the dark and scary entrance to a karst or Hong in Thailand to emerge into a central pool of sunlight filtering through fluttering leaves.

Snorkelling through coloured fish and corals in the South Pacific was a delight. Eating fish and crabs we have caught ourselves and feeling self sufficient as we eat them with our own fresh bread, baked on board. It is exciting to apprehensively row ashore to a remote island with a little gift of a bar of scented soap, a small screwdriver or pencils and being welcomed by an Islander who invites us into his/her home. It is very special to arrive at a Polynesian Island to hear the sound of guitars, ukuleles, and melodious singing wafting across the lagoon, and smell the welcome of the strong perfume of tiare and frangipani blossom.

I enjoy being behind the wheel barefoot and scantily clad with the spinnaker up in light airs and seeing if I can make our staid old boat pick up here skirts and dance for me; or the excitement of a gale, clutching the wheel, feet braced on deck trying to control her skid down an angry grey breaking wave.

There is unparallel joy and satisfaction of landing on the other side of an ocean having relied on our own skills and perseverance; of being in charge of our own destiny and responsible for all our decisions. On the ocean, as we glide through the sea, there is time to sit and watch each bubble of foam swirl around within the vortex of its ephemeral short life.

Looking down into the Aegean blue often the direct gospel light of God penetrated into the depths resembling those beams of hope which shine down from behind a dark cloud in religious pictures.

Sailing close inshore along Crete's craggy coastline we noticed the clefts in the bold cliffs

Sailing in paradise across the Pacific.

crammed with oleander like a waterfall of pink blossom tumbling down into the sea..

Fortunately, with much patience on both sides, we have completed our quarter of a century on board, having voyaged over 65,000 miles to 56 different countries and are closer and more in love now than we ever dared hope. In fact, we don't like to be parted for more than a few hours which is going to bring its own problems, but hopefully not too soon.

INDEX